D1593653

R. K. Narayan:
Contemporary Critical Perspectives

R. K. Narayan:
Contemporary Critical Perspectives

Edited, and with an Introduction

by

GEOFFREY KAIN

Michigan State University Press
East Lansing
1993

Copyright © 1993 Geoffrey Kain

All Michigan State University Press books are produced on paper which meets the requirements of American National Standard of Information Sciences—Permanence of paper for printed materials ANSI Z23.48-1984.

Printed in the United States of America

Michigan State University Press
East Lansing, Michigan 48823-5202

Library of Congress Cataloging-in-Publication Data

R.K. Narayan : contemporary critical perspectives / edited, and with an
   introduction by Geoffrey R. Kain.
      p.   cm.
   Includes bibliographical references (p.) and index.
   ISBN 0-87013-330-6 (alk.paper)
   1. Narayan, R. K., 1906-   —Criticism and interpretation.
2. India in literature. I. Kain, Geoffrey R.
PR9499.3. N3Z842 1993
823—dc20
                                                          93-29080
                                                             CIP

Errata: Pushpa Naidu Parekh's biographical entry on page xiii should read as follows:

Pushpa Naidu Parekh teaches world literature at Spelman College in Atlanta, Georgia. She received her B.A. in English, with honors, from Panjab University, Chandigarh, India; her M.A. in English from the University of Madras; and her M. Phil. in English from Panjab University (her thesis having been selected as the best in English in 1980); and her Ph.D. in English from Louisiana State University. Professor Parekh has a keen interest in Narayan and has lately been engaged in various projects concerning his writings.

For Lisa

Contents

Acknowledgments

Special thanks to Dr. Elinor Miller, Chair, Department of Humanities & Social Sciences at Embry-Riddle Aeronautical University, for her advice, interest, and financial support of this project. Warmest regards to Dr. Warren French in response to his interested and interesting correspondence. I am grateful, also, to Dr. Fred Bohm, Director, and to Julie Loehr, Chief Editor, of the Michigan State University Press for their personable interest in this endeavor. Thanks, also, to John Iliff and Lynn Prine of the Embry-Riddle Library staff for their gracious assistance in filling seemingly impossible reference gaps in the text. Special thanks to Carol Liptak for her prompt and cheerful service in helping to prepare this manuscript, and to Dr. Reinhold Schlieper for his aid and expertise. Finally, my gratitude to artist Martin Hoffman for his valued advice on preparing the cover illustration.

Notes on Contributors

Fakrul Alam taught English and American literature at Clemson University from August 1989 to May 1991 as Fulbright Lecturer. He is associate professor in English at the University of Dhaka, Bangladesh. He did graduate studies at Simon Fraser University and the University of British Columbia. Author of *Daniel Defoe: Colonial Propagandist* (Dhaka, Bangladesh: University of Dhaka Publications, 1989), he has also published essays on Daniel Defoe, Herman Melville, D.H. Lawrence, Salman Rushdie, and American literary history.

Warren French is honorary professor of American Studies at the University College of Swansea, Wales, who retired from Indiana University at Indianapolis in 1986. He was chair of the English Department at the University of Missouri-Kansas City from 1966 to 1970. He has published and edited a number of books and articles, principally on John Steinbeck, J. D. Salinger, the Beat Generation, and American films.

Geoffrey Kain received his Bachelor's and Master's degrees in English, with honors, from Rosary College in Chicago; he also attended the University of London (under the auspices of Rosary College) while working toward his Master's degree. He received his Doctor of Arts degree in English, with a dual focus on rhetoric and modern literature, from Idaho State University in 1984. His critical essays have appeared in a variety of journals, including the *Language Quarterly, The Nathaniel Hawthorne Review, The Quarterly of Research and Practice, The Journal of Foreign Languages* (Shanghai), and *Teacher Education Quarterly.* He has also published personal essays and poetry, and has served as technical editor, textbook editor, film script editor, and film narrator. His teaching has taken him from Idaho State University and the University of Wisconsin-Marinette to Fuzhou and Xiamen Universities in the People's Republic of China where he lived with his wife Lisa and son Julian and taught for three years as a Foreign Expert in English Language and Literature. Currently, Professor Kain teaches World Literature (with an emphasis on Asian and Third World contributions), Western Humanities, and various writing and literature courses at Embry-Riddle Aeronautical University in Daytona Beach, Florida, where he also serves as associate chair in the Department of Humanities and Social Sciences.

Rosanne Kanhai-Brunton is a native and citizen of Trinidad and Tobago. She received her B.A. in English (1980) and Master of Philosophy in English (1985) from the University of the West Indies in Trinidad. She graduated with a Ph.D. in Comparative Literature from Pennsylvania State University in 1990. She is now employed as a specialist in Postcolonial Literature and Feminist Theory and Criticism at Western Washington University. Previous publications include creative writing as well as scholarly publications on writers such as V.S. Naipaul, Shiva Naipaul, Bessie Head, and Simone Schwarz-Bart. She is currently working on a text that articulates and discusses the creative expressions of Indo-Caribbean women.

Shantha Krishnaswamy is a professor in the Literature Department at De La Salle University in Manila, Philippines. She received her Mittel Stufe in German language and literature from the Goethe Institute in Brussels, Belgium; her Diplome Superieur in French from the Universite Libre of Brussels; her B.A. in Philosophy from Kerala University, Trevandru, India; her M.A. in English language and literature from Kerala University; and her Ph.D. from the University of the Philippines. She has published one book (*Glimpses of Women in Indian Fiction*), a number of articles, and several poems.

John Lowe has taught at Columbia, Saint Mary's College (South Bend), and Harvard University, where he was an Andrew W. Mellon Fellow in the Humanities. He was a Fulbright Scholar in India in 1983. He is the author of articles which have appeared in *American Quarterly, Studies in Native American Literatures, Appalachian Journal,* and other periodicals. He is also the author of the forthcoming *Jump at the Sun: Zora Neale Hurston's Cosmic Comedy,* editor of *Redefining Southern Culture,* and coeditor (with Jefferson Humphries) of *The Future of Southern Letters.* He is currently on the graduate English faculty at Louisiana State University in Baton Rouge.

Ganeswar Mishra was educated at Utkal, Kent, and London Universities. He is currently professor and head of the Department of English, Utkal University, Bhubaneswar (India). He has published a number of research articles on aspects of Indian and Commonwealth literature and has participated in national and international seminars. Besides being an academic, he is an eminent creative writer in Oriya with fifteen books (both fiction and non-fiction) to his credit.

Gideon Nteere M'Marete has recently completed his Ph.D. at Massey University in New Zealand, as a Commonwealth scholarship recipient from Kenya. A high-school teacher and senior master at a school in Nairobi before traveling to New Zealand, he has been engaged in analyzing more than twenty works of Indian, African, and Caribbean literature.

Pushpa Naidu Parekh teaches world literature at Spelman College in Atlanta, Georgia. He received his B.A. in English, with honors, from Panjab University, Chandigarh, India; his M.A. in English from The University of Madras; and his M.Phil. in English from Panjab University (his thesis having been selected as the best in English in 1980); and his Ph.D. in English in 1986 from Louisiana State University. Professor Parekh has a keen interest in Narayan and has lately been engaged in various projects concerning his writing.

Sadhana Allison Puranik graduated from the University of Tennessee, Knoxville, in 1988 after completing a thesis which analyzed the issues of ethnicity and displacement in five books of V.S. Naipaul. She has completed her M.Phil. in English at Oxford University which deals with the connection between frontiers and individuality in the novels of R. K. Narayan and Anita Desai.

Javaid Qazi is a native of Pakistan who, after receiving a Ph.D. in English Renaissance literature from Arizona State University, has worked principally around San Jose, California, as a technical writer and editor in the computer industry.

Gita Rajan is an assistant professor of English at the University of New Orleans where she teaches nineteenth-century British literature, literary criticism and theory, and post-colonial literature. She has published in critical theory, feminist poetics, and nineteenth-century and post-colonial discourse. She is currently working on an interdisciplinary manuscript for a university press on Pater entitled *"Ecriture Feminine as Autobiography in Walter Pater."*

Suresh Raval is a professor of English at the University of Arizona. He received his Bachelor's and Master's degrees from Bombay University, another Master's (American literature) from the University of New Orleans, and a Ph.D. from the University of Washington. He is the author of two books and numerous critical articles and reviews.

Sr. Mary Beatina Rayen received her Ph.D. in English from Loyola University of Chicago in 1989; her dissertation concerned the work of R. K. Narayan. She currently teaches at St. Mary's College, Tuticorin, South India, where she has instructed since 1974 (after receiving St. Mary's top student award in 1974, upon completing her Master's in English). Her articles on various topics appear in local magazines (in both English and Tamil), and her talks on women are broadcast by regional radio stations.

D. A. Shankar is chairman of the Department of Post-graduate Studies in English, University of Mysore, India. He has contributed a number of critical articles to various journals and has published a book on

Cleanth Brooks, as well as a translation of a central Sahitya Academy award winning Kannada novel, *Carvallo.* He has also to his credit Kannada translations of Camus's *The Outsider,* Mulk Raj Anand's *Untouchable,* Voltaire's *Candide,* and Tolstoy's non-fictional prose. He is currently engaged in bringing out a translation of the short stories of U.R. Anantha Murthy.

Kirpal Singh is a senior lecturer in the Department of English Language and Literature at the National University of Singapore. A scholar with committed interest in Commonwealth literature (of India and Australia, primarily), he has published a host of books—among them *Through Different Eyes: Responses to Indian Literature* (Writers Workshop) and *The Writer's Sense of the Past* (Singapore University Press)—articles, and reviews.

Rajini Srikanth received her B.A. in English from Bangalore University, and her Ph.D. in English in 1987 from the State University of New York at Buffalo. Aside from her work on Narayan and William Faulkner, Professor Srikanth has worked as an editor and writing and editing consultant, as well as co-producer of several documentary films.

M. N. Sundararaman is a professor and Head of the Department of English, St. Joseph's College, Tiruchirapalli, Tamil Nadu, South India. He received his M.A. in English Literature from Benares Hindu University, a Post-Graduate Certificate in the Teaching of English from the Central Institute of English and Foreign Languages in Hyderabad, and his Ph.D. (focusing on Indian drama in English) from Madras University. He has also served as Dean of Arts and Humanities and as Chairman of the Board of Studies in English at St. Joseph's College. His publications include *Mosaic,* an anthology of Indian English plays which he edited, and a number of critical articles.

Introduction

Fortunately when he was unable to locate a willing publisher for *Swami and Friends*, the young man whom R. K. Narayan urged to throw the manuscript into the Thames did not heed his friend's advice but sought further among the English for an appreciative eye—and found it with author Graham Greene who, the often recounted tale goes, was so immediately and strongly impressed by the quality of the narrative that he personally saw to its publication. Greene thereafter became an enthusiastic standard-bearer for Narayan's work, claiming at one point that he did not hesitate to name Narayan in the company of such as Leo Tolstoy, Henry James, Ivan Turgenev, Anton Chekhov, and Joseph Conrad (v). Surely Narayan and those of us who have invited into our imaginations the characters, shops, and streets of Malgudi and its environs feel for Greene a very deep debt of gratitude, yet too much can easily be made of Greene's role in Narayan's success. Even if that as-yet unpublished novel of *Swami and Friends* had been chucked into the Thames, we feel certain that the rich horde of ensuing works would still have come into the hands of readers across the globe (and in addition to their availability to readers throughout the English-speaking world, Narayan's work has been translated into a number of other languages) because R. K. Narayan is a natural, a born teller of tales. In fact, the very anecdote of Narayan's early frustration in publishing works well in itself as classic Narayan narrative: a hopeful endeavor deteriorates into an individual crisis, a frustration of the individual will (which now, held against the conclusion, appears more comic than cause for sympathy), and then a series of events unfolds that in the end suggests the reassuringly inevitable.

In any case, following the various publishers' refusals and Graham Greene's personal commitment to Narayan's work, we have seen a long and consistent contribution from Narayan's hand. From the publication of *Swami and Friends* in 1935 to *The World of Nagaraj* in 1990, Narayan has remained primarily committed to exploring and evoking the familiar world in and around the fictional South Indian town of Malgudi. He has revealed that world, chiefly, by focusing on the experiences of individual characters, as the titles of the novels suggest: *The English Teacher, The Financial Expert, The Guide, Mr. Sampath, The Painter of Signs, The Vendor of Sweets, Talkative Man, The World of Nagaraj.* It is the fourteen novels and nine volumes of short stories that are centered almost exclusively in Malgudi with which the majority of Narayan's readers will be most familiar. His recasting of tales from the *Ramayana* and *Mahabharata* add depth and breadth to his writing and underscore the importance to the author (and to his other work) of his native religious and mythic tradition, while his collections of travel essays and his autobiographical material afford the reader some additional insight into this modest writer's sense of self.

The comic touch, the ironic exposure of character's motivations and aspirations, the smoothly concise portrayal of shifts in fortune, the clarity and informal simplicity of style are by now Narayan's trademarks and serve as the basis for much of what has been written about his work over the years. Critical investigations of his fiction have been rather uniformly positive although there have been some notable and interesting points of contention. Primary among these is what might be regarded as the author's "world view" as it is implied by his fiction. The "world view" discussions ordinarily surround the author's "ironic detachment" from his characters and his seemingly cheerful acceptance of people and events as they are.

As early as 1961 William Walsh centered on Narayan's dispassionate recording of life, and saw in this approach a cause not for censure but for praise:

> "Accepting" indeed is the word which best defines his attitude . . . . "Welcome" would be too shrill and hearty, "resignation" too passive and submissive. . . . His acceptance, a kind of piety toward existence, isn't simply an inherited temperament with its corresponding technique of passive reflection. It is something which has to be worked towards, grown up to, gradually matured. Nor is it . . . in any way rapt or mystical. It includes delight in the expressive variety of life, cognisance of its absurdities, mockery at its pretensions, and acknowledgement of its difficulties. (97–98)

Narayan's depiction of people and things as they are, not because the author encourages us to realize rather how they might or should be, but because this is simply how he finds them, is that quality of seeing and offering the particular while implying the general or universal that many readers will confess to be one of Narayan's major points of attraction as a writer.

Narayan's way of seeing has led some, Graham Greene among them, to cite the author's ability to communicate an essence of "what it is like to be Indian" (v). But that way of seeing or depicting, that India that

Narayan conveys, has been pointed to by others as incomplete or misdi-
rected. V. S. Naipaul has remarked that while Narayan's novels had so
well exposed "the lesser life" of the Indian community he knew while
growing up in Trinidad, they

> . . . did not prepare me for the distress of India. As a writer he had
> succeeded almost too well . . . .The small town he had staked out as
> his fictional territory was, I knew, a creation of art and therefore to
> some extent artificial, a simplification of reality. But the reality was
> cruel and overwhelming. In the books his India had seemed accessi-
> ble; in India it remained hidden. . . . I did not lose my admiration for
> Narayan; but I felt that his comedy and irony were part of a Hindu
> response to the world, a response I could no longer share. And it
> has . . . become clear to me . . . that, for all their delight in human
> oddity, Narayan's novels are less the purely social comedies I had
> once taken them to be than religious books, at times religious fables,
> and intensely Hindu. (12–13)

The re-created reality of Narayan's fiction, as Naipaul understands it,
is actually bound to an "inherited temperament" (Walsh's words), an
attitude that recognizes that "every man with ideals, plans, and illusions
is Quixotic and funny, because these plans will come into collision with
the fixed and determined" (Holmstrom, 125).

Whatever the particular sources and nature of his apparent disinterestedness or detachment, Narayan has been a source of frustration for some
who regard his focus on the internal changes of his characters to be out
of keeping with the pressing social concerns of contemporary India. The
point at which tradition meets the pressures of the modern is precisely
the point at which we are to find the greatest division among his critics
over the significance of his contribution. As M. M. Mahood has rightly
observed,

> Narayan's technique as a story-teller is the source of that luminous
> quality which to his cult-followers is so comforting a sign of his
> serene fatalism, and to others so uncomfortably a sign of his social
> unawareness. (94)

The pressures of the modern are not to be strictly associated with
poverty and squalor ("the distress of India"), but also with the post-colonial legacy of the West as it vies for personal and social primacy with the
ancient beliefs, modes of behavior, and family responsibilities that have
gone toward defining Indian culture. Of course, Narayan has never
avoided treating this central aspect of modern Indian life. The intersec-
tion of the British/Western and the Hindu is evident in virtually all of
Narayan's fiction (not least in the act of his writing in English); in

"Malgudi the two worlds are indissolubly linked" but while on the surface it displays evidence of its colonialism—its street plans, its school and colleges, its government, its printing presses, mills, and railways— "on the private level it has remained loyal to the Hindu past, to the traditions that embody the essential genius of India and to which its people return when the world's attractions grow dim" (Woodcock, 16).

Anita Desai notes Narayan's tendency to retreat to "the essential. . . India," and echoes some of Naipaul's observations about the lack of correlation that then necessarily results between the fiction and the immediately tangible surface of much of contemporary Indian life:

> . . . in the 50 years that Narayan has been writing his tranquil fiction, his "rootedness" has become as unique in India as it is in the West, the traditional structure of rural existence that he celebrates having given way and collapsed irrevocably under the manifold pressures of an industrialized, urbanized and above all uncontrollable population. There are many of Narayan's readers who feel that his fiction does not reflect the chaos, the drift, the angst that characterizes a society in transition and that his "rootedness" is a relic of another, pastoral era now shaken and threatened beyond recovery. (3)

But as Desai goes on to establish (in her discussion of *A Tiger for Malgudi*), "Signs of outer development are only reflections of inner evolution . . . hence the superficial impression given of all change being too trivial to be of any note . . ." (3). Desai's assessment reminds us that, again, for Narayan what is of true significance is the response and evolution of the inner self.

Nevertheless, while one may be able to convince himself that a socially concerned Narayan "appears to cry inwardly while he laughs outwardly" at the foibles of various characters (Raizada, 164), to another even Narayan's emphasis on spiritual growth is escapist and essentially unreal:

> Faith in the transcendental, in the mysterious fate or karma and in self-knowledge without cultivating a positive spiritual stance in tackling problems caused in the main by an unjust man-made establishment—is, in a sense, a turning away from life's realities . . . . (Singh, 108)

Clearly, the claim that Narayan's fiction displays a deficient social and/or political concern and ignores some of the most vital realities of his own milieu has enjoyed some currency, yet those who express it typically value his work nonetheless. Narayan has enjoyed unusually strong acclaim—consistently—for decades. And I think that to deplore what his fiction might lack can distract from precisely what it does offer us.

Narayan's artistic commitment to the individual and his experience within the limited, private sphere of family and acquaintances allows us to become engaged in the immediate, contemporary relevance and value of traditionalism. A sense of inevitability permeates the works, yet they never come off as having been designed as vehicles for this purpose. We come to some insight into the fusion, the workings of the whole by observing the struggles, puzzles, and indirections on the level of the particular. George Woodcock has observed that, despite how many readers tend to categorize him,

> Narayan is not primarily a satirist: the comic irony through which he sees his characters suggests no strong desire to change them. Perhaps his Hinduism emerges most strongly in this limitation: the people he describes are what their karmas made them, and in accepting their weaknesses all we hope is that by following out their destinies they may transcend them.(23)

Narayan's work shows us, and the critical assessments remind us, that we should not come to R. K. Narayan in search of a literature that delves into and exposes cultural ailments in topical narratives; rather, we should anticipate light and subtly ironic tales of provincial middle-class individuals who often delight because of their naivete and fallibility and who, despite their local immediacy, remind all readers of our limited capacity for gaining and maintaining control of all that affects us.

The discussions of Narayan's work to be found in this volume add significantly to the bulk of Narayan criticism, the general tenor of which I have sketched in above. This collection is representative of the general field of Narayan criticism in that it provides both positive and negative assessments; but, more importantly, it breaks new ground. Several of the essays offer new readings or encourage re-readings of familiar material. Narayan's *The Painter of Signs* is approached from a feminist perspective in Shantha Krishnaswamy's "Daisy Paints Her Signs Otherwise," in which the author identifies a "tragic negation beneath the surface humor" as the rebellious Daisy finds it impossible to freely realize her feminine nature within the Malgudian context; nevertheless, she "alerts us to far-reaching institutional implications" by perhaps originating for women "a whole process of reassessment." Gita Rajan, in her "Colonial Literature as Oppositional: R. K. Narayan's Unconscious Specular Register," turns Narayan criticism in a new direction also as she approaches *Swami and Friends* from a culture studies perspective, analyzing the contradiction or ambivalence in Narayan's pre-Independence narrative discourse as it both affirms and resists its colonial identification. In her "*The Painter of Signs*: Breaking the Frontier," Sadhana Allison Puranik opens yet another (parallel) path that others may now likely extend as she assesses the implications of colonization/decolonization for Narayan's work, establishing through her analysis of the novel that the genre of the novel itself proves to be "Narayan's frontier between Britain and India, and the writer himself stands out as an example of the Indian paradox he outlines—the condition of simultaneously occupying the margins and the center of Indian life."

These essays chart new directions for Narayan criticism while others are intended to provide more detailed or extended analyses along lines of inquiry previously opened by others; all are valuable for the newer insights or alternative emphases they contribute to the existing discussions. Ganeswar Mishra's "The Novel as Purana: A Study of *The Man-Eater of Malgudi* and *Kanthapura*" and Rosanne Kanhai-Brunton's "Kali as Man-Eater and as Goddess: Myth-Making in R. K. Narayan's *The Man-Eater of Malgudi*" both explore Narayan's incorporation of traditional Indian motifs, Mishra pointing to structural elements of Narayan's narrative that place it clearly within the puranic tradition, Kanhai-Brunton seeing in *Man-Eater* the author's invocation of Kali as "an affirmation of Indian nationalism" and his recognition thereby that the experience of decolonization will necessarily realize its cycle of destruction, creation, and preservation.

Other essays that extend the boundaries of established critical opinion include Mishra's "The Holy Man in R. K. Narayan's Novels," Sr. Mary Beatina Rayen's "*The Guide:* A Study in Transcendence," Suresh Raval's "Irony, Structure, and Storytelling in R. K. Narayan's *The Financial Expert,*" and my "Eternal, Insatiable Appetite: the Irony of R. K. Narayan's Baited Hero."

Gideon Nteere M'Marete surprises us with "Kirshnan's Jasmine-Scented Quest" as he cogently explores the significance of the jasmine motif in *The English Teacher* and argues effectively for the viability of the novel's metaphysical elements; his perspective is original and invites us to revisit the novel with an enhanced awareness. The same is true of Fakrul Alam's "Plot and Character in R. K. Narayan's *The Man-Eater of Malgudi*: A Reassessment."

Two of the essays in the collection point to elements in Narayan's work that they consider to be less than positive. Kirpal Singh recognizes Narayan's technical excellence while he is especially troubled that the author "does not allow the average and the ordinary to transcend their situations," and he claims, further, that Narayan is "incapacitated by his ironic vision to see beyond ridicule and ambiguity"; Singh's position, that Narayan's irony is largely ineffective because it necessarily distances him from the "average" humanity he portrays, stands apart from that prominent strain of Narayan criticism which finds fault with the author for his passive acceptance of whatever life may proffer.

Like Singh, D. A. Shankar ("The Absence of Caste in R. K. Narayan and Its Implications for Indian Writing in English") feels that there is "something missing" from Narayan's fiction that leaves him dissatisfied. That "something" for Shankar is Narayan's failure to depict how sub-caste shapes characters and defines their interactions.

Two of the essays (Pushpa Parekh's "The Dialectics of Opposing Forces in *The World of Nagaraj* and Rajini Srikanth's "*The World of Nagaraj*: Narayan's Metanovel") deal with Narayan's latest novel, two of them recount personal encounters with Narayan (John Lowe's "A Meeting in Malgudi" and Warren French and Javaid Qazi's "Some Notes on 'Reluctant Guru'"), and one alerts us to a rarely recognized side of Narayan, "R. K. Narayan, The Dramatist" (M. N. Sundararaman).

It is especially gratifying that these essays be published by Michigan State University Press since, after having served as the original American publisher of *The Bachelor of Arts, The English Teacher, Mr. Sampath, The Financial Expert,* and *Waiting for the Mahatama,* the Press now re-establishes its commitment to Mr. Narayan. Every essay represented here has been forwarded to me by the authors—both men and women—from various nations. In one response to my call for papers, India's formidable literary scholar and friend of Narayan, C. D. Narasimhaiah, gracefully declined to contribute (citing a host of other concurrent commitments), but added that "I know Mr. Narayan will be pleased to learn of this volume, though he protests at times that he is not interested in what the critics think of his work." While I am aware of Narayan's indifference to academic considerations of his art, I have been conscious to select those critical essays that even Mr. Narayan might find intriguing and illuminating, fair and insightful discussions of his creations. As this collection testifies, Narayan continues to encourage discussion from men and women across national boundaries, and I believe that his work gains in strength through its assessment from such diverse critical perspectives as we encounter here.

Works Cited

Desai, Anita. "R. K. Narayan and the Grand Malgudi Circus." *The Washington Post Book World* (4 September 1983): 3, 9.

Greene, Graham. Introduction to *The Bachelor of Art.*. London: Heinemann, 1978.

Holmstrom, Lakshmi. *The Novels of R. K. Narayan.* Calcutta: Writers Workshop, 1973.

Mahood, M. M. "The Marriage of Krishna: Narayan's *The Man-Eater of Malgudi*." *The Colonial Encounter: A Reading of Six Novels*. London: Collings, 1977, 92–114.

Naipaul, V. S. *India: A Wounded Civilization*. New York: Vintage Books, 1977.

Raizada, Harish. *R. K. Narayan: A Critical Study of His Works*. New Dehli: Young Asia Publications, 1969.

Singh, Satyanarain. "A Note on the World View of R. K. Narayan." *Indian Literature* 24, no.1 (1981): 104–9.

Walsh, William. "The Intricate Alliance: The Novels of R. K. Narayan." *A Review of English Literature* 2, no. 4 (October 1961): 91–99.

Woodcock, George. "Two Great Commonwealth Novelists: R. K. Narayan and V. S. Naipaul." *Sewanee Review* 87 (1979): 1–28.

The Novel as Purana:
A Study of the Form of The Man-Eater of Malgudi and Kanthapura

GANESWAR MISHRA

I

Though the novel as a literary form was borrowed from the West by Indian authors in the mid-nineteenth century, traditional forms of narrative such as the *purana* and the folktale have considerably influenced its growth in India. Critics, both Indian and Western, have generally failed to notice the impact of traditional forms on the Indian novel, and this has led to unfavorable comments both on the Indo-Anglian and the Indian-language novel. Several critics have complained about the aimlessness and lack of organization of the Indian novel. Bhupal Singh, the first Indian critic of Indo-Anglian literature, complained that:

> they [Indo-Anglian novelists] do not seem to realize that prose fiction, in spite of its freedom is subject to definite laws. In plot construction they are weak, and in characterization weaker still. Their leanings towards didacticism and allegory is a further obstacle to their success as novelists. (310)

M.E. Derrett observes:

> Borrowing from the West is more obvious in form . . . than elsewhere. . . .Form, at least initially, must conform to the general current usages in the West if the work is to be read outside India so that a taste for this fiction can be cultivated. Although the majority of these authors have chosen to write in the traditional (i.e. nineteenth century) form of the novel one feels that an apparent formlessness may be more natural to the Indian. (91)

Dorothy M. Spencer thinks that "some considerable degree of reorientation in the Indian world view would have had to precede or accompany the novel in that country" (10).

It is not my intention here to suggest that Indian novelists are masters of the novel form, or that they have already succeeded in blending their indigenous forms of narrative with the Western ones. However, I would emphasize that comments on the form of the Indian novel must take into account the impact of the *purana* and the folktale, and that the Western novel form need not always provide the standard by which an Indian novel is judged.

Several Indian novelists have realized the inadequacy or inappropriateness of the Western novel form for expressing an Indian ethos and sensibility. Novelists like Raja Rao and R.K. Narayan have made attempts to incorporate traditional forms of narrative in their works. It is interesting that Ruth Prawer Jhabvala, though with her Polish and British background she may not be in a position to realize the inappropriateness of the Western novel form to present an Indian reality as much as Rao and Narayan do, is aware that the novel in India, to reflect faithfully an Indian reality, must embody certain Indian characteristics:

> [The Indian novel] would be bits of prose-poetry, anecdotes, lots of philosophizing and musing, an oblique kind of wit, and an ultimate self-surrender, a sinking back into formlessness, into eternity. . . something like Indian music. (Derrett, 94)

Many Indian-language novelists have perhaps made similar attempts, though our information regarding their experiments in the novel form is scanty. Meenakshi Mukherjee has recently suggested that three Bengali novels, Bibhutibhushan Banerji's *Pather Panchali* (1929), Manik Bandopadhyaya's *Putul Nacher Itikatha* (1936), and Tarashankar Banerjee's *Hansuli Banker Upakatha* (1947), which are considered classics in modern Bengali fiction, clearly imply their authors' concern for the form of the novel.[1] In fact, the titles of these novels suggest the novelists' awareness of the traditional forms: Panchali (a traditional devotional song); Upakatha and Itikatha (legends or folktales). Translators of the UNESCO version of *Pather Panchali* have so misunderstood the form of the novel as to delete completely the last of the novel's three sections. The novel, which conforms to a *Panchali* or religious song, corresponds to the mythical journey of Krishna to Brindavan. By failing to recognize this, the translators have distorted the basic theme and form of the novel. (Many translators have taken similar liberty with Indian-language texts.) K.C. Panigrahi's Oriya novel *Matira Manisha* (1931), as rightly pointed out by a reviewer in *Quest*, reads more like a folktale than a novel in the Western sense (Myadas).

The Indo-Anglian novelists' indebtedness to Hindu myths has been suggested by several critics. In her essay "Myth as Technique," Mrs. Mukherjee has analyzed a number of novels by Rao, Narayan, Anand, and Ghose to suggest their mythical structure. The structure of a myth, as that of a folktale, may not be very different from the structure of a *purana*. Narayan's *The Man-Eater of Malgudi*, modeled after the myth of Bhasmasura, is significantly close to the structure of the *purana*. In his article on Narayan, Edwin Gerow aptly suggests the similarities between the story of Shaktideva in *Dashakumarcharita* and *The Man-Eater*: "Point of view aside, the plot structures are fundamentally similar" (9). He even suggests that Narayan is closer to the Indian narrative tradition than Indian-language novelists like Bankim Chandra Chatterjee and Tagore (17). K.S. Ramamurthy presumably having access to Tamil, Narayan's mother tongue, recognizes the similarity in technique between *The Guide* and a Tamil epic, "The narrative technique of *The Guide* reminds us of that employed in the mythical Tamil epic, *Manimekalai*, a technique that takes us backwards and forwards through time" (45).

Even Mulk Raj Anand, who with his Marxist bias often shows religious organizations and custodians of traditional values as corrupt, has modeled the plot structure of his novel *The Old Woman and the Cow* after the myth of the banishment of Sita.

II

I will examine here *The Man-Eater* and *Kanthapura* which retain to a considerable extent the traditional form of the *purana*. Raja Rao himself in his Foreword to *Kanthapura* suggests that he has followed, in his style, the tradition of *sthala-purana* (vii); critics have justifiably emphasized *Kanthapura* as an experiment in the novel form, some even going so far as to suggest that Rao's is the form most suitable for Indian fiction.[2] Rao adopts the puranic form more obviously than Narayan does, following the literary devices of the *purana* such as the invocation to gods and goddesses, the employment of religious images and metaphors, and the retention of the stylistic features of the oral form of storytelling; and *Kanthapura* is perhaps closer to the *purana* than *The Man-Eater*.

But *The Man-Eater* is also an experiment in the puranic rendering of a story of modern India. Though critics like Edwin Gerow and Meenakshi Mukherjee have suggested the mythical structure of the novel, and M.M. Mahood and M.K. Naik have studied it as an allegory, both political and social, they have not emphasized adequately the fact that *The Man-Eater* should be primarily appreciated and understood in the context of the puranic tradition.

Narayan's method of employing the puranic devices in his work is more subtle than Rao's, and Narayan seems to aim at retaining the spirit and essence of the *purana* rather than its extrinsic formal and stylistic features. Narayan does not claim, like Rao, that he is adopting a puranic form or world view; for that matter, no other Indo-Anglian has made such a claim in regard to any of his or her work. But puranic elements are not rare in Narayan's works, or in Indo-Anglian fiction in general. We can study *The Man-Eater* and *Kanthapura* with reference to any of the *puranas* to see where and how the novelists retain the puranic tradition. My purpose here is to analyze both the novels with reference to the *Vishnu Purana*, to show the affinity between the novels and the *purana*, and to suggest how Rao, in *Kanthapura*, follows the puranic tradition more closely than Narayan does in *The Man-Eater*.

Narayan's puranic approach to theme, structure and characterization in *The Man-Eater* is evident from the opening passage of the novel:

> I could have profitably rented out the little room in front of my press on Market Road, with a view of the fountain; it was coveted by every would-be shopkeeper in our town. I was considered a fool for not getting my money's worth out of it, since all the space I needed for my press and its personnel was at the back, beyond the blue curtain. But I could not explain myself to sordid and calculating people. I hung up a framed picture of Goddess Laxmi poised on her lotus, holding aloft the bounties of earth in her four hands, and through her grace I did not do too badly. My son, little Babu, went to Albert Mission School, and he felt quite adequately supplied with toys, books, sweets and any other odds and ends he fancied. My wife, every Deepavali, gave herself a new silk sari glittering with lace, not to mention the ones she bought for no particular reason at other times. She kept the pantry well-stocked and our kitchen fire aglow, continuing the traditions of our ancient home in Kabir Street. (1)

A number of important points may be noted in the passage: the stability and continuity of the Malgudi world and its ancient traditions are emphasized; Lakshmi, the Goddess of Wealth, is referred to; the narrative starts in the first person, and so on. One can see the similarity between the opening passage of a *purana* and that of his novel. The *puranas*, being religious in nature, invariably invoke gods and goddesses in the beginning. The *Vishnu Purana*, for instance, starts with "OM! Glory to Vasudeva-Victory be to thee, . . ." and as H.H. Wilson, whose translation and commentary of the said work is considered authentic, notes, "An address of this kind, to one or other Hindu divinity, usually introduces Sanskrit compositions, especially those considered sacred"

(1). Narayan introduces his narrator, Nataraj, as a worshipper of Lakshmi, the Goddess of Wealth (and the wife of Vishnu), and suggests a puranic beginning. The reference to the framed picture of Goddess Lakshmi is not incidental to the theme of the novel. In fact Nataraj, being a businessman, is a worshiper of Lakshmi (a famous Sanskrit proverb says Lakshmi presides over business) and we may remember that in the opening passage of *The Vendor of Sweets* Narayan introduces Jagan as a worshipper of Lakshmi: "Jagan sat under the framed picture of the goddess Lakshmi hanging on the wall, and offered prayers first thing in the day. . ." (13). The very first sentence of *The Man-Eater*, showing that Nataraj is not very businesslike in not renting out the little room in front of his press, suggests the flaw in his worship of the Goddess of Wealth; and later, when his suffering starts with Vasu's arrival in Malgudi, we can see the Hindu view of *karma* being reflected in the course of the story as Nataraj is punished for this flaw.

Narayan retains the spirit of the puranic device of eulogizing a god or goddess by praising his or her virtues and powers. This is how Vishnu is eulogized in the beginning of the *Vishnu Purana*:

> May that Vishnu, who is the existent, imperishable, Brahma who is Iswara, who is spirit, who with the three qualities is the cause of creation, preservation and destruction; who is the parent of nature, intellect, and other ingredients of the universe; be to us the bestower of understanding, wealth and final emancipation. (2)

And Narayan eulogizes Lakshmi in two ways. First, Nataraj's prosperity is attributed to the kindness of Lakshmi. "Lakshmi poised on her lotus, holding aloft the bounties of each in her four hands" symbolizes the stability and prosperity of the world, the Malgudi world, that is. And Nataraj is sure that he did not do too badly "through her grace." Secondly, "the blue curtain," which is a recurring symbol in the novel, is employed to suggest the ocean, the citadel of Lakshmi. Lakshmi, according to myth, was born out of the ocean when gods and demons churned the ocean by Mount Meru[3] (another name of Lakshmi is Sindhu-suta, the daughter of the ocean). In traditional Hindu paintings, Lakshmi is usually shown against the background of the ocean. The blue curtain that divides the parlor and the press in a way marks the difference between the two worlds: the world of mundane reality, the world of Sens preoccupied with Nehru's foreign policy, the Heidelberg machine, and the endless mad crowd of the Market Road; and the world of peace and wisdom, the world of Nataraj at peace with himself, and Sastri, more interested in sacred Sanskrit texts than in printing K.J.'s labels. When Vasu stirs the curtain and the "unusual thing" happens, it is in a way a violation of the natural order of keeping the two worlds apart. Vasu, by stirring the blue curtain intrudes into the world of Lakshmi and Vishnu; and it is but natural—and again we see *karma* at work—that he be punished by Vishnu, the God with whom rests the preservation of the world order.

If the invocation of Goddess Lakshmi in the opening passage of *The Man-Eater* is suggested rather than overtly stated, in *Kanthapura*, the invocation to the Goddess Kenchamma is clearly made in the manner of the *Vishnu Purana*:

> Kenchamma is our goddess. Great and bounteous is she. She killed a demon ages, ages ago, a demon that had come to demand our young sons as food and our young women as wives, Kenchamma came from the Heavens—it was the sage Tripura who had made penances to bring her down—and she waged such a battle and she fought so many a night that the blood soaked and soaked into the earth, and that is why the Kenchamma Hill is all red. If not, tell me, sister, why should it be red only from the Tippur stream upwards, . . . (2)

The myth of Kenchamma descending down from the heaven in response to the penance of a sage is obviously in the tradition of puranic myths. Several Hindu myths suggest the descending of gods and goddesses, as the result of the penance of sages, to save humanity from demons. The Goddess Durga (or Devi, who is adored in the *Devi Purana*) came down to earth to destroy the demon Mahisha[4] and the Goddess Ganga descended to earth as the result of the penance of Bhagiratha, the noble king (and Ganga is also known as Bhagirathi, after that king).[5] In fact, in most of the *puranas* we can see this conventional pattern of the descent of gods and goddesses as the result of the penance of sages, to save humanity. This puranic motif is very important to a full understanding of *Kanthapura* as well as *The Man-Eater*; and the invocation to Goddess Kenchamma has far greater significance in the novel than simply to give a puranic flavor to the story. But it is necessary to be aware, at this point, of two facts: first, in the *puranas* and myths, gods and goddesses are also shown descending to earth to bestow boons on demons if the demons undergo the necessary penance and suffering. Thus all the powers of the demons are also derived from divine sources. Demons like Mahisha and Ravana derive their great strength and power from Brahma, the Supreme God, though later they are killed by Durga and Rama, incarnations of Devi and Vishnu, who come down to earth. To forget that both the demon and the sage in the *purana* are shown as deriving their power from the same source is to misunderstand the philosophy behind the *puranas*, and to see novels like *Kanthapura* and *The Man-Eater*, which are so immersed in the puranic setting, in the wrong perspective. Secondly, Rao, in *Kanthapura*, combines both the puranic and folktale elements from the other; and Rao in the foreword to his novel talks not of *purana* but of *sthala-purana*. The story of Kenchamma's descent to earth to kill a demon is puranic; but when the narrator connects that story with the color of the Kenchamma hill, the elements of legend and *purana* get blended together as to make the story a *sthala-purana* (*sthala* means local). A *sthala-purana* can be said to be the local version—and therefore a considerably debased form—of a *purana*. The innumerable digressions in the narrative ("If not, tell me, sister, . . . " etc.) are clearly part of oral forms of storytelling, and belong to the folk rather than the puranic tradition. The *puranakara*, in his interpretation, does digress from the main theme, but usually he does so to preach a moral.

In his introduction to *Gods, Demons, and Others*, Narayan writes about the setting of the *purana*:

> Most narratives begin in a poetic setting, generally a cool grove on the banks of a river or forest retreat, in which are assembled sages at the end of a period of fruitful penance. A visitor comes from afar. After honoring the guest, the sages will ask, "Where are you coming from? What was noteworthy at such-and-such a king's sacrifice? Tell us whatever is worth hearing." And the visitor will begin his tale. (7–8)

And thus two important motifs are suggested in the opening of the *purana*: first, the world seems peaceful and tranquil to the sages until the visitor arrives and disturbs that peace by narrating stories of demons and so forth; secondly, the narrative invariably assumes the form of a dialogue. In the opening lines of the *Vishnu Purana*, Maitreya is shown adoring Vishnu and the world seems peaceful and glorious. The narrative begins when the sage Parasara arrives and Maitreya asks metaphysical questions about creation and destruction, good and evil, time and history, gods and others, such as:

> . . .I am now desirous, oh thou who art profound in piety! to hear from thee, how this world was, and how in future it will be? What is its substance, oh Brahman, and whence proceeded animate and inanimate things? Into what has it been resolved, and into what will its dissolution again occur? How were the elements manifested? When proceeded the gods and other beings? . . .What are the families of the gods and others, the Manus, the periods called Manvantaras, those termed Kalpas, and their subdivisions, and the four ages: the events that happen at the close of a Kalpa, and the terminations of the several ages. . .? (3)

Parasara replies:

> . . .I had heard that my father had been devoured by a Rakshasa
> employed by Visvamitra: violent anger seized me, and I commenced
> a sacrifice for the destruction of the Rakshasa: hundreds of them
> were reduced to ashes by the rite, when, as they were about to be
> entirely extirpated, my grandfather Vashishtha, thus spake to me:
> Enough, my child; let thy wrath be appeased: The Rakshasas are not
> culpable: thy father's death was the work of destiny. . . .Every man
> reaps the consequences of his own acts. . . .(4).

The purpose of quoting the above two passages is not only to show how
the narrative, from the beginning, takes the form of dialogue, but also to
suggest the nature of its theme.

The emphasis on the stability and continuity of the ancient traditions—the observance of the Deepavali, for instance—in the opening
passage of *The Man-Eater* is puranic; and we realize the significance of
this emphasis only when we see this stability and ancient traditions
shaken to their roots by the arrival of a traveler from afar, Vasu. Vasu,
the Parasara in the *Vishnu Purana*, is not of course the narrator of the
story; he is the protagonist of the story. But this is not uncommon in the
puranas and epics that the narrator becomes a participant, sometimes a
major participant, in the action of the story. Thus, as we can see in the
brief passage quoted earlier, Parasara narrates the story in which he is
the hero. The classic example is, of course, Valmiki, who is the narrator
of the *Ramayana*, and one of the characters in the narrative. Narayan
retains the puranic tradition by making Vasu, who traveled to Malgudi
from Junagadh, the protagonist of the narrative. Had he made Vasu
rather than Nataraj the narrator of the story, he would not have retained
its puranic nature; for all the *puranas* are narrated by sages who symbolize ancient Hindu wisdom (the term *purana* literally means 'ancient'),
and never by demons. It is, however, possible that a demon is the most
important character in a *purana*, and such a *purana* is called the *Purana* of
Darkness (*Tamasa Purana*).[6] Nataraj, the South Indian Brahmin (like
Narayan himself) owes his ancestry to Hindu sages and it is apt that the
novel to be presented from a puranic standpoint be narrated by him.

Raja Rao, in the opening paragraphs of *Kanthapura*, both invokes
Goddess Kenchamma and emphasizes the stability and ancient tradi-
tions of Kanthapura, much more elaborately than Narayan does in *The
Man-Eater*:

> Our village—I don't think you have ever heard about it—Kantha-
> pura is its name, and it is in the province of Kara. High on the Ghats
> is it, high up the steep mountains that face the cool Arabian seas, up

the Malabar coast is it, up Mangalore and Puttur and many a centre of cardamom and coffee, rice and sugarcane. Roads, narrow, dusty, rut-covered roads, wind through the forest of teak and of jack, of sandal and of sal, and hanging over bellowing gorges and leaping over elephant-haunted valleys, they turn now to the left and now to the right and bring you through the Alambe and Champa and Mena and Kola passes into the great granaries of trade. There, on the blue waters, they say, our carted cardamoms and coffee get onto the ships Red-men bring, and, so they say, they go across the seven oceans into the countries where our rulers live.

Cart after cart groans through the roads of Kanthapura, and on many a night, before the eyes are shut, the last lights we see are those of the train of carts, and the last voice we hear is that of the cartman who signs through the hollows of the night. The carts pass through the main street and through the Potters' lane, and then they turn by Chinnaya's pond, and up they go, up the passes into the morning that will rise over the sea. Sometimes when Rama Chetty or Subba Chetty has merchandise, the carts stop and there are greetings, and in every house we can hear Subba Chetty's 350-rupee bulls ringing their bells as they get under the yoke. "Ho," says Subba Chetty, "ho-ho," and the bulls shiver and start. The slow moving carts begin to grind and to rumble, and then we hear the long harsh monotony of the carts' axles through the darkness. And once they are on the other side of the Tippur hill the noise dies into the night and the soft hiss of the Himavathy rises into the air. Sometimes people say to themselves, the Goddess of the river plays through the night with the Goddess of the hill. Kenchamma is the mother of Himavathy. May the goddess bless us! (1–2)

It is clear that Kanthapura is viewed as a prosperous, peaceful and noble place. The first passage with its minute description of the setting of Kanthapura, in the midst of mountains, the cool Arabian seas, and the tropical forest, reminds us of the forest retreat and the poetic setting invariably described or suggested in the opening of the *puranas*. The second passage describes the wealth and commerce of the villagers, and the Goddess Kenchamma (who, in the past, killed a terrible demon) is in a smiling pose, much like the Goddess of Wealth on the wall of Nataraj's printing press—"poised on her lotus, holding aloft the bounties of earth in her four hands." Though there is a reference to the "Red Man" and the alien rule, and we later see that Gandhi's message which violently disturbs the peace and prosperity of Kanthapura is meant to end this alien rule, no bitterness is implied in the reference to the 'Red Man' in the opening passage. The river is the source of all the wealth and prosperity of Kanthapura; and Kenchamma presides over the moral destiny of

Kanthapura and protects it from evil. The harmony between the Goddess of the River and the Goddess of the hill (that is, Kenchamma) suggests absolute peace, prosperity, and stability.

Rao repeatedly emphasizes the stability and continuity of Kanthapura
traditions by referring to various religious rituals and ceremonies such as
the Sankara-Jayanthi, and so on; and only when Jayaramachar, the
Harikatha man, arrives on the scene and narrates the story of Mohandas,
and is himself arrested by the police, do we realize that the stability of
Kanthapura is at stake (Policeman Bade Khan comes to live in Kanthapura two days after Jayarmachar's arrest). Jayaramachar is closer to the
sage-narrator of the *puranas* than Nataraj or Vasu. Jayarmachar, like
Parasara of the *Vishnu Purana*, is both the narrator and a participant in the
narrative; he is wise and, as his name and occupation suggest, is a Brahmin. (He was to perform the camphor ceremony at the end of the
Harikatha, which, in his absence, was performed by Moothy, another
Brahmin.) Though Rao retains the puranic pattern by suggesting that the
Brahmin-narrator coming from afar (Jayaramachar, apparently, did not
belong to Kanthapura for he was 'invited' to perform the *Harikatha*) disturbs the peace and stability of the village, he deviates from the pattern
in the sense that the narrator is a woman—a Brahmin woman, and not a
peasant woman as some critics mistakenly believe[7]—and as a result, the
narrative tends rather to the form of a folktale.

Both *The Man-Eater* and *Kanthapura* are first person narratives; and
this stylistic device clearly resembles the puranic form of narrative.
About the stylistic devices of the *purana*, H.H. Wilson observes:

> The invariable form of the puranas is that of a dialogue, in which
> some person relates its contents in reply to the inquiries of another.
> This dialogue is interwoven with others, which are repeated as hav-
> ing been held on other occasions between different individuals, in
> consequence of similar questions having been asked. (x)

In narrating the story in the first person, Narayan is closer to the puranic
style than he would have been had he adopted an impersonal narrative
method. As stated earlier, the choice of Nataraj as the narrator rather
than Vasu is significant; and the story is presented through the perspective of puranic world view. The character of Nataraj is roughly that of
the sage-narrator, Parasara, who is undoubtedly a participant in the
action of the story he narrates. Sastri and the Poet may be considered the
two other sage-companions of Nataraj. The dialogue that takes place
between Nataraj and Sastri, like the dialogue between Parasara and
Maitreya in the *Vishnu Purana*, occasionally seems to aim at understanding the metaphysical nature of reality, and makes us feel that the
Nataraj-Vasu conflict is symbolic and significant:

"How can I do any work with a wolf and a whatnot staring at me? And there's a python hanging down the handrail of the stairs."(94)

...Every *rakshasa* gets swollen with his ego. He thinks he is invincible, beyond every law. But sooner or later something or other will destroy him. (96)

Nataraj's innocuous questions, when answered by the learned Sastri in puranic terms, no longer seem so. We identify Vasu with the puranic demon, Bhasmasura; Rangi, the temple prostitute, becomes associated with the Mohini incarnation of Vishnu; Nataraj, Sastri, Sen the journalist, and Kumar can be seen as innocent beings under the oppression of a demon. We do not find any significant difference in the world views of Nataraj and Sastri, and long before Sastri compares Vasu with a *rakshasa*, Nataraj is aware of Vasu's demonic qualities. The Poet is innocent, religious, among Nataraj's "constant companions," preoccupied with writing the life of Lord Krishna in monosyllabic verse; and so belongs to the world of Nataraj and Sastri, the world of sages and Brahmins. Sen the journalist, the forester, Muthu the tea-seller, and Kumar belong neither to the world of Vasus nor of Natarajs; they belong to the mundane world of humanity. They are mostly victimized by the demon, and saved by the god. They are hardly aware of their predicament.

In *Kanthapura*, Rao's method of storytelling is much more puranic than Narayan's in *The Man-Eater*. The old Brahmin woman who narrates the story is shown as a guest in a neighboring village, Kashipura; and she starts narrating the story (in which she herself is a participant), when the women of Kashipura gather around her in the evenings and ask her about Kanthapura and all that happened in that village:

> . . . And Timmamma and I, we live in Jodidar Seetharamiah's house, and they say always, "Are your prayers finished, aunt? Are your ablutions finished, aunt?" before every meal. "Aunt, aunt, aunt," they always call us for this and that, and the children say, "The Mahatma has sent us his relations. There is the aunt who tells such nice stories," and that is me, "and the aunt of the pancakes," and that's Timmamma, and they all laugh.
>
> In the afternoons we all gather on the veranda pressing cotton wicks and hearing the Upanishads. . . . They say Rangamma is to be released soon. And maybe my poor Seenu too, though they have sent him to a northern jail. . . .(179–80)

Both the narrator-audience situation and the atmosphere in which the story is related are puranic. The narrator is a traveler from Kanthapura to Kashipura, and is treated hospitably in Kashipura. She starts her narrative when Kashipura women show interest as to what happened in

Kanthapura, and the narrator starts: "Our village—I don't think you have
ever heard about it—Kanthapura is its name. . . ."(1). The last chapter in
Rao's novel, when the narrator is shown as a guest among Kashipura
women and is asked questions is parallel to the opening passage of a
purana when sages (or a sage, as a Maitreya in the *Vishnu Purana*) ask the
traveler about good and evil, etc. Rao starts the novel where the sage-
narrator of a *purana* would start narrating the story in reply to the questions asked by the host-sage or sages. Thus, the puranic method of
narrating the story in the form of a dialogue is retained in *Kanthapura*
with considerable skill.

The atmosphere no less than the situation is puranic. We may compare R.K. Narayan's description of the atmosphere in which a *purana* is
read out in a village, with that in which Rao's narrator starts her story:

> All day the men and women are active in the fields,. . . .At seven
> o'clock (or in the afternoon if a man-eater is reported to be about)
> everyone is home.

> Looking at them from outside, one may think that they lack the
> amenities of modern life; but actually they have no sense of missing
> much; on the contrary, they give an impression of living in a state of
> secret enchantment. The source of enchantment is the storyteller in
> their midst, a grand old man who seldom stirs from his ancestral
> home on the edge of the village, the orbit of his movements being
> the vegetable patch at the back and a few coconut palms in his front
> yard, except on some very special occasion calling for his priestly
> services in a village home. Sitting bolt upright, cross-legged on the
> cool clay-washed floor of his house, he may be seen any afternoon
> poring over a ponderous volume in the Sanskrit language mounted
> on a wooden reading stand, or tilting towards the sunlight at the
> doorway some old palm-leaf manuscript. When people want a
> story, at the end of their day's labours in the fields, they silently
> assemble in front of his home, especially on evenings when the
> moon shines through the coconut palms.

> On such occasions the storyteller will dress himself for the part by
> smearing sacred ash on his forehead and wrapping himself in a green
> shawl, while his helpers set up a framed picture of some god on a
> pedestal in the veranda, decorate it with jasmine garlands, and light
> incense to it. After these preparations, when the storyteller enters to
> seat himself in front of the lamps, he looks imperious and in com-
> plete control of the situation. He begins the session with a prayer,
> prolonging it until the others join and the valleys echo with the
> chants,. . . .(1–2)

Both Narayan's Pandit (the reader of the *purana*, literally meaning "wise") and Rao's narrator find themselves and their audience in the same sort of atmosphere. The time is evening; the villagers, after their day's work, gather to listen to the story; and the villagers look to the storyteller with a sense both of affection and religious reverence. Narayan's Pandit is a "grand old man," a Sanskrit scholar, the "source of secret enchantment" to the villagers and is "in complete control of the situation" in the midst of his audience. He is immensely religious and starts his puranic reading only after elaborate prayers are offered to the gods. Rao's narrator, similarly, is an old Brahmin woman (of the "*Veda Sastra Pravina* Krishna Sastri's family"); she is referred to as 'aunt' by the villagers and is reverentially asked if her 'prayers' and 'ablutions' are finished; and she narrates the story only after the *Upanishads* are recited. The time, of course, is in the evening, when Kashipura women, after their day's work, gather around her.

We can further extend the puranic parallelism in *Kanthapura* by dividing the characters into two groups: the narrator and her audience, on the one hand, and the participants in the freedom struggle, on the other. The first group of characters to some extent resembles the sages of the *purana* who gather in the forest retreat and discuss gods, demons, and the nature of their conflict. It is interesting that before the narrator in *Kanthapura* starts her story, the *Upanishads* are read out. The *Upanishads* (literally meaning "sitting down opposite") are a series of dialogues among sages, and sometimes women participate in such dialogues. The narrator-audience situation in *Kanthapura* is, in some ways, Upanishadic. The second group of characters considerably resembles the gods and demons of the *purana*. The conflict between the opposite forces—between Moorthy and Bade Khan, Moorthy and his mother, Gandhi and Sadhu Narayan, the Skeffington Coffee Estate sahib and the Brahmin Seetharam—is suggested throughout the novel with complexity and ambivalence, as is the conflict between the gods and demons in the *purana*. The two groups of characters, "the sages" and "gods and demons," however, are not mutually exclusive.

While I would emphasize the puranic situation and atmosphere in *Kanthapura*, it is also important to suggest where and how Rao deviates from the puranic norm. As stated earlier, Rao intends to write a *sthala-purana* rather than a *purana* in *Kanthapura*, and the puranic and the folktale elements are skillfully inter-blended throughout the novel. Comparison of the situation and atmosphere in which Narayan's Pandit narrates his *purana*, with the situation and atmosphere in which Rao's narrator tells her story, can give us a clue to understanding the difference between the two important literary forms, the *purana* and the folktale. The most important difference in the situations of the two narrators is that the Pandit reads out a written or printed text, while the old woman tells us the story from memory. Though the Pandit does interpret the story in his language and sometimes makes topical reference and entertains his audience ("The films have taken away all the fiddlers and crooners, who have no time nowadays to stand at the back of an old storyteller," the Pandit often comments), generally he has to follow the text and cannot take too much liberty with it. On the other hand, Rao's narrator, because she is narrating the story from memory, is free to make as many digressions, repetitions and distortions as she likes. Thus, though conforming generally to the puranic pattern, Rao liberally introduces elements of oral storytelling in *Kanthapura*. We may also notice that the reading of the *purana* by the Pandit is purely a ritual (he smears sacred ash on his forehead), whereas the old woman-narrator, though she starts with prayers, views the storytelling act as outside the religious duty, and starts her story after the "prayers" and "ablutions" are finished; the Pandit is a Sanskrit scholar, and the old woman, though she belongs to a family of Sanskrit scholars ("*Veda Sastra Pravina*" means "expert in the *Vedas*"), is not a scholar herself; and the audience of the old woman consists only of women, whereas that of the Pandit consists of men and women or, presumably, of men only. All these factors must help determine the form and content of the narratives. *Kanthapura*, though generally puranic, does deviate from the puranic norm in being less religious, less scholarly, more intimate and informal—sometimes not different from feminine gossip—and thus, considerably resembling the folktale.

Notes

1. *Pather Panchali* and *Putul Nacher Itikatha* have already been translated into English, under the sponsorship of UNESCO; *Hansuli Banker Upakatha* has been approved for translation by UNESCO, but not yet translated.

2. "Indian fiction in English can, it seems to me," writes C.D. Narasimhaiah, "make headway by continuing the Raja Rao line. . . ." (294).

3. The churning of the ocean is the Hindu myth of creation. Lakshmi was born when the gods and demons churned the ocean to get nectar. (See *Hindu Myths*, Penguin 1975), 273–78.

4. See "Devi," *Gods, Demons, and Others* (New York, 1964).

5. See Heinrich Zimmer's *Myths and Symbols in Indian Art and Civilization* (New York, 1962), 110–14.

6. Traditionally, the *puranas* are classified according to the predominance of one of these qualities: *satva* (purity), *raja* (passion), and *tamasa* (darkness). See The *Vishnu Purana*, xii.

7. Among others, C.D. Narasimhaiah mistakes the village woman-narrator for a peasant woman. "Here is a distinctive Indian sensibility, a peasant sensibility, to be precise,. . .", he says (290). The caste of the narrator is not a minor fact in the novel, as it might appear to some. The puranic nature of the novel derives largely from the fact that the novel is presented through the perspective of a Brahmin widow, a member of the *"Veda Sastra Pravina* Krishna Sastri's family"* (Rao, 5). Markandaya's *Nectar in a Sieve*, on the other hand, is a novel in which the story is narrated by a peasant woman, and there is almost no element of *purana* in it. It is not difficult to see that the religious world view of Rao's narrator is hardly shared by Markandaya's narrator.

Works Cited

Derrett, M.E. *The Modern Indian Novel in English*. Brussels: University Libre, 1966.

Gerow, Edwin. "The Quintessential Narayan." *Literature East and West* 10, no. 1–2 (1966), 1–18.

Mahood, M.M. *The Colonial Encounter: A Reading of Six Novels*. London: Collings, 1977.

Mukherjee, Meenakshi. *The Twice-Born Fiction: Themes and Techniques of the Indian Novel in English*. New Delhi: Heinemann, 1971.

Myadas, Loony. "Review of *A House Undivided*." *Quest* 85 (Nov.-Dec. 1973), 91.

Naik, M.K. "Theme and form in R.K. Narayan's *The Man-Eater of Malgudi*." *Journal of Commonwealth Literature* 10, no. 3 (April 1976): 65–72.

Narasimhaiah, C.D. *Critical Essays*. 1968. Dharwar: South Asia Books, 1977.

Narayan, R.K. *Gods, Demons, and Others*. New York: Viking Press, 1964.

_____. *The Man-Eater of Malgudi*. New York: Viking Press, 1961.

Ramamurthy, K.S. "The Puranic Tradition and Modern Indo-Anglican Fiction." *Indian Writing Today* 11 (Jan.-March 1970), 42–46.

Rao, Raja. *Kanthapura*. New York: New Directions, 1967.

Singh, Bhupal. *A Survey of Anglo-Indian Fiction*. London: Heinemann, 1974.

Spencer, Dorothy M. *Indian Fiction in English*. Westport, Conn.: Greenwood Press, 1960.

The Vishnu Purana. Transl. H.H. Wilson. Calcutta: Punthi Pastak.

Colonial Literature as Oppositional: R. K. Narayan's Unconscious Specular Register

GITA RAJAN

To write a critical essay on R.K. Narayan's work for a collection of Narayan criticism raises important questions behind the ideology of such an endeavor. Is one to assume that such a critical evaluation would be aimed at making R.K. Narayan more readable?[1] This would allow the reader to assume a critical position vis-a-vis the project and create a series of "explications" for a collection of R.K. Narayan's works. Or one could assume a "culture studies" stance, and read R.K. Narayan as a storyteller who narrates his own position as other to a central, Imperial culture in his works. I opt for the second position as reader, i.e., I will read R.K. Narayan's *Swami and Friends*[2] as a cultural artifact and, thus, reveal the semiosis[3] behind his text. This means that I will show how meaning is created in Narayan's text through his careful structuring of language, historical events and cultural contexts. More importantly, the meaning posited through such an analysis will unmask the unstable ideological position of the author in circulating such a text in society.

To engage in such an analysis, I will situate Narayan inside his text; i.e., show that his writing in English, albeit Indian English, is a political move that places him in opposition to the British writers writing in English. Even though his works may follow traditional, thematic patterns, he contextualizes his narrative incidents differently. Consequently, his narrative signals create definite historical implications. For example, *Swami*, written in 1935, just thirteen years before India gained independence, must be read vis-a-vis this struggle. It is necessary to emphasize this historical fact because the Indian freedom struggle was gaining momentum at this point—political demonstrations, both actual and intellectual, were the norm rather than the anomaly. Through this historicizing of the text—framing the text within the Indian political scene—I will show how Narayan's oppositional stance (desire to be accepted into the canonical traditional) and his patriotic fervor (desire to reject the creators of the canon) evokes a certain "ambivalence" in the text. This, in turn, signals an unconscious specular register. By this I mean that Narayan's text mirrors his hopes and fears about a free India. Homi K. Bhabha in *Nation and Narration* examines the effect of patriotism or "nationness" on narrative discourse in colonial literatures, and points out that the kind of cultural ambivalence, as will be seen in Narayan, is produced because authors are straddling a "transitional history,. . .[and hence] waver between vocabularies" (2).[4] The issue of transition is important because around the time *Swami* was written, even though India was a British colony, the effort to break away from foreign domination was becoming a viable option.

Theoretical Outline

To read colonial literature as oppositional to Imperial literary traditions simultaneously validates the authority of the political oppressor as central, and acknowledges colonial discourse as always marginal, robbed of its souffle at the very moment of its inception. R.K. Narayan's *Swami* becomes the site for locating the cultural traditions of colonial India as a socially marketable product, markedly, the Indian struggle for independence; in this position the text is patriotic. Yet, it also reveals a certain admiration for replications of Imperial power structures; in this it is anti-patriotic. In my reading then, *Swami* is constituted ideologically and historically, through this contradiction. While critics see Narayan exhibiting an elite Brahmin sensibility, quite different from other Indian writers of his cultural milieu, I posit that it is more than that—it is an unconscious rewriting of British authority. By domesticating (foreign) authority in this fashion, i.e., unconsciously validating British power structures, Narayan mirrors the tyranny of a colonized India. His text, at one level, forbids debate and denatures a potentially political situation. Gayatri Chakravorty Spivak suggests in "Can the Subaltern Speak?"[5] that the colonized subject (woman), is unable to speak because she lacks agency. More importantly, Spivak shows how the oppressed person is a ventriloquist's dummy—capable only of voicing the master's desires. However, using Spivak's idea of the "subaltern" in conjunction with Homi Bhabha's hypothesis of "ambivalence" grants colonial discourse a degree of latitude and fluidity in analysis. Such a critical move would allow the text and its interpretation to be situated on the very cusp of the opposition between Imperial (central) and colonial (marginal) space. Bhabha addresses this opposition in his comment that "the boundary is Janus-faced and the problem of outside/inside must always itself be a process of hybridity, . . .generating other sites of meaning, and, inevitably, in the political process, producing unmanned sites of political antagonism and unpredictable forces for political representation" (4). My argument, accordingly, will also be "Janus-faced," looking at points in Narayan's text that reveal an allegiance to Imperial authority (inside), and insurgence against this oppression (outside) in *Swami*, and see how the subaltern subject situates himself.

Allegiance

Swami is a Dickensian story about a boy growing up in Malgudi, a village in South India, in 1935. Historically this was a time of insurgence in India, yet the story is untouched by the general political mood of the country.[6] In fact, it was a tumultuous time in the Indian nationalist movement, but the work is impervious to the political climate. The text seems more emphatic about tracing Swami's infantile trajectory as he moves from elementary to high school. Swami, the textual subject, is polarized in this opposition, torn between admiration for representatives of "colonial power" and disdain for abject "victims" of this power. For example, he has a strange respect for his father, a symbol of patriarchal power who, incidentally, as court attorney, also stands in for (Imperial) judicial power. He idolizes Rajam, the Police Superintendent's son, because the Superintendent symbolizes direct, Imperial state power. And Swami is in awe of Mani, the village bully who attempts to arrogate local power in every situation, so that he symbolizes brute, oedipal power. He chides himself continually for not being more like these figures, thus revealing his desire to share in the structures of domination. In contrast, he is insolent with his "granny" and his mother because they are submissive. As Brahmin women, they are subjugated by cultural/gender conditions. He is also deliberately rude to the servants in the house who are necessarily subjugated by socio-economic conditions. His attitude toward the second group—members of his household (in itself an ironic metaphor of inferiority)—reveals Swami's contempt for people who do not fight columns of oppression. Lest the reader impute a cowardly exercise of power in Swami's interaction with his "granny" or his mother, the text incorporates incidents where Swami asks these women to "stand up" for their rights against his father. (Surprising and short though these moments are, they reveal the insurgent potential of the overall text.) And because they fail to do so, he shows his disdain through his insolence toward them. Swami's relationship to the various characters in the text can be read either through his admiration or contempt for them. This shows how clearly he is conscious of the master-slave dialectic, both in himself and in society, and allows himself to be analyzed as a "subaltern."[7]

The "subaltern," loosely defined for the purposes of this argument, is a person who is appointed by the ruling class to act as a liaison between their power and the ruled class. It is important to point out that the "subaltern" would have the responsibility of carrying out the dictates of the ruling class without the privilege of mandating decisions independently. The ruling class, in this instance, would include the British potentate or their substitutes like Swami's father or Rajam's father. When these figures, either directly or indirectly, grant Swami certain powers to act on their behalf, Swami turns into a "subaltern" character.

From a cultural/political perspective, Swami, as a Brahmin boy, has the same authority over the women and servants in the household as his father, albeit in his father's absence. Similarly, from a socio-political perspective, Swami, as Rajam's friend (who borrows his father's authority), acts as a policing agent in controlling his classmates against their nationalistic ideas and actions. Swami is not coerced in either perspective; he seems very eager to please. But, the other side of the Janus-faced reading shows that the ruled class in the text would, again, include Swami himself, his granny, his mother, and the servants. Swami joins the ranks of the "ruled" because he seems to obey his father or Rajam throughout the work, he has no independent identity. Once more, we see the master-slave dialectic and Swami's bi-level stance as both subaltern (empowered) and not-subaltern (disempowered).

But the very invocation of the term "subaltern" must be accompanied by Spivak's warning that "the subaltern must be seen only as a vehicle of greater meaning" (Spivak, 244). In order to contextualize the "subaltern" and get "greater meaning," Narayan's *Swami* must also be read as a signification of the Indian struggle for independence. Just as Swami struggles to overcome hurdles in life and to be recognized as an independent identity, so too India is fighting to free herself from Imperial power. But, to read *Swami* as a mere metaphoric signification of nationalism with emancipatory implications would be trivializing the epistemology or method of knowing behind Narayan's discourse. Ironically, this line of reasoning, i.e., reading *Swami* as basically a liberatory text, is awkward. Because, when one looks at the base to trace the epistemology of the narrative, Narayan's text contradicts such a political assault, and becomes an expression of Imperial hegemony.

The above statement presupposes that I appropriate the position of the subject reading Swami as object, and I must clarify not only his investment in furthering a master-slave dialectic, but I must also expose the underlying ideology of Narayan's position.[8] Ideology is a problematic term to use but Pierre Macherey gives an appropriate definition that will serve our purposes. He writes:

> What is important in a work is what it does not say—that is not the same as the careless notation "what it refuses to say" although that would in itself be interesting; a method might be built on it with the task of measuring silences whether acknowledged or unacknowledged. But, . . .what the work cannot say is important, because there the elaboration of the utterance is carried out, in a sort of a journey of silence. (87)[9]

From a deconstructive stance, what Narayan and his subaltern subject Swami "do not" and "cannot say" is important. By highlighting both negative gestures concurrently, one can see that what Narayan does say gets muffled in the text. Because Swami constantly validates Imperial power, he refuses to articulate the Indian independence struggle and the unspoken rings louder than his words. Some critics, in amplifying the muffled message, erase the tracings of *Swami's* obvious endorsement of British authority. While it is plausible to suggest a postcolonial nostalgia in reading Narayan's work, and posit that his lack of political commitment indicates the nascent immaturity of the independence struggle itself, the text signals otherwise. I propose that Swami's denial of a space from which to articulate this revolution is symptomatic of his unconscious desire to replicate the very power that he thinks he wants to overthrow. In reading the semiotics behind the social, cultural context, Narayan's lack of utterance signals his inability to act against Imperial authority. This is the Janus-faced discourse that Bhabha sees inherent in the articulation of a colonial consciousness that is faced with a history in transition. Because of India's turbulent state of insurgence, Narayan's text attempts to overtly deny this "political antagonism" (Bhabha, 4) in its narrativity. But a cultural critique can point out that Narayan envisions his text between two registers: the colonial and the Imperial. The first register is the absolute, primal State of a free India; and the second is also the absolute, but corrupt, State of a British India.

Narayan's "ambivalence" and his gesture of acquiescence to Imperial power can be proven with three clear examples from the text. I choose these examples from innumerable others in the text with the intention of signaling the historico-cultural ambiance of the work. The first example of such behavior is seen during a small demonstration against the British in Swami's village school, where his intentions for getting involved are highly questionable. Even though the school building can be read as a metaphor for the intrusive British influence, Narayan aborts its significance. Swami, swayed by the violent mob, is spurred on to break the glass panes in the school building not in anger born out of patriotism, but because the incident will give the children a holiday from the drudgery of class work. Rajam's father, the Police Superintendent, gives orders to crush the demonstration—which usually means beating the Indians into submission. Swami flees the scene lest he be recognized as a demonstrator by the police, especially Rajam. Instead of feeling enraged at Rajam's father's unpatriotic stance, he is embarrassed and apologizes to Rajam for "his own nationalistic outburst" (38). If *Swami* is to be seen as a metaphor for the country struggling for freedom, Narayan equivocates, on a crucial issue, the central character's conscious will to fight. Not only does Swami deflect the villagers' insurgence to reflect his own boyish prank, he categorically denies political opposition to a representative of Imperial authority.

In another instance, Swami rebels against the headmaster of his high school, a substitutive symbol of authority, and rushes off to the forest. The text narrates Swami's terror and misery in being lost in the forest for three horrifying days and night. The imagery is fantastic with traditional, literary evocations of mazes, mysteriously frightening shapes in the dark, and intense moments of self doubt/worth. It is a literary trope that Narayan uses from the canonical storehouse to suggest a rite of passage, and again he systematically aborts Swami's initiation. The scene ends with a teary-eyed Swami being rescued and taken to "the father and not father person of the District Forest Officer" (104). If indeed Narayan is signaling India through Swami, and is narrating the independence struggle—a fight against British authority—he bankrupts the attempt by allowing Swami to be lost in the forest. The semantics behind the emphasis on the "father-person" mentioned thrice in the span of two pages shows that Narayan is conscious of the oedipal power structures in checking rebellion. The scene ends with Swami returning eagerly to the safe-haven of "the father person" and erasing the earlier, textual reference to "not father person." What is even more ironic in the concluding scene in this sequence is that the Police Superintendent (Rajam's father) is the "authority" who is called in to identify Swami as a constituent of his village, and is repeatedly invoked as the benevolent savior (109). The suggestion that Swami (and, by extension India) is incapable of traversing a new destiny as independent agent, and therefore must be rescued by Imperial authority (who is simultaneously father/not father and strict but fair), is resoundingly clear. The "not" preceding the "father-person," evokes at one level, at least, the foreignness of the District Officer in Swami's life. Yet, that very foreignness is denatured when the Superintendent brings the errant boy back into the village fold. And Swami abandons his hopes and fears quite willingly to merge into this dubious oedipal/imperial figure. Not only is Swami's gesture of defiance aborted, he is taken home by his father and Rajam's father who conflate/strengthen the original oppressive power configurations.

The last example of Swami's allegiance to Imperial authority is his frantic effort to win the respect of the Anglicized Rajam. Rajam's household is not the typical Brahmin home—the text describes how Rajam dressed differently, used tableware, and had a retinue of servants in the way that the English (*sahibs* and *memsahibs*) did in India. Rajam's aesthetic sensibilities were definitely Anglicized. Swami consciously tries to emulate Rajam's ways, even to the point of ordering his "granny" and servants to "behave" when Rajam visits him (52). One afternoon, Swami invites Rajam to high-tea, has the servants prepare elaborate snacks, and waits anxiously, but Rajam forgets to come. Swami transfers this disappointment onto the members of his household by lashing out at them. The desire to please, even appease Rajam, is an undercurrent throughout the narrative—it is also a desire that remains unfulfilled. The story closes on the same note with a distraught Swami running down the railway platform clutching a copy of "Anderson's *Fairy Tales*" (181) desperately trying to say goodbye to Rajam who is leaving town. Rajam remains stoically unmoved through this drama of emotion and almost becomes a caricature of the "stiff upper lip" Imperialist imagery. In contrast, Swami remains completely native, poignantly attempting to engender Rajam's love and respect. This is one more gesture of wish fulfillment on Swami's part. The contrast between the two boys—one Anglicized and the other Indian—is striking and pathetic. It is tempting to read Rajam's exit as a signification of Imperial evacuation. Sadly, Swami remains loyal to the Raj, even though the Raj leaves him behind. One wonders if this is a warning against the 1935 bravado, of calls by the Indians to revolt against British occupation. With the incremental, pro-British, narrative connotations structured thus far in the text, is it possible to suggest that Narayan is indeed attempting a stern critique of the "Quit India" slogan? After all, this cry was resonating throughout the country at the time. Since *Swami* closes with this haunting image, the question becomes more than rhetorical and the historical significance of the incidence transcends the actual boundaries of the text.

Insurgence

Yet, it is a gross injustice to deny Narayan a patriotic voice when he is one of the few Indian writers expressing a public opinion in the politically volatile climate of pre-independence India. By circulating his text at

this historical time Narayan is taking a risk. The very fact that he can fic-
tionalize the independence struggle is itself a mark of insurgence, and his
attempt to raise political awareness. His literary text which makes a
virtue of submission, ironically calls attention to British oppression.
Through careful self-reflexiveness, Narayan highlights the conflicting
registers of such a dilemma in his text. His "ambivalence" itself becomes
a trope of unimaginable, illegitimate display of authority, and serves as
his patriotic gesture. As Macherey has show in other contexts, Narayan's
insurgence is articulated through "what he does not say" (Macherey, 87).
While the commentary on the three examples presented above suggest
that Swami is unwilling to take a patriotic stand, the meta-commentary
shows that the text must not be taken at face value. I will attempt, again
by using three examples, to show the text reveals insurgence, and my
argument too will be Janus-faced, much like Narayan's text.

The first example is at the very beginning of the narrative, where
Ebenezar, the "scripture master" in Swami's school, gets carried away by
his missionary zeal and beats him for being impertinent. Swami's father,
upon hearing of the incident, writes a stiff note to the headmaster: "the
one conclusion that I can come to is that you do not want non-Christian
boys in your school. If that is so, you may kindly inform us as we are
quite willing to withdraw our boys and send them elsewhere" (5).
Though this is a very brief intrusion, and gets obliterated in the vast
detail of Swami's general apathy towards schooling, it is nonetheless
important. As is well known, the desire to educate and reform the bar-
baric Indians was a primary agenda behind colonization, and perhaps its
most effective tool. Missionary schools could shape the minds of the
young Indians along Anglicized, Christian lines, such that India's cultural
and religious history could be rewritten. And Swami's father's brief
recognition of this evil is worth noting. The second example is a faint
glimmer of patriotic rebellion on Swami's part. While studying for his
final exams, he "opened the political map of Europe and sat gazing at it".
He wonders how "those map-makers find out what the shape of the
country was?" (55). Narayan raises this very significant question of
appropriating land and using cartography—a scientific measure of
land—which also gives a *reasonable* explanation of colonization, to hint
at the insidious power behind Imperial practices. But, as with the first
example, this too is only a suggestion of interrogation—it is not a full-
fledged inquiry into Imperial hegemony.

The last example that I use is, perhaps, the most blatant of Narayan's
insurgent gestures. Swami accidentally attends an anti-British rally, where
the speaker attacks oppressive, Imperial trade/economic policies. In the
general cry of "burn Lancashire and Manchester cloth, as the owners of

those mills had cut off the thumbs of the weavers of Dacca muslin, for which India was famous" (96), Swami feels impelled to take a stand, impelled to act. Boyish and rowdy though Swami is, he throws his cap into the "bonfire of foreign cloth" as part of the anti-British demonstration. Immediately, of course, he is contrite because he has to explain this wasteful and excessive behavior to his father, but for one brief moment, Swami joins the core of patriots struggling to free India. It is intriguing to read the semiosis behind Narayan's narrative scheme, because it seems to suggest that he is using Swami as an agent, albeit a naive agent, of India's desire to be free. While the above examples show a certain will to fight, more emphatically they reveal Swami's perplexity in analyzing very powerful colonizing practices, i.e., education, land appropriation, and economic sanctions. Indeed, the text must be now seen as an ironic gesture of defiance.

It is here that we must re-examine Spivak's position regarding the "subaltern subject" and incorporate Bhabha's concept of "ambivalence" in colonial discourse. Spivak in her "Subaltern" essay explains a certain "contradiction" in the subaltern subject that allows for the kind of doubleness that we have seen in Swami. Spivak, theorizing from a deconstructive/Marxist position,[10] says that the very formation of the subject in society is fractured or fissured. The importance of Spivak's observation is that this contradiction is not meant to be resolved, but is actually present as class representation at any given moment. There is a suggestion in Spivak's argument that the subject is not capable of active agency. While Bhabha makes a similar point about the indeterminacy of the subject's agency in colonial discourse, he has a different reading of the situation. Bhabha emphasizes the destabilizing effect of history which "produces unpredictable sites of meaning [and] political representation" (Bhabha, 4). Spivak, on the other hand, emphasizes the debilitating effect of ideology on the subject.

By reading the difference in these two theorists' positions at one glance, one can see a new critical perspective. Spivak's subaltern reading makes it impossible for Swami to act, but Bhabha's reading makes it impossible for Swami to act consistently. This means that Swami's intentions are not always governed by his will to act, but by his indecisiveness to move between overt and covert discourse practices. In our context, Swami as subaltern, is a contradictory subject, and this irresolvable factor is not a fluctuation at the moment of crisis, but is a legacy of his social position at a particular point in history. Thus, Swami is situated simultaneously on both sides of the ideological boundary: capable of understanding the emancipatory possibilities of a public utterance, but also governed by the need to police this very utterance to neutralize it.

Swami thus, by refusing to vocalize the independence metaphor, calls attention to it through his contradictory subject position. The subaltern manages to articulate the horrors of Imperial hegemony precisely because he cannot speak about it. By re-reading Swami through the colonial registers of subject "contradiction," or discourse "ambivalence," one can trace the ontology of Narayan's desire to write a "revolutionary" narrative.[11] Thus, while the first reading of *Swami and Friends* moved away from the obvious explanation of patriotism to reveal the duplicitous encoding of hegemony, the second reading reverses the trajectory to argue for a high sense of subject awareness. This becomes Narayan's plea for independence for India.[12]

Notes

1. Roland Barthes proposes in *S/Z*, a theory of reading literature that is based on two modes: the "readerly" and the "writerly." He explains that "readerly" can be seen as a category of "classical" texts that have created a place for themselves, both in the culture and ideology (or value structure) of a civilization. The "writerly" he uses to describe the more "modern" texts that are purely experimental in nature. He goes on to clarify that there are, as yet, no "writerly" texts in literature—there is no written language that does not succumb to ideology, or genre, or criticism—which mean one thing rather than another. In other words, texts can be classified according to their level of readerliness. Criticism finds its proper place between these two extremes, in the range of "the more or less parsimonious" making "plural meanings:" its job is the "differentiation" of the mass of meaning thus engendered (*S/Z*, 5). The critical task, then, is to make works "readable," and demand a debate about the meaning behind the words and the intention of the author in circulating such a text in society. For more on this, see Roland Barthes *S/Z*, trans. Richard Miller (New York: Hill and Wang, 1974).

2. R.K. Narayan, *Swami and Friends* (Chicago: University of Chicago Press, 1944). All further references to the work will be made parenthetically in the body of the essay.

3. Semiosis is a practice by which the critic reveals how the words come to mean what they do. All language is a sign system, and writers make use of different signs to articulate their ideas. What is interesting about semiotics is that it allows the critic to go beyond the surface meaning, examine what images and contexts the writer uses to suggest his intended meaning and, thus, reveal the ideological position of the writer. My reading of Narayan's text draws from deconstructive, Marxist, and semiotic schools of thought to suggest radical interpretations of cultural dynamics that operate in the work.

4. Homi K. Bhabha, ed., *Nation and Narration* (London and New York: Routledge, 1990), 2. Bhabha in his introduction to the book makes the point about "ambivalence" in most authors' intention in colonial literature a factor of the transitory history of their native country. This means that even though colonial authors may consciously aim at patriotic discourse, sometimes they are

incapable of it. However, Bhabha does not use Narayan as an example. Bhabha addresses the "ambivalence" issue in two other articles, namely, "Of Mimicry and Man: The Ambivalence of Colonial Discourse" in *October* 28 (1984): 125–33, and "Sly Civility" in *October* 35 (1985): 71–80.

5. See Gayatri Chakravorty Spivak's "Can the Subaltern Speak? in *Marxism and the Interpretation of Culture*, eds. Cary Nelson and Lawrence Grossberg, (Urbana and Chicago: University of Illinois Press, 1988), 271–313. See also Jenny Sharp's "Figures of Colonial Discourse" in *Modern Fiction Stds.* 35, no. 1 (Spring 1989): 137–55, for a clear summary of Spivak's arguments. Benita Parry's "Problems in Current Theories of Colonial Discourse" in *Oxford Lit. Rev.* 9, no. 1–2 (1987): 27–58 also provides a useful discussion on this topic.

6. I raise this point about overt patriotic writing because two other, prolific South Indian artists come to mind—poet Bharatiyar, and novelist K.K. Krishnamachary.

7. From the Latin subalternus = sub= below + alternus = alternate, > alter. *The American Heritage Dictionary*, 2nd. ed., (Boston: Houghton Mifflin, 1982). The term "subaltern" is used consciously by critics of colonial discourse to show how Imperial governments created pockets of empty power in colonized states to force local people to govern their own countrymen in keeping with Imperial policy. This means that certain Indians would be given judicial or police status to carry out the dictates of the British against the Indians. However, their power remained ultimately governed by Imperial authorities.

8. My critical or subject stance robs Narayan of his own subject position in his text, and relegates him to an object status. I am conscious of Spivak's warning in such a critical endeavor. In her "Subaltern" essay, she specifically calls attention to Foucault and Deluez, etc., for using a Western, Eurocentric perspective for reading cultural/colonial texts and negating the authority of those native texts through their appropriating the subject position. My deconstructive reading of Narayan will be different, in that I show instances where his subject position remains intact in certain places in the text.

9. I introduce Macherey here because Spivak uses it as an example to show how the subaltern subject lacks agency. For more on this argument, see Spivak's work cited above. While Spivak focuses explicitly on Macherey's notion of "what the work cannot say through the subaltern subject" due to a lack of agency, I will focus concurrently on "what the work does not and cannot say."

10. Spivak's explanation of "contradiction" in the subject is crucial to understanding the structuration of the subaltern subject. She uses the example from *The Eighteenth Brumaire of Louis Bonaparte*, where Marx analyzes French, nineteenth century working class subjects. Marx claims that there is a paradox in class-formation, and consequently, in subject consciousness, and says: "insofar as millions of families live under economic conditions of existence that separate their mode of life from the ruling class. . .they form one class. . .[yet] insofar as the identity of their interests fails to produce a feeling of community, they do not form a class" (Spivak, 248). The point that Spivak makes in her essay is that the subject is simultaneously occupying two sides of the ideological line—the privileged and the unprivileged class.

11. Recent work on analyzing post-colonial literatures is vast and fascinating. *The Empire Writes Back* is one such text that is useful for furthering critical interpretation in this field, and has an exhaustive bibliography. See *The Empire Writes Back: Theory and Practice in Post-Colonial Literatures*, Bill Ashcroft, Gareth Griffith, and Helen Triffin, London and New York: Routledge, 1989. See also Gauri Viswanathan's "The Beginnings of English Literary Study in British India," *Oxford Literary Review* 9, nos. 1 & 2 (1987): 2-26.

12. I wish to thank Gurudev and Radhika Mohanram for their help while writing this article.

Works Cited

Barthes, Roland. *S/Z*. Trans. Richard Miller. New York: Hill and Wang, 1974.

Bhabha, Homi K., ed. *Nation and Narration*. London and New York: Routledge, 1990.

Macherey, Pierre. *A Theory of Literary Production*. Trans. Geoffrey Wall. London: Routledge, 1978.

Narayan, R.K. *Swami and Friends*. Chicago: University of Chicago Press, 1980.

Spivak, Gayatri Chakravorty. "Can the Subaltern Speak?" in *Marxism and the Interpretation of Culture,* eds. Cary, Nelson and Lawrence. Urbana and Chicago: University of Illinois Press, 1988, 271-313.

Krishnan's Jasmine-Scented Quest

GIDEON NTEERE M'MARETE

Central to a full understanding of Narayan's autobiographical work, *The English Teacher* (1935)[1] must be a deep appreciation of the part played by the jasmine motif in the novel. The usual critical controversy centers around the non-mimetic second half of this work which some critics believe ruins Narayan's novel. Though we do not ignore this controversy, our purpose is not to raise more dust with demand for realism, but rather to study the work focusing on the jasmine motif in order to explicate the other side of Narayan which William Walsh has referred to as "the poet of Indian domestic life" (*Critical Appreciation*, 51). Krishnan's search for an ideal home is what we have called here the jasmine-scented quest.

Bored indifference on the part of the main character, the near-thirty Krishna, is the note on which the novel starts. Trudging on in life with "a sense of something missing" (10) and a restlessness that remains uncured by the work at the Albert Mission College, which he thinks should get him feeling fulfilled, identifies in Krishnan the need for something more profound than work. The missing link in his life cannot be leisure—the walks and the bathing in the river have left his real need undiscerned. Narayan refuses to simplify life into a life-leisure formula, insisting that commitment to a family must complement careers and leisure. Thus the introduction of a wife as the missing link in Krishnan's life falls right in place as what he has not been able to discern all along.

The jasmine image that pervades the entire novel symbolizes, among other things, the romance of married love between Krishnan and his wife Susila: theirs is a jasmine-scented relationship. *The English Teacher* is a work where Narayan hopes to make the reader appreciate his story by a constant stimulation of two senses—sight and smell—in order to make him receptive to his jasmine-scented story. This, however, is not done in an exotic manner.

The jasmine image is introduced quite casually, the evening Krishnan receives two letters; one is from his wife. Just as the author invites the reader to share his hero's loneliness caused by his wife's absence, so does he call upon him to partake of his experience of how missing his wife gets relieved by his substitution for seeing her—the smell that has come to symbolize her existence: the jasmine smell. Thus on the letter is born a jasmine smell that "surrounded her and all possessions ever since I had known her" (18). But Krishnan's love for jasmine as a symbol of good things in life does not begin this evening. It goes back ten years when as a student, in spite of being laughed at, he took special interest in the growth of a jasmine bush outside the hostel and trained it up a bamboo bower.

Jasmine, however, over the years, has come to transcend its Indian religious significance as a fragrance for celebrating the Vinayaka festival at the hostel. It has become a multi-faceted image, symbolic of everything that is worthwhile in life. How symbolic it has become is underscored by the fact that as he contemplates vacating the hostel, it is the only thing he feels sad to have to leave. This is not to mean that Krishnan will miss nothing else: he will miss the buildings, his colleagues, and the scenery. The joint care he and Singaram have given the jasmine bush has paid off. On his way to the bathroom he notices that although all else has been scorched by the sun, the jasmine—the epitome of his ideals in life—stands outside the hostel untouched by the fierce sun of Malgudi, "I sighed as I passed it, the only object of any beauty here-abouts. The rest of the quadrangle was mere mud, scorched by Malgudi sun" (19).

Between Tain's *History of Literature* and his wife's letter, it is the jasmine-scented stationery of Susila's letter that proves irresistible to Krishnan. His abandonment of the scentless Tain to pick up the letter, smell and read it once more word for word, is Narayan's way of stating how important Krishnan's setting out soon after, in search of a house to settle his family in, must be at this point in the novel. In the symbolic act of smelling the letter, we see the jasmine quest, which begins with caring for a jasmine bush at the hostel transformed into a new commitment to his family. The work-leisure formula offered at the beginning of the novel which leaves Krishnan with "a sense of something missing" (1) is deftly replaced by a work-family-leisure alternative with the family at the center of his cares, and the sources of his fulfillment.

As the poet of Indian domestic life in this novel, Narayan begins celebrating the place of the home in Indian society by portraying Krishnan henceforth as ill-at-ease in the hostel.[2] The queue at the bathrooms, which hitherto has not bothered him, now makes him feel like one undergoing an endless torture while the mirror, once he is back in his room after a bath, cannot stay in position for his use—it keeps dazzling his eyes with light that appears too intense not to be a nuisance. But these annoyances will soon vanish when Krishnan's jasmine-scented home soon becomes a reality with the arrival of his family. The central place that his family is beginning to occupy in his life, which was not possible while they were away in rural India, begins to stand in telling contrast to the impersonal lectures Krishnan sometimes delivers at the College. Nothing is implied to the effect that Krishnan does not up to this point love his family: rather, distance is singled out as having wrenched the family out of their central place in his life—something he remains oblivious of until his father-in-law brings it to his attention.

With the transfer of the jasmine-scented quest from its deprived hostel environment (stated in terms of the scorching Malgudi sun) to the home just about to come into being, the authorial perspective focuses on the anticipated arrival of Susila and Leela. The account of the reunion of Krishnan with his wife and child at the Malgudi railway station seems to omit as being redundant the jasmine motif. Furthermore, Narayan goes for not only what is authentically Indian (by keeping the husband-wife reunion undemonstrative in public) but also what is artistically effective. For this he uses his characteristic understatement. Susila's freshness and beauty, her indigo-colored silk saree, and her unmentioned jasmine-scented aroma, all make Krishnan gaze upon her with more love than is openly expressed. The most he can manage after looking at his wife and his child is "once again in this saree, still so fond of it" (33).

The search for authenticity in depicting traditional Indian romance is not confined to the Malgudi station incident. The attitude of not being publicly demonstrative on matters of love is examined in much more detail. Susila is depicted as managing to put across a concealed gesture of love by waiting for Krishnan in the garden of their house when he comes from school in the evenings—under the pretext of minding Leela. This soon becomes her habitual unspoken appreciation of his arrival home. We see in this gesture Susila gracing their garden the way the jasmine bush decorates the sun-burnt grounds of the hostel.

But Narayan is too much of a realist to give the reader the impression that Krishnan's relationship with his wife—drawn from his own experience—is jasmine-scented all through with no ups and downs that shake marriages to pieces in the real world. The scorching sun of Malgudi that bares the hostel ground surely does singe a leaf or flower on the jasmine plant although Krishnan manages to keep it generally green and beautiful. The first time the Krishnan-Susila relationship is not jasmine-scented is occasioned by Krishnan's alteration of the grocery list during shopping and his going far away in a hired jutka to patronize the National Provisions Store which he likes, regardless of the expenses involved. It happens next when he resents his being rid of old paper and a dilapidated clock. The "orthodox milieu of Indian Society" (Narayan, *My Days* 119),[3] in which the man wishes to be left unanswerable to anyone after misusing the family income and inconveniencing his family with quite inconsequential and dispensable things in the manner of Krishnan, is the sun that destroys the jasmine relationship between couples. Both times in their soured romance it is Krishnan who has placed in jeopardy the chances of realizing his quest of harmonious marital relationship with his wife. The orthodoxy of his conduct at home must be pruned in order for him to see the sense in Susila's opinions regarding their domestic disharmony.

Fortunately for the jasmine quest, Krishnan is a man who can swallow his pride—even to the point of feeling that he has acted like a savage during the paper-and-clock incident. Since leisure now exists for the sake of the family, Krishnan takes his wife to a Tarzan movie in Variety Hall where their bitterness is purged, their feelings are mellowed, and the jasmine fragrance is restored. In the first clash Krishnan comes around to seeing that altering the grocery list means wasteful excesses of provisions for lack of storage. Next, he realizes that paying cart hire to South Extension, when the Cooperative Store is just nearby, is an unnecessary expense. This adds a new momentum to the jasmine quest as the orthodoxy of the Indian world begins to crumble to accommodate more consideration in the husband-wife relationship.

Lakshmi Holmstrom has observed that the relationship between Krishnan and Susila is "one of the most delicately stated ones in Narayan's work" (49). Part of his success in depicting this relationship she attributes to his use of an articulate poet-narrator. Besides having no problems whatsoever in evaluating his motives and actions, Krishnan is also a narrator who knows how to place his wife in proper perspective in the quest for a perfect home. He registers in articulate detail every new feeling about his wife, and when it is not immodest by Indian standards we are generously treated to these responses. Highly elated by his wife's appearance on their way to Lawley Extension, Krishnan cannot contain any longer his long-withheld decision to name his wife "Jasmine" to celebrate their married romance. But the visual image of Susila is deemed as important as the jasmine smell she carries in greater amounts this particular day of searching for a new house. She appears, in their old house, "at the kitchen doorway, like a vision, clad in her indigo-colored saree, her hair gleaming and jasmine covered" (55).

It is not difficult to agree with K.R. Iyengar that the married life of Krishnan and his wife is a prose lyric on which Narayan has lavished his best gifts as a writer (357). He manages to cultivate a unique balance between lyrical effusion and down-to-earth realism in the first half of

The English Teacher where his concern is to embody, in a couple, certain Indian domestic ideals without making their relationship idealistic. The couple is constantly engaged in adding new dimensions to their relationship. No easy pathways exist for the smooth progress of their relationship. They have to master their own selves to make themselves maximally productive in their supportive roles in the quest.

The discovery of the ideal house in Lawley Extension where Indian married romance can blossom further is not stated in terms of Cinderella-type palatial find. The buffalo image that is used to describe the person who would be unable to appreciate its beauty is an afterthought that follows the lyrical understatement which spells out the hoped-for location of their jasmine-scented quest, "I would like to call this the Jasmine Home, its perfume greets us even as we enter" (64).

The work-leisure dichotomy that polarizes Indian domestic activities is harmonized by a symbolic Jasmine Home in which Susila is to be a human flower, a jasmine plant deserving the utmost care by a husband originally orthodox in domestic ideas. Not to see the jasmine creepers at the gate as predictors of the tenderness that is meant to saturate the relationship at the couple's new residence is, perhaps, to miss too much in one's reading of the story.

Predictions do not always come true, however. Furthermore, it is a characteristic of danger to often strike at what was thought most secure in its destructive ambushes on humanity. It is not Leela, the couple's daughter, who falls as her father fears might happen (during his inspection of the parapets to make sure that they can hold her in the event of danger). In Susila's fall, which eventually proves fatal, Narayan is not simply reproducing the biographical fact of his wife's death. He is documenting the elusive nature of life in a world fraught with danger. The ironic twist in circumstances from this point on highlights the uncertainties of life which hitherto have remained hidden to Krishnan who, though not naive, probably looks at existence in a literal manner. In Susila's fall and contraction of a fatal illness on the very day of locating for her the home of his dream, we see Narayan scoring an ironic point against his hero in a manner that comes to full fruition in *The Guide* (1958).[4]

There is an economic angle to the loss depicted in Narayan's story. Contractors do not build houses to sell to people footing bills incurred by the sick. This point, which is only casually made, is not a minor one in the set of circumstances that conspire to destroy the possibility of happiness in the story. Fighting on two fronts—to save the life of a bed-ridden wife and to pay for a house—is an impossible task for someone of Krishnan's means.

The English Teacher is about the disintegration of a vision—the jasmine vision. But it is also concerned with gathering up the pieces of a shattered vision to replace the broken one in an effort to counter the numbing effects of unexpected loss.

The loss begins with the termination of the Jasmine Home deal. It is a blow that does more than leave a foreboding gap in the anticipated domestic bliss. In the tragic economy of the novel, it heralds the loss of the one at the center of the cherished jasmine vision: Susila. Krishnan's fruitless endeavor to reduce her escalating temperature becomes an alarming pointer to the inevitability of tragedy, "But so far it is not the fever which cools. But the ice that melts" (95).

The catastrophic typhoid, the bug that destroys Krishnan's jasmine flower, defies medication. Narayan's sense of irony at this point is more profound than a cursory glance at the book will reveal.[5] Krishnan has already, quite inadvertently, using Wordsworth's poem, sung of Susila as a phantom of delight, a momentary companion who has gleamed upon his sight just for a time:

> A lovely apparition, sent
> To be a *moment's ornament*
> (49) [emphasis mine]

Narayan's work deals with the crumbling up of the temporal jasmine vision and the subsequent substitution of a psychic one in its place. In an examination of Narayan's miscellaneous writing, S.C. Harrex in his *Fire and the Offering* sees the fictional world of Narayan as abounding with images of turbulence, an observation that may be deemed rather inaccurate with regard to a writer who rarely records physical violence. Yet few events in Narayan's entire corpus can match the turbulent shattering of Krishnan's jasmine vision by the violent hand of death. Violence, then, is not foreign to Narayan's fiction after all, though what is pertinent here is the violence of nature rather than of man. Is this not likely to be part of the violence Harrex would have been pointing to?

But Narayan's art comes out as strongly in checking chaos as it does in depicting turbulence. Narayan has such a keen dislike for tragedy that he will fight tooth and nail to patch up the tragic. The building up of a psychic jasmine experience through the occult needs to be seen as Narayan's rejection of the tragic as the ultimate in life. There is not much left of the original ingredients of the vision out of which to build a new one. As the cremation party approaches the burial ground, the dead Susila lies face upwards, the tragedy having reduced the protagonist's vision to a mere string tied somewhere about her head (105). To K.R. Iyengar the psychic experience in *The English Teacher* introduces a whimsical and fantastic element to a story that has so far been true to life. A lot of critical controversy centers around the book's non-mimetic second half, to which Iyengar adds his own fuel. The objections to the second part of the work are, however, not always of a literary kind, legitimate as they might be. C.D. Narasimhaiah's, for instance, is that Narayan "turns to the occult rather than the profoundly spiritual which his own heritage could have offered in abundance" (*The Swan and the Eagle,* 146). The non-mimetic element is not Narasimhaiah's concern as it is for Iyengar.

Raja Rao's *The Serpent and the Rope* offers an example of profound spirituality that is culturally acceptable by Indian standards. Rao's narrator, Ramaswamy, affirms his belief in reincarnation when he speaks about his mother having had a death-bed dream in which she saw his past lives: "She saw three of my past lives, and in each of them I was a son, and of course I was always her eldest born, tall, slim, deep-voiced, deferential and beautiful" (10) The psychic experience in Narayan's work is not sought through the Indian reincarnation cycle. The task at hand, however, is not to delve into Indian religious thought but to appreciate a work of art purely on the basis of what it presents. Hence the need to return to the jasmine quest.

A paradoxical graduation from adulthood to childhood is what Narayan posits as a major prerequisite to the protagonist's experiencing contact with the invisible. Adult insensitivity to spiritual presences must be eliminated through psychic experiments before a breakthrough can be made. Major non-mimetic incidents in the work include the invisible presence of Susila with a jasmine in her hair during the sitting at the end of chapter five. But the most significant of these is the jasmine garland incident at the end of the novel. In a rapturous intoxication, as a result of his new childlike acceptance of spiritual presences, Krishnan is finally initiated by a hypnotic melody into the other world where Susila is sitting on his bed, "still jasmine-scented" (213). These incidents form part of what some critics have called the other half of the story that will never be believed. This is an age that does not take kindly to the non-mimetic, unless perhaps, in science fiction where the conventions are understood from the start to have nothing to do with credibility.

Narayan will not, however, be easily dismissed on the grounds of credibility. In *My Days,* he has contended that except for the controversial second half, he would not have written the novel. To him, the claims that the domestic life of Krishnan in the first half is used as a bait to draw the reader into impossible speculations is not a viable critical stance (135). The psychic training sessions presented in the work, he asserts, need to be seen as credible accounts since he personally underwent similar ones. It is not Narayan's art that is in question. He is no doubt a master of form. What claims that art makes is at the center of the controversy. As the merits and demerits of non-mimetic art are not the main concern of this discussion, it is necessary to concentrate on the jasmine quest.

There is a sense in which the re-issued title of *Grateful to Life and Death* (1953) is a more accurate one than the original *The English Teacher* (1945). It points more directly to the obliteration of the barrier between life and death which the psychic experience is meant to convey. The integrating principle of the novel is founded on the duality of physical existence in this world and the inevitable transmutation by death into a purely spiritual state which Susila represents. The jasmine motif is built into the novel on a cosmic scale as a symbol of the beauty of life in both states of existence, though no detailed portrayal of Indian metaphysics is given.

Narayan's is the story of a man who decides that death should not spell the end of his married romance. P.S. Sundaram in *R.K. Narayan* argues that this romance story is told from Leela's point of view. But according a child its rightful place in the homes does not necessarily make a home child-centered. In life and death, the Krishnan-Susila relationship is the focal point from which the story is told and the hinge on which the novel turns. Leela becomes the embodiment of sensitive innocence needed for one to penetrate non-physical reality. Married romance remains the central theme of the novel throughout the narrative. A woman of mystical simplicity,[6] Susila can be an elusive character, with more in her than is apparent at a casual glance. Lakshmi Holmstrom's objection to Narayan's story as inconsistent in theme and character portrayal in the post-tragedy episodes, is based on what appears to be an inaccurate reading of Susila's character. For her, Susila is too simple to be the articulate coach of Krishnan that we meet in the psychic sessions. But if it is remembered that before her death, there are times when her husband finds her impenetrably enigmatic, it becomes easier to understand why she is no longer the learner but the coach. Also this apparent reversal of roles is occasioned by the acquiescence of the articulate poet-narrator, who is more accustomed to telling than hearing, to a listener's position. Death having numbed his tongue, he has really no choice but to sit and receive instruction.

Few critics of *The English Teacher* confine themselves to purely artistic concerns, which is probably responsible for many negative comments about Narayan's work. The question of the occult belongs more to religion than art. The most a critic can do—being neither guru nor preacher—is simply raise an objection against the occult or ignore it altogether. But the inclusion of what would not be considered part of legitimate Hindu spirituality cannot be the sole basis for judging this so controversial a work. To an impartial critic such as William Walsh, most of the heat-generating matters recede into the background as purely critical standards are brought into play. Walsh is able to say what few other critics—if any at all—have been able to say about Narayan's work. He sees him as having succeeded in persuading the reader to accept Krishnan's contact with his wife: "a feat unprecedented in realistic fiction" (13). What Walsh realizes is that an author can combine the mimetic and the fantastic with compelling effect. It is the jasmine quest that requires this combination with the passing of Susila. Realism, which remains the predominant mode of narration, is effectually counterpointed with non-mimetic incidents during the psychic sessions. Readers often fall into the trap of seeking and demanding pure forms in art. But few writers are willing to work within the narrow confines of non-counterpointed art, though they may not postulate radical non-mimetic positions like Narayan's in *The English Teacher*. Raja Rao appears even more averse to being detained in the world of the real for too long. His works reveal a constant concern to want to come to terms with the Indian Metaphysical.

The jasmine quest is a negation of a resignation to the fate of loneliness after a disaster. The new hope that a future capable of alleviating loss is possible is embodied in the dawn that Krishnan and Susila wake up to, if we accept dawn here as both literal and symbolic: "The first purple of day came through the window, and faintly touched the walls of our room. 'Dawn!' she whispered and rose to her feet" (213). It is not uncommon for plots to get assimilated into the seasonal, solar, water-state or the human organic cycle as expressed in generations[7] to adduce independent evidence for the statements on life being made in a work of art. Narayan uses two of these to negate the tragic in favor of a tragi-comedy that affirms the continuity of life in new beginnings. Leela is the evidence that the Indian home will weather the storms of life and come through to a better dawn. No wonder, then, that she is depicted as an exact replica of her mother. No obligation exists for any author to state explicitly the cycle or cycles he employs to compose or counterpoint his plot. Northrop Frye has amply demonstrated that it does facilitate the task of criticism if the cyclic archetypes can be identified for critical attention. In the jasmine-scented quest of the couple in Narayan's work, the solar and human archetypal motifs are so casually stated that they could easily be missed.

In *The English Teacher*, as in other works of Narayan, the force of rhetoric resides more in the juxtaposition of incidents, detached parodic humor, and a penchant for portrayal of idiosyncratic human behavior than in the sway of eloquence. Not even Krishnan's mother, who belongs to the category of Indian mothers whom M.E. Derrett observes are drawn in Indian literature with reverential care (74), escapes Narayan's parody of middle class decorum. In *The Ironic Vision*, M.K. Naik's otherwise perceptive analysis of *The English Teacher* lacks one thing: the recognition that there is no justifiable reason to compare it with *Macbeth*. His finding the novel deficient in compelling diction equal to the task of communicating the supernatural experience it is meant to convey, is based on the assumption that nothing short of Shakespearean eloquence can effectively articulate the supernatural.[8] Evidence that Narayan's story-telling ethos is of another kind can never be lacking. That vast subject, however, lies outside of this discussion.

In our view Narayan's novel succeeds. After all, the main point is not how well he depicts the European rose but how melodiously he sings of Indian jasmine.

Notes

1. The American version of *The English Teacher* is *Grateful to Life and Death* published by Michigan State College Press, 1953. This title is excerpted from the last sentence in Narayan's work. All further references and quotations are from this version.

2. Institutions such as the school are not satirically portrayed in this work. But the theme of the family as the central unit in Indian society makes the others look peripheral.

3. Narayan in this autobiography discusses in depth his attitude to the mistreatment of the Indian woman and how it influenced his writing of *The Dark Room*.

4. For more on Narayan's masterly use of irony as a mode of fiction, see M.K. Naik's *The Ironic Vision: A Study of the Fiction of R.K. Narayan*.

5. Narayan in *My Days* reveals that he dislikes being deliberate in writing and he is not impressed by authors who try to be so. The result is that he often uses narrative techniques such as understatement which can easily escape the eye of the casual reader. In his study of Narayan's ironic techniques, M.K. Naik reports that *The Times Literary Supplement* (1967) asked for nominations for the most underrated author in the previous seventy-five years. In my view, D.J. Enright's nomination of Narayan proves the point we are making here: that for a proper understading of Narayan, more than cursory perusals through his apparently straightforward works are required.

6. The phrase "mystical simplicity" needs some attention. I use it to summarize the traits that make the paradoxical character of Susila. She appears simple but possesses a depth which the author makes a part of her religious inclination.

7. See chapter three of Frye's *Anatomy of Criticism* for more on the affinity that exists between narrative plots and cyclic archetypes. By 'water-state' we mean the forms in which water exists—dew, vapor, ice and snow, for example.

8. To accept Naik's view would require subscription to the idea of poetic diction which European Romanticism challenged. Their moulding up of poetic diction out of ordinary language was a reaction against eloquence that did more mimicking than communicating. Narayan's language is tailored to communicate, not to imitate.

Work Cited

Derrett, M.E. *The Modern Novel in English*. Universite Libre de Buxelles, 1966.

Frye, Northrop. *Anatomy of Criticism*. 1957. Princeton: Princeton University Press, 1973.

Harrex, S.C. *Fire and the Offering: The English Language Novel of India 1935–1970*. Thompson, Connecticut: Calcutta Writers Workshop, 1978.

Holmstrom, Lakshmi. *The Novels of R.K. Narayan*. Calcutta Writers Workshop, 1973.

Iyengar, K.R. *Indian Writing in English*. New Delhi: Sterling, 1962.

Naik, M.K. *The Ironic Vision: A Study of the Fiction of R.K. Narayan*. New Delhi: Sterling, 1983.

Narasimhaiah, C.D., ed. *Fiction and the Reading Public in India*. Mysore, India: University of Mysore, 1967.

_____. *The Swan and the Eagle*. Simla, India: Indian Institute of Advanced Study, 1979.

Narayan, R.K. *Grateful to Life and Death*. 1935. East Lansing, Michigan: Michigan State College Press, 1953.

_____. *The Financial Expert*. 1953. New York: The Noonday Press, 1964.

_____. *The Guide*. 1958. Mysore, India: Wesley Press, 1980.

_____. *My Days*. London: Chatto and Windus, 1975.

Puess, John,. ed. *Commonwealth Literature*. London: Heinemann, 1965. Conference at University of Leeds, 1964.

Rao, K.S. *World Literature Written in English*, 14 1975.

Rao, Raja. *The Serpent and the Rope*. London: John Murray, 1960.

Sundaram, P.S. *R.K. Narayan*. New Delhi: Arnold-Heinemann, 1973.

Walsh, William. *R.K. Narayan: Writers and their Work*, No. 224. London: Longman, 1971.

_____. *R.K. Narayan: A Critical Appreciation*. London: Heinemann, 1982.

The Absence of Caste in R. K. Narayan and Its Implications for Indian Writing in English

D. A. SHANKAR

In this short note, I have a twofold purpose: one, to present as clearly and textually as I can, the way caste figures in R.K. Narayan; and two, to give my reading of Narayan's fiction a broader, a more general theoretical validity. And before I get into the text, let me make a confession. Of all the Indian writers in English, Narayan, to me, is the finest and most authentic creative writer. There is hardly ever anything that is unreal about the India that he presents in his fiction. Narayan, again, may be the only genuinely profound writer that we have among our Indian writers in English. And yet—this is the confessional part—there is "something" that is wanting in him, and this something that is wanting in Narayan is that "something" which is wanting in all our Indian writers in English. I hope to make clear in the course of this note what that "something" is.

Perhaps "Fellow Feeling" is the only story of Narayan where caste is allowed to operate freely, uninhibitedly at the verbal level. While traveling by the Madras-Bangalore Express, Rajam Iyer ("Iyer" is indicative of caste. It is a Brahmin suffix. It is interesting to note that proper nouns in Narayan become neutral in his late writings. Cf Raju, Raman, Sriram, etc.) is annoyed by the rudeness displayed by a co-passenger and he tries to make him behave himself. At this point, the following conversation ensues:

> "Just try and be more courteous, it is your duty". . . . "You are a Brahmin, I see. Learn, Sir, that your days are over. Don't think you can bully us as you have been bullying us all these years." "What has it to do with beastly conduct to this gentleman?"

> The newcomer assumed a tone of mock humility and said: "Shall I take the dust from your feet, O Holy Brahmin? Oh, Brahmin, Brahmin . . . Your days are over. I should like to see you trying a bit of bossing on us."

"Whose master is who?" asked Rajam Iyer philosophically. The newcomer went on with no obvious relevance. "The cost of mutton has gone up out of all proportion . . . yes, and why? . . . Because Brahmins have begun to eat meat and they pay high prices to get it secretly . . . I have with my own eyes seen Brahmins, Pukkah Brahmins with sacred threads on their bodies, carrying fish under their arms, of course all wrapped up in a towel . . . ." (53–55)

The fact that Rajam Iyer, the Brahmin, in the end, triumphs over the muscularly-built non-Brahmin may not be irrelevant for a discussion of Narayan's attitude to caste, though even here it is, as it normally is with Narayan, ambivalent. When Rajam Iyer boasts that he has driven the bully away, Narayan says that a few passengers looked skeptically at him.

In *The Financial Expert,* we have Balu throwing away Margayya's account book in to the gutter. With the loss of the book Margayya loses his hold on his creditors, and then a thought crosses his mind: "Suppose he announced a reward to any scavenger who might salvage it? Even if it was salvaged what was the use? How was it to be touched again and read!" (37). I shall only say here that Margayya appears to belong to a community which is orthodox, which is generally governed by accepted notions of pollution and purity.

A little later, when Margayya is about to secure for his son, Balu, the daughter of a wealthy man of a respectable family, thoughts about his own caste surface in him: "There was a family secret about his caste which stirred uneasily at the back of his mind" (150). His ancestors were corpse-bearers. His father and his uncle were known as "Corpse Brothers." But in course of time—it took two or three generations—they became agriculturists, landed men, and people forgot about the origin of the family, though there's an aunt who kept saying: It's written on their faces—where can it go, even if you allow a hundred years to elapse" (151). But now Margayya's "own financial reputation overshadowed anything else" (151). I pause here to remark that this upward mobility of a family in the Indian caste hierarchy that Narayan registers is sociologically interesting. But you will see that there isn't connection made in the novel between the two passages I have cited. That is, notions of pollution and purity play little or no role in the interrelationships between characters. They are just there, in midair as it were.

There is a fairly realistic picture of the area where the outcastes live in *Waiting for the Mahatma*: "This was one of the dozen huts belonging to the city sweepers who lived on the banks of the river. It was probably the worst area in the town, and an exaggeration even to call them huts; they were just hovels, put together with rags, tin-sheets, and shreds of coconut matting, all crowded in anyhow, with scratchy fowls cackling about and children growing in the street dust" (23). There are, however, certain jarring notes here. When we read: "The municipal services were neither extended *nor missed* (italics mine); and, "each had a considerable income by Malgudi standards" (31), and when we remember it is the novelist speaking, it makes us uncomfortable. There is also a passage (31) where the Municipal Chairman tries to befriend a Harijan boy, but his inner feeling is not any different from Margayya's recorded earlier.

Rosie of *The Guide* is said to belong to the caste of temple dancers. And it is interesting to note that when Raman of *The Painter of Signs* and Raju of *The Guide* fall in love with women who do not belong to their caste, their mothers make an almost identical response: Raman's mother goes away to Kashi and Raju's to her brother's place. Both disapprove of marriage outside the caste and have little or no consideration for their daughters-in-law.

The passages make it obvious that Narayan is aware of caste and the hold it has on men and women. But when we try to see what relationship it bears to characters and their actions we are in for a disappointment. Caste, in fact, has little or no bearing on the psyche of Narayan's characters: there isn't any structural or organic relationship between the characters and their caste.

Margayya's rise and fall, the growth that we see in Sriram, Raju's success—if it can be called that—are in no way related to their caste affiliation. The characters work out their life independently of their vaguely suggested caste moorings. I say 'suggested' because one is never sure of the exact caste position of any of Narayan's characters. We are only vaguely or in a very general sense made to feel, to assume that Sriram, Raman, and Raju belong to an upper caste, more or less in the same sense in which we are made to feel that Annamalai and Muni do not. Through a scattering of an aura of certain set, general beliefs and observances, Narayan endows his characters with their caste status and achieves authenticity. The vagueness and generalness are exploited to subserve authenticity of realization.

I do not say that it is not possible to argue that behind the de-linking of characters from their caste there is a deliberate fictional strategy involved. The strategy—if it really is one—appears to be this: Narayan seems to allow caste to enter fictional works only in its broadest, most general aspect so that it does not tie him down to too much actuality. Somebody might well ask: "If this helps one succeed, as Narayan surely seems to, in achieving an authentic portrayal of life, why bother? Why complain that there isn't enough 'Caste' in Narayan?"

But the heart of the problem is this. In India, what is important is not caste but sub-caste. It is not merely that *Varna* terms like *Brahim*, *Kshtriya*, etc., do not have any social content, even broad caste terms like

Brahmin, Vokkaliga and *Idngayat* do not have adequate social content. They really belong to the world of Nominalism, with no real, objective referents. It is not possible in actual life to come across a *Brahmin*; one can only come across a *Smartha*, a *Madhva*, a *Hoysala Karnataka* or a *Kamme*. And it is the subcaste which decisively defines a man's caste status and moulds his attitudes, his social biases, in fact, his being itself.

Narayan, by choosing to work with non-existent broad types of caste, is forced to leave out all the little local details that go with an individual's actual living which is co-extensive with this subcaste status. When details get left out, the writing becomes thin. Its social content or rather the density, variety and richness of an individual's societal activities and relationships—all these are lost and there remains in the writings only a pathetically thin-looking social reality.

I shall briefly deviate only to come back to Narayan. Consider Raja Rao's Ramaswamy. We know that he is a devotee of Shankara, an *advaitin*, etc., but that is not much of a help. For he is the amorphous Brahmin of the *Varna* system which is socially non-existent. And pan-Indian *Brahmin* is no *Brahmin* at all, i.e., in terms of social reality. We are not told what his subcaste is and, therefore, instead of specific local details we have only a metaphysic.

I have a feeling that most of our writers who write in English ignore sub-castes and choose to operate with *Varna* types, and thereby hangs the tale of that "something" I spoke of earlier.

The absence of subcaste brings upon Indian writing in English a twin disability. They are (1) a thinness of social content leading to lack of complexity, and (2) a too-easy transcendence of the actualities of a subcaste structured society, resulting in a corresponding thinness of texture.

The thinness of social content of a novel in Indian writing in English becomes obvious the moment it is placed beside a regional novel like Kuvempu's *Malegalli Madumagalu*, Karanth's *Nambidavara Naka Naraka*, U.R. Ananthamurthy's *Samskara*, or Chaduranga's *Vaishaka*. What gives a rich cultural density of meaning to regional writing is its direct living touch with the subcastes. The actions of characters stem from and are directed by the particular code of subcaste which governs them. Moments of crisis put not only the characters' minds but their whole value system to test. And the characters either transcend the subcaste barriers and become shaping spirits of new-value based society or they crumble, and point to the enormous power subcaste structures can bring to bear on their actions. Or, in other words, characters in the regional novel belong to specific socio-cultural groups; but they also become or try to reach toward the typical, the representative. It is a process of interacting, or growing and becoming, and therefore dramatic in terms of the social content itself.

Not only do novels written in English lack dramatic social reality; they have another drawback. They begin with "transcendence," with ready-made types of the *varna* system, and this deprives the novelist of an opportunity of working with what is obviously a potential creative theme.

Side-stepping or transcending the subcaste forces the Indian-writing-in-English novelist to make the main motive of his characters psychological or metaphysical or economic. He cannot locate the central motive in the societal being of individuals. This is why the urges of Narayan's main characters like Margayya, Vasu, Raju, and others are almost wholly psychological; of Raja Rao's Ramaswamy and Nair almost wholly metaphysical, and of Mulk Raj's almost wholly economic. The Indian writers in English make their characters work out their salvation with least reference to the society that is around them, whereas the regional language writers locate the central motive of their characters simultaneously in the social, psychological, and metaphysical. These are, as is obvious, interrelated, and consequently the writing comes to possess a richer, a denser texture. This is why there is even in our best Indian writers in English a thinness of social content and texture, and hence its unsatisfactory authenticity.

Raja Rao's *Kanthapura* and Mulk Raj Anand's *Untouchable* are, to an extent, exceptions but exceptions do only prove a rule anyway.

Works Cited

Narayan, R.K. "Fellow Feeling." *An Astrologer's Day and Other Stories.* London: Eyre & Spottiswoode, 1947, 53–55.
_____. *The Financial Expert.* New Delhi: Indian Thought Publications, 1953.
_____. *Waiting for the Mahatma.* East Lansing: Michigan State University Press, 1955.

The Guide: *A Study in Transcendence*

SR. MARY BEATINA RAYEN, O.S.M.

R. K. Narayan, the Indian English novelist, has often been highly com-
mended for his realistic portrayal of his characters' "joys and sorrows,
aspirations and achievement, feelings and failures and above all their
human foibles" (Ranganath, 62). But his realism far surpasses mere
detailed presentation of the concrete and the material. Realism has found
varied expressions in literature. Social realism intends the visible and the
concrete to function as incitements to social change. Realism is rushed
further into the psychological realm by attempting to reproduce the
underlying process of thought. Narayan's realism, however, portrays the
reality of the inner vision which transcends and transforms the mundane
to realize the sacramentality of life, and leads to something beyond—
the mundane-transcendent interactions which liberate man from fear
and grant him freedom of spirit. Thus, Narayan's realism differs from
that of the Western tradition which sometimes swings to the extreme of
unrelenting pessimism in viewing man as totally impotent in a hostile
universe.

The most disputed but also the most acclaimed of Narayan's novels,
The Guide (1958), demonstrates the realism that leads to mundane-transcendent interactions and liberation. This novel is more complex than his
other novels in both technique and content; it thus raises questions
about all the features of transcendence that commonly appear in
Narayan's fiction.

The "mundane" in this article acquires a more complex meaning than
the ordinary one, for example, "earthly" or "worldly." The mundane here
refers to simple, ordinary, sometimes raw or frail human nature of
immense potential to be fully alive and dynamic, which is not to be
abhorred or destroyed but to be led and moved toward the transcendent.

Regarding the discussion here of the "transcendent," what we find in
Narayan's fiction is a form of spiritual experience usually accompanied
by religious elements, which most novelists in the realist tradition do not
attempt to portray. Hence, the "transcendent" in Narayan implies not

necessarily any visionary experience or *nirvana,* but a getting beyond the expected, a spiritual discovery. A sense of dissatisfaction and restlessness with a mundane life—often egoistic—initiates a step into a radically different world, a world that stuns the character and seems in many cases to be beyond the character's limits. The character does or experiences something that is "out of character" and, in a realistic novel, may verge upon the unconvincing—the typically Narayan risk. This step into another world always involves a spiritual experience—the kind of experience that would normally be called "transcendent," and yet the experience that follows the transcendent experience often seems more genuinely spiritual than the conventionally religious or conventionally "other worldly" experience itself. This wider and richer form of transcendence occurs when the character brings the transcendent experience to bear upon the mundane world. It is difficult to say precisely where the larger transcendence begins and the mundane leaves off because the two are inseparably mixed. Although there are no clear boundaries, the transcendence is identifiable. The result is, however, that our concept of the spiritual and the transcendent is enlarged and enriched.

To do justice to a Narayan novel, one must therefore acknowledge two kinds of transcendence, which commonly appear together. The first is easily recognizable—an encounter with the gods, the donning of holy garb, the telling of religious fables, etc. However, few readers are likely to finish a Narayan novel with the idea that these are the most important or the most transcendent events. For, flowing out of these events are the larger, richer, and more "realistic" events that nonetheless place the character in a world beyond that which the novel has led us to expect such a character could enter. The study here undertaken is necessary precisely because this larger mode of transcendence, this larger sense of what counts as spiritual, needs careful explanation. At one end it is anchored in a conventionally spiritual experience; at the other it is anchored in the mundane. The multiple interactions between the transcendent (in both senses) and the mundane deserve our closest attention.

The term "liberation" refers to an aspect of transcendence—the spiritual experience that liberates the self of its pettiness, allowing it to move toward a richer and wider horizon. Hence, any so-called freedom, which is not accompanied by spiritual experience and does not liberate the self, is here regarded as mundane, and Narayan commonly makes it clear that such "freedom" is a kind of license. Likewise, any discipline (exterior or interior) that does not lead the self to some spiritual experience or to liberation is mundane.

The process of movement with and from the mundane to the transcendent involves struggle and pain in every individual. Narayan's extraordinary skill in revealing the complex relationships between the mundane and the transcendent, and depicting the movement from and with the mundane to the transcendent, elevates him not only to the level of a great novelist in the world of Indian English Literature, but also qualifies him to rank high in World Literature in English itself.

Raju's behavior in *The Guide* may puzzle any reader. Of all Narayan's characters, Raju is the most controversial. It is comparatively easier to study the mundane-transcendent interactions of other characters in Narayan's fiction than that of Raju because Raju is an exceptionally complex human being. Moreover, the traditional notions of family and profession are brought to question in Raju.

Balarama Gupta labels Raju as "a selfish swindler, an adroit actor, and a perfidious megalomanic" in his article, "A Sinner is a Sinner is a Sinner—A Study of Raju" (135). On the other hand, C.D. Narasimhaiah also canonizes Raju as a saint: "with all his limitations Raju's is a rich and complex life—achieving integration at last. It is worthwhile studying this singular success of the novelist's creation. It is obviously not very easy to make a saint out of a sinner, especially for one with a comic vision of life" (186). These are two extreme views. It is better to bear constantly two things in mind while discussing the transcendent. First, in Narayan's fiction, there is no absolute integration or liberation; it is therefore misleading to speak of saints and sinners, as though such categories are mutually exclusive. Second, Narayan is not interested in presenting good or bad characters, but in tracing the reactions and vibrations that may affect the inner Self of a person during the process of integration through ordinary events. What counts is the process, not any absolute or final outcome.

Raju's life occurs in three phases: his position as a tourist guide, "Railway Raju"; his adventure with the dancer Rosie and her husband Marco; and finally his life at the village, Mangala. He never settles down with a family life. The remarkable and recurrent features in Raju's life in all three phases are several: his innate tendency to accommodate and please others ("I have to play the part expected of me. There is no escape" [45]); his gregarious nature and his love of public attention ("It is something to become so famous, isn't it, instead of handing out matches and tobacco?" [52]); the complex co-existence of the mundane and the transcendent— "self deception and sincerity" (Walsh, 114); and finally, whatever his pretense and ambiguities may be, his concern for the welfare of those whom he serves, even though this concern is often self-serving.

Raju begins as the son of an ordinary shopkeeper at Malgudi who must occasionally tend his father's shop. He enjoys the position of a salesman in meeting a variety of people. When the railways come to Malgudi, Raju is urbanized, and also with some unique intuition he attains great fame and position in Malgudi and environs as "the guide":

"Tourists who recommend him to each other would say at one time, 'If you are lucky enough to be guided by Raju, you will know everything. He will not only show you all the worthwhile places, but also will help you in every way'" (80). Raju is a helper by nature. His humble beginnings in no way indicate any possibility of his later becoming an "omniscient humanist":

> You may ask me why I became a guide or when. It is for the same reason that someone else is a signaller, porter or guard. It is fated thus. Don't laugh at my railway associations. The railway got into my blood very early in life. Engines with their tremendous clanging and smoke ensnared my senses. I felt at home on the railway platform and considered the station-master and porter the best company for man, and their railway talk the most enlightened. I grew up in their midst. Ours was a small house opposite the Malgudi station. The house had been built by my father with his own hands long before the trains were thought of. (10)

From the time his father handed over the small shop at the station to Raju, Raju has been growing amidst the thrill he derives from the modernity and bustle of the environment. He enjoys company: "I liked to talk to people. I liked to hear people talk" (43). In order to accommodate himself to others and to meet the expectations of others, he equips himself in many ways: "I read stuff that interested me, bored me, baffled me, and dozed off in my seat. I read stuff that picked up a noble thought, a philosophy that appealed, I gazed on pictures . . . I learnt much from scrap" (44). He is never left alone: "Although I never looked for acquaintances, they somehow came looking for me" (49). When people come with inquiries or to seek his help, Raju is unable to say "no" to anyone:

> I never said, "I don't know." Not in my nature, I suppose. If I had the inclination to say "I don't know what you are talking about," my life would have taken a different turn. Instead, I said, "Oh, yes, a fascinating place. Haven't you seen it? You must find the time to visit it, otherwise your whole trip here would be a waste." I am sorry I said it, an utter piece of falsehood. It was not because I wanted to utter a falsehood, but only because I wanted to be pleasant. (49)

Without giving serious thought to the inquiries or the subject, Raju furnishes the information in order to please the inquirer, and to accommodate himself to any situation.

Thus, from the beginning of his career, he is an accommodator: "So extreme a degree of accommodation means that Raju's sincerity consists in being false, and his positive existence is being a vacancy filled by others" (Walsh 122). What Walsh ignores, however, is that Raju's attempts to accommodate, mundane as they are, nonetheless prepare him for the transcendent life he eventually achieves. Raju accommodates as a product of others' interests and needs. Raju's personality is shaped as a kind of "selfless detachment," sacrificing self and identity to please others—this is also an essential quality for good business. Such detachment and sacrifice can lead to a loss of genuine identity. It can lead, however, to transcendence.

One day a scholar named Marco and his wife, Rosie, arrive in Malgudi as tourists. Life takes many unexpected turns for Raju after Marco's appearance. "Enigmatic" and "a queer abstraction of a man," Marco has his interests in "collecting and annotating ancient art," and has little appreciation for Rosie's talents as a classical dancer, or indeed any other interest: "Anything that interested her seemed to irritate him" (67). With his humanitarian and tactful approach, Raju easily gains Marco's confidence: "I was accepted by Marco as a member of the family. From guiding tourists I seemed to have come to a sort of concentrated guiding of a single family" (100).

Marco's scholarly preoccupation with the ruined temples (reminiscent of totally secularized and insensitive teachers and scholars in Narayan's other works) and Rosie's loneliness and dazzling beauty initiate Raju into an affair with Marco's discontented wife. "Their relationship," as Walsh observes, "both at the beginning and later when she breaks off with Marco and comes to live with Raju, appears to be much more one of feeling than sensuality, a temperamental rather than a passionate union" (123). Rosie is the only woman Raju is infatuated with, though temporarily, and is the only woman in his life, save his mother, to warn him on his vanity. But Raju accommodates Rosie, and—as always—takes an interest in what most interests her, namely, classical dance.

Dance in India is a religious ritual because it is an archetype of the dance of Shiva, "the god whose primal dance created the vibrations that set the world in motion" (108). By caste Rosie is a temple dancer, familiar with the *Natya Shastra of Bharat Muni* (a thousand-year-old treatise on dance by sage Bharat). Besides her studious reading at least a couple of hours every forenoon in the ancient works of art ("to keep the purity of the classical forms"), she wishes to be helped by some expert who can read and explain to her "episodes from *Ramayana* and *Mahabharata,* because they are a treasure house, and we can pick up so many ideas for new compositions from them" (108). She further demonstrates to Raju not only her skill, but her religious commitment to this ancient art. One day, standing at one end of the hall, she sings in a soft undertone a song from an ancient Sanskrit composition of a lover and a lass:

When she lightly raised her foot and let it down, allowing her ankles to jingle, I felt thrilled. Though I was an ignoramus, I felt moved by the movements, rhythm, and time, although I did not quite follow the meaning of the words . . . "Lover means always God," and she took the trouble to explain to me the intricacies of its rhythm . . . I could see, through her effort, the magnificence of the composition, its symbolism, the boyhood of a very young youth to decay, but the heart remaining ever fresh like a lotus on a pond. When she indicated the lotus with her fingers, you could almost hear the ripple of water around it. She held the performance for nearly an hour; it filled me with the greatest pleasure on earth. I could honestly declare that while I watched her perform, my mind was free, for once, from all carnal thoughts; I viewed her as a pure abstraction. (110–11)

On seeing the brilliant performance, and on hearing Rosie's eloquence and her earnestness on this subject, Raju feels that:

he should immediately pick up and cultivate the necessary jargon. I felt silly to be watching her and listening to her, absolutely tongue-tied. There were, of course, two ways open: to bluff one's way through and trust to luck, or to make a clean breast of it all. I listened to her talk for two days and finally confessed to her, "I am a layman, not knowing much the technicalities of the dance; I'd like you to teach me something of it." I didn't want her to interpret it as an aversion on my part to the art. That might drive her back to the arms of her husband, and so I took care to maintain the emphasis on my passion for the art. (109)

It is obvious how sincerity and self deception, a caution not to offend or displease Rosie, an anxiety to be on a par in taste and knowledge, and a fear of losing this beautiful woman—all co-exist in Raju. The mundane pull is strong yet, as so often in Narayan's fiction, inextricably mixed with the sacred. But only because Rosie is in her own way a devout young woman, completely devoted to her art, can she serve as an improbable step in Raju's journey toward the transcendence of his own mundane and multifarious life. Raju, it may be said, has no mind of his own; he lives at the whim of others about him and his own transient emotion. Rosie does have a mind of her own, and together they embark on the most persistent and single-minded project imaginable for Raju.

Although Rosie makes many good efforts to stay with her husband, and stabilize her love and marriage, Marco deserts her during their second trip to Malgudi: "The word 'dance' always stung him" (130). Dance, and other fine arts in India, originated in the temple. Almost every composition or choreography of south Indian classical pieces of performing and fine arts is a form of prayer. Art was a form of *bhakti* (devotion), prayerful articulations of devotion to the Absolute godhead. But in Marco's opinion, dance is nothing more than some "street-acrobatics." Marco's dislike has some grounds, owing to the numerous scandals of lechery caused by some of the temple authorities and dancers. Hence, he is very much infuriated on hearing Rosie argue:

> "Everyone except you likes it."

> "For instance?"

> "Well, Raju saw me do it, and he was transported. . . ."

> . . . .

> ". . . you are not my wife. You are a woman who will go to bed with anyone who flatters your antics. . . ." (132–34)

With this argument, Marco makes up his mind to leave Rosie. When Marco leaves Malgudi, Rosie takes refuge in Raju's house in order to nurture her art. He consoles her on hearing her sorry plight: "'You are in the right place. Forget all your past. We will teach that cad a lesson by and by.' I made a grandiose announcement. 'First, I'll make the world recognize you as the greatest artist of the age'" (135). Raju's spontaneous promises and emotional utterances to console and help the other party are not surprising, since he has shaped himself to be an accommodator.

His widowed mother doesn't approve of Rosie's presence in the house, and warns him of the danger that might follow when a married girl, especially a dancer, deserted by her husband, stays with a bachelor in the same house. The role of women in Narayan's novels in enhancing the transcendence of the protagonists is vital. Here, Raju, a self-made man, pays little heed to his helpless mother, and her sacred and traditional values: "Don't interfere, Mother. I am an adult. I know what I am doing. . . . I don't care for their [his uncle's and cousin's] opinion. Just don't bother about such things" (135-36). Encouraged by Raju, Rosie starts her dance practice: "She got up at five in the morning, bathed and prayed before the picture of a god in my mother's niche, and began the practice session which went on for nearly three hours. The house rang with the jingling of her anklets" (136).

Raju's mother keeps insisting to him that Rosie ought to go to her husband and "fall at his feet" (137). She instructs Rosie, too, with anecdotes on the varieties of husbands, "good husbands, mad husbands, reasonable husbands, unreasonable ones, savage ones, slightly deranged ones, moody ones, and so on and so forth; but it was always the wife, by her doggedness, perseverance, and patience, that brought him round" (137). Such instructions to Rosie from Raju's mother increase day by day. She also "quoted numerous mythological stories of Savitri, Seetha, and all well-known heroines" (137). Raju turns a deaf ear to his mother's traditional views, and Rosie is torn between her passion for art and an indifferent husband. With finances not so well off, Raju, though he wishes, is not in a position to keep Rosie in any hotel. Hence, Raju is forced to face gossip and insults from his people and creditors, and has to stay with his mother in the same house.

Rosie continues to be a devoted artist though, in the beginning, Raju tries to use her just to satiate his carnal emotions and passions, in order to forget his worries and troubles. As for Rosie, "She was a devoted artist, her passion for physical love was falling into place, and had ceased to be a primary obsession with her" (145). Raju never ponders over the sacredness of tradition and morality. The women in his life are not able to effect his transcendence. Although Raju's mother tries to adjust to Raju's ways "as an unmitigated loafer," the arrival of her elder brother brings matters to a close. Finally, despite his pleas, his mother leaves him and Malgudi in order to live with her brother in another village. She reminds him as she leaves, "'Don't fail to light the lamps in the God's niche. . . . Be careful with your health" (155).

After his mother's departure, Raju and Rosie are "a married couple to all appearances" (155). Rosie manages the housekeeping in addition to her dance practices. Raju is prone to steep himself "in an all-absorbing romanticism, until I woke up to the fact she was getting tired of it all" (155). Rosie insists on further plans as she is now ready for public performance, "a show for four hours" (157). The deteriorating financial position compels Raju to awaken from his licentious slumber.

One day, his creditor, a wholesale merchant, calls on Raju. Raju owes the merchant a good sum of money. Within a week Raju has to appear in court regarding his debts. With no friends left, except the taxi driver, Gaffur, Raju shares with him his new vision of Rosie: "'She is a gold-mine' I cried. 'If I had money to start her with—oh!' My visions soared. I said to him, 'You know *Bharat Natyam* is the greatest art-business today. There is such a craze for it that people will pay anything to see the best'. . . ." (144). Raju's efforts, combined with Rosie's brilliance in and devotion to her art, open new gates to fame and money.

Once Rosie's talent and genius as a dancer are recognized by the public, "rocket-like she soared" (162). Raju's relationship with Rosie alters "from being personal to functional or official." With the change of her name to "Nalini," Raju is now "less the lover and more the manager, trainer and agent of Rosie" (Walsh, 124). Living now in a world of show-manship,

> [they are] going through a set of mechanical actions day in and day out—the same receptions at the same station, fussy organizers, encounters, and warnings, the same middle sofa in the first row, speeches and remarks and smiles, polite conversation, garlands and flash photos, congratulations, and off to catch the train—pocketing the most important thing, the cheque . . . . I demanded the highest fee, and got it, of anyone in India. I treated those that came to ask for a show as supplicants. I had an enormous monthly income, I spent an enormous amount of income tax. Yet I found Nalini accepting it all with a touch of resignation rather than bouncing contentment. (172)

Rosie's interest declines once Raju commercializes her art. Although by caste a temple dancer, and now a woman living away from her husband with another man, Rosie's sense of values is not entirely wiped out. Raju has no sense of any values of his own. With no awareness as to how his inner self is affected, he revels in publicity, money, and busy schedules. The experience with Rosie, though potentially transcendent, thus turns out to be a false start—as so often happens in Narayan's work.

The world of fortune and fame collapses as suddenly as it came about. One day, a bulky letter addressed to Rosie from a lawyer's firm in Madras arrives by registered mail. Raju wavers for a moment, deciding whether to open it himself or give it to Rosie. The mundane wins. He opens the letter and learns that Rosie's lawyer has sent an application to be duly signed by his client and her husband Marco, for the release of her jewels from the bank. The mundane in Raju rejoices at the thought of more jewels, and prompts him first to delay handing over the letter to Rosie and finally to keep Rosie in ignorance of the letter and its contents. The lawyer's instruction, "Per return post," urges Raju to act fast, not through honest means, but to forge Rosie's signature. Whether Raju acted deliberately or "out of some muddled system of motives, a mixture of curiosity, jealousy, good will, sheer love of the devious, and the habit of doing things for no adequate reason at all" (Walsh, 124), Raju is soon prosecuted for forgery, and sentenced to two years imprisonment. With this event, the second phase of his career terminates.

In jail, however, Raju's leadership among his fellow convicts as "model prisoner" keeps him busy as a public person:

> I visited all departments of the prison as a sort of benevolent super-visor. I got on well with all the wardens. . . .Whether they were homicides or cut-throats or highwaymen, they [the prisoners] all lis-tened to me, and I could talk them out of their blackest moods.

> When there was a respite, I told them stories and philosophies and what not. And they came to refer to me as *vadhyar*—that is, teacher. There were five hundred prisoners in that building and I could claim to have established a fairly widespread intimacy with most of them. (202–3)

The amazing vitality with which Raju could face the grim situation, and do positive things for his fellow convicts, cannot be dismissed. Raju does not allow either his spirits or those of the other prisoners to sink into hopelessness. Quite unaware, he is able to liberate the prisoners from their "blackest moods." Here too, he is a guide, a *guru,* a teacher. Whatever his personal shortcomings, now in this environment, where men are locked up so as to undergo remorse, alienation, and loneliness, Raju gives them rays of hope. Raju had rendered the same kind of assistance to Rosie whenever her spirits got shattered by her indifferent husband.

After rendering his services to his fellow prisoners, Raju spends some time in solitude with nature and work in the vegetable garden:

> I loved every piece of this work, the blue sky and sunshine, and the shade of the house in which I sat and worked, the feel of cold water; it produced in me a luxurious sensation. Oh, it seemed to be so good to be alive and feeling all this—the smell of freshly turned earth filled me with the greatest delight. (203–4)

Raju has the unique capacity to love life wherever he is, and to relish things around him. Despite his unedifying past, he lives the present in its every moment and accepts everything it offers. Instead of brooding over things past and lost, he is in harmony with nature, and enjoys the luxury of blue sky, sunshine, shade, and the earth. In fact he feels sorry to be released after his term, since he finds the prison "not a bad place," except "to be awakened every morning at five," which he hated (8).

After his release from prison, the third phase commences at a neglected temple on the outskirts of a little village, Mangala, where Raju seeks shelter. He spends the night here and awakes the next morning to find a peasant, Velan, staring at him intensely. Velan is the first peasant to discover Raju by the sacred precincts: "Raju welcomed the intrusion— something to relieve the loneliness of the place. The man stood gazing reverentially on his face. Raju felt amused and embarrassed" (5). Velan associates the temple and the river flowing beneath it, the sacred symbols of India, with Raju. After that day, the rustics unquestioningly impose reverence and devotion on Raju, and consider him a divine oracle: "The villager on the lower step looked up at his face with devotion, which irked Raju (8). Raju asks brusquely, "Why do you look at me like that?" to which the man replies, "I don't know" (8). Thus, Raju is raised to the level of a spiritual leader without any effort on his part. Raju is astonished, and so he "stroked his chin thoughtfully to make sure that an apostolic beard had not suddenly grown there" (6).

Raju wants to tell them that he is at their village because he has nowhere else to go, and that he is "not as great" as they "imagine" but just an "ordinary" man, but whenever he attempts to articulate this truth something or other hinders him. First, Velan seriously seeks Raju's guidance in dealing with a problem. Now "the old, old habit of affording guidance to others" asserts itself, and so Raju inquires about the problem without uttering the truth he wanted to. It is also "his nature to get involved in other people's interests and activities" (8). When the naive rustics approach him with problems, Raju nods his head and adds, "'So has everyone,' in a sudden access of pontificality. Ever since the moment this man [Velan] had come and sat before him, gazing on his face, he [Raju] had experienced a feeling of importance" (13). This time his role is that of a "spiritual guide." The extreme simplicity of Velan and companions, "the stuff disciples are made of" (17), which Balarama Gupta calls "idiotic" (130), enhances the role of Raju. But in these simple folks, intellect is subordinated to intuition, and dogma to experience, and hence, they fail to probe the authenticity of any *guru* or *sanyasi* (one who has renounced the world). Thereafter, Raju feels "like an actor who was always expected to utter the right sentence" (14).

The gifts of food brought by the villagers solve Raju's immediate problem of satisfying his hunger, whereas Chandran's (the protagonist in Narayan's *The Bachelor of Arts* [1937]) sense of remorse is provoked by the very sight of the gifts brought by the villagers. Chandran, too, takes the easy guise of a *sanyasi* to live amidst the villagers. But his choice is an alternative to suicide, and once he realizes his folly he gives up the guise and returns home. Yet in both cases, the villagers benefit by strengthening their own religious sensibilities. In Raju, Narayan presents "the ironic treatment of a hallowed Indian prototype whose *avatars* (incarnations) continue to beguile Indians and mystify Westerners . . ." [Kantak, 42]. But Narayan's irony in Raju "becomes something like a new perspective because his sympathies are as deeply engaged by the genuine component of that prototype as his derision is aroused by the imposture often foisted upon it" [Kantak, 42]. It is easier to brand Raju as a sinner than to wait with immense patience and compassion to trace the effects of such imposed spiritual leadership.

Narayan's comic art and subtle irony are at their height in these episodes, and doubtless many readers do (and should) enjoy them for that reason alone. But there is a deeper level, as we see Raju once again drawn willy-nilly, by a naive single-mindedness akin to Rosie's, into an ambiguously sacred role. He is compelled, by the will of others simpler even than he is, to rise above his limitation—or more precisely, to make the most of his talents and what by now must be called his long schooling in both unselfish dedication and shameless showmanship.

Ordinary utterances and simple guesses of Raju are sufficient to provoke the rustics' admiration, and to increase their pious sentiments. Velan comes one day and tells Raju of his worry concerning his step-sister:

> "As the head of the family, I have given her every comfort at home, provided her with all the jewellery and clothes a girl needs, but . . . ." He paused slightly before bringing out the big surprise. But Raju completed the sentence for him, "The girl shows no gratitude."
>
> "Absolutely, sir!" said the man.
>
> "And she shall not accept your plans for her marriage?"
>
> "Oh, too true, sir," Velan said, wonderstruck. (14)

Now, after this conversation, Velan has no doubts about the prophetic abilities of Raju.

Whenever Raju makes earnest attempts to make his position clear, and to erase their faith in him, he not only fails, but makes the reverence soar higher than before. Raju tells Velan sharply, "There is nothing extraordinary in my guess," and promptly comes the reply from Velan: "Not for you to say that, sir. Things may look easy enough for a giant, but ordinary poor mortals like us can never know what goes on in other people's minds" (27).

Sivaramakrishna points out that "the basic structural polarity of the novel, in terms of characters, is built around the villager Velan (or villagers) and the urbanized Raju . . ." (71). Here is a principle of double effects—the uncritical faith of the simple villagers acts as a compelling force for Raju to continue amidst their company. The fine compliments and simple faith that well from the hearts of the people bewilder Raju, yet his uneasiness is only within him, and he never makes any bold attempt to clear the place on account of his second thoughts about his economy and identity which fare well near the temple, river, and village. Although he is aware of the false role imposed on him, he "acquiesces" in it.

Raju adjusts his physical appearance to suit the role—acquiring beard and beads—for which Balarama Gupta calls Raju "a classic example of a counterfeit guru, a hypocrite masquerading as a saint, a sinner in saffron" (31). However, Raju is amazed "at the amount of wisdom welling from the depths of his being" (41). No wonder "the Yogi is still a mysterious figure and a source of satirical portraiture in the hands of the Western novelist" (Narasimhaiah 182). There is a general tendency in most Westerners to associate Yogi or the mysticism of the East only with some rigorous and bizarre exotic exercises of the body.

Some Eastern crooks and vagabonds reinforce this general tendency by posing as astrologers, yoga masters, saffron-robed *sanyasis* with "beard and beads," etc., for monetary purposes. Spirituality or religious sensibility can nowhere be commercialized. Narayan brings in these different figures and counterfeits to contrast with the genuine religious sensibility and culture of India. Raju, undoubtedly, is a fake *sanyasi* at this moment though he doesn't perform any of the exotic feats. Another important observation regarding Raju is that though he is far from any genuine sage, he never misguides these simple folks. On the contrary, he works toward their unity and their well-being.

One day when the children of the village throng around him and gaze in awe, Raju, in the manner of big men in cities, asks the small boys about their school and classes. On hearing that they have no school in the village and that the boys minded the cattle all day, "Raju clicked his tongue in disapproval" (39). His emotions and gestures, though often not genuine, have an infectious effect on his audience: "The gathering looked pained and anxious" (39). As usual, Raju explains grandly the importance of education, and inspires them with the suggestion of an evening school. Raju of course is a well-educated man, though largely self-educated, through his indiscriminate reading, his expertise as a tour guide, and his interest in Rosie's sacred arts. The next afternoon, a school master meets with Raju to talk about the difficulties of an evening school, but Raju says with authority: "'I like to see young boys become literate and intelligent.' He added with fervor because it sounded nice. 'It's our duty to make everyone happy and wise.' This overwhelming altruism was too much for the teacher. 'I'll do anything,' he said, 'under your guidance'" (41). The teacher goes back to the village "a changed man." Himself not yet liberated, still he helps the children of a village to liberation—from ignorance to knowledge.

The following evening, a dozen children of the village gather in the ruined temple for their education. The teacher points out to Raju the reason for the small attendance: "They are afraid of crossing the river in the dark; they have heard of a crocodile hereabouts" (41). Raju's eloquent lecture on courage and fearlessness is very effective:

> "What can a crocodile do to you if your mind is clear and your conscience is untroubled?" Raju said grandly. It was a wonderful sentiment to express. . . . "Keep your ears open and mouth shut, that'll take you far," hitting upon a brilliant aphorism. (41–44)

Pouring out fine sentiments, often without realizing their seriousness, has become quite habitual for Raju. Courage and fearlessness are the fruits of transcendence, but the aphorisms Raju utters to the simple villagers are not those of a transcended Raju; he merely poses as a *guru* as if witnessing to the spirit and some disinterested virtues. Yet the villagers' genuine faith in his spiritual guidance and fine sentiments always moves the villagers themselves towards liberation, and Raju's mundane virtues begin to take on sacred value. At the teacher's request, Raju talks to the small boys on godliness, cleanliness, *Ramayana*, and the epics. It is an irony to hear him speak of "clear mind" and untroubled conscience. Yet, his eloquence does effect courage and fearlessness in them; the "upturned faces of the children" shone in the half light as they listened to Raju.

Day by day his name and fame grow enormously: ". . . his prestige had grown beyond his wildest dreams. His life had lost its personal limitations; his gatherings had become so large that they overflowed into the outer corridors. . ." (47). Things proceed smoothly till a drought hits Mangala, when hunger, poverty, loss, and petty quarrels between villages increase with time. Raju reflects and decides: "The village people do not know how to remain peaceful. They are becoming more and more agitated. At this rate, I think I'll look for a new place" (84).

Narayan allows his readers to draw whatever implications they will from his relentless and comic exposure of Raju. It has often been observed that Raju is full of rather universal human qualities. In the character of Raju, Narayan portrays the enormous proportion of the mundane in every man, which is constantly in conflict with transcendent urges, and attempts to postpone or delay the integration to the very end.

Balarama Gupta accuses Narayan of being "less scathing and more covert" in his attacks on Raju, "because he [Narayan] can laugh at human follies and absurdities without any great involvement or a well-defined commitment to human values" (135). But Narayan, as Narasimhaiah states, knows:

> his men and his women; he knows their pettiness as well as their ideals and aspirations, and above all, the little ironies of their lives. He looks at all of them with a tenderness and a compassion more like a Jane Austen than a George Eliot, much less as a Hardy. (175)

At any rate, Raju grows, "against serious odds . . ." (Narasimhaiah, 187). His fame and position as a *guru* are well established, yet they carry with them an enormous responsibility, especially in the bad times. Raju dreads any serious responsibility, particularly when it concerns his own liberation from his deep rooted "self-deception," yet he cannot escape the situation at Mangala which grows worse with time. "His life," as Narayan explicitly indicates, "had lost its personal limitations."

He cannot exercise his charisma to control nature, as he did with the simple folks. The rains fail. The wells dry up. The cattle are found dead. People quarrel at the water-hole for priorities, and there is "fear, desperation and lamentation in their voices." Raju, "on observing the growing violence in the village, and the villagers' fights with other neighboring villagers for commodities," feels it "impossible to lecture on the ethics of peace, and so merely says, 'No one should fight'" (87). With selfish motives he reflects: "He did not like the idea of commotion. It might affect the isolation of the place, and bring the police on the scene. He did not want anyone to come to the village" (87).

While Raju is alarmed over growing unrest in the village, though with selfish apprehensions, Velan's younger brother, "one of the lesser intelligences of the village, brings news about a serious fight between the villagers. Raju feels too wary to reason with this "semi-moron," hence he grips the boy's arm and says:

> "Tell your brother, immediately, wherever he may be, that unless they are good I'll never eat."
>
> "Eat what?" asked the boy, rather puzzled.
>
> "Say that I'll not eat. Don't ask what. I'll not eat unless they are good."
>
> . . . .
>
> This was frankly beyond the comprehension of the boy. . . . His eyes opened wide. He could not connect the fight and this man's food. (87)

Raju never foresees that the message he delivers to Velan's younger brother can undergo such an enormous distortion.

Velan and company hear the message: "The Swami, the Swami, does not want food anymore . . . because . . . it doesn't rain" (88-89). The message is mistaken for a fast, and so the villagers start prostrating before Raju. They tell him: "You are not a human being. You are a Mahatma. We should consider ourselves blessed indeed to be able to touch the dust of your feet" (93).

Much against his will and expectation, another great title is conferred on Raju, "Mahatma" (great soul), which implies in this context fast and sacrifice. Gandhi is always addressed as "Mahatma Gandhi" because of his greatness. Shortly before his death in 1948, Gandhi undertook a fast to end communal disturbances and pleaded for brotherhood and understanding. So the undertaking of fast to bring peace and unity by great people is well known even to these illiterate simple folks of Mangala.

The whole countryside is now in a happy ferment "because a great soul had agreed to go through the trial" (95). The villagers are edified by the sacrifice Raju is to undertake on their behalf: "They gazed on his face and kept looking up in a new manner; there was a greater solemnity in the air than he had ever known before," and "Raju felt really touched by this attitude" (93-95). Here, the villagers' faith and reverence infect him, and his old habit of complying and accommodating now compel him to serve them according to their wishes. The villagers' spontaneous remarks reveal and affirm the exalted regard they have for Raju:

> "This Mangala is a blessed country to have a man like the Swami in our midst. No bad thing will come to us as long as he is with us. He is like Mahatma. When Mahatma Gandhi went without food, how many things happened in India! This is a man like that. If he fasts there will be rain. Out of his love for us he is undertaking it. This will surely bring rain and help us . . ." The atmosphere became electrified. They forgot the fight, and all their trouble and bickering. (90)

The villagers may appear idiotic in their blind faith in Raju because "whatever the battle Gandhi might be engaged in, his weapons were always *ahimsa* ('non-violence, the refusal to hurt any living thing'), truthfulness, courtesy, and love" (Zaehner, 173).

Raju, the reader knows, is far from the essential Gandhian ideologies which emphasized even during the freedom struggle that "until the Indians had freed themselves from egoistic passions, they would never free themselves from the British" (Zaehner, 177). Raju's ego is still deeply satiated, though at times with apprehension, in the veneration he receives from the simple folks. Once this is acknowledged, one still must say that Raju's *way* of stroking his ego brings wonder, beauty, and liberation to the villagers—moreover, with hindsight, we can see that he has been doing this sort of thing throughout his life, and that his checkered career has even been a preparation for his ambiguously holy life.

Velan says that a Saviour should "stand in knee-deep water, look to the skies, and utter the prayer lines for two weeks, completely fasting during the period . . ." (95). Raju realizes "the enormity of his own creation," and the "giant" he has created with his "puny self" (96). His realization leads to no remorse, rather it impels him to ponder on his imprudent calculations. If he had known that his pious suggestions would be applied to him, "he might have probably given a different formula" (97). Even now he is "perhaps ready to take the risk, if there was half the chance of getting away," yet he is moved "by the recollection of the big crowd of women and children touching his feet," and "by the thought of their gratitude" (97).

The earnestness with which the villagers express their sentiment and faith "brought tears to Raju's eyes" (95). He feels deeply that "after all the time had come for him to be serious—to attach value to his own words. He needed time—and solitude to think over the whole matter" (96). As he tries to speak, "his tone hushed with real humility and fear; his manner was earnest" (96).

Balarama Gupta may view *The Guide* as a "delightful" exposure of the "ignorance ridden Indian rural society as well as of typically Indian pseudo saints" (135) but the veneration, not the imprudence, of these simple folks, "with unswerving faith in God and the goodness of man (Narasimhaiah, 178), for "Raju the sanyasi," can be attributed to their cultural heritage:

> From the beginning of her history India has adored and idealized, not soldiers and statesmen, not men of science and leaders of industry, not even poets and philosophers . . . but men who have stamped infinity on the thought and life of the country, men who have added to the invisible forces of goodness in the world. (Radhakrishnan, 35)

There is a reversal of role here. While the villagers believe that Raju is their *guru*, Raju is now their disciple. Their faith and piety impel Raju to transform himself. In the end, Raju's resolution to keep away from food gives him "a peculiar strength," and his strength develops on these reflections: "If by avoiding food I should help the trees bloom, and the grass grow, why not do it thoroughly?" (213). Narayan comments:

> For the first time in his life he was making an earnest effort, for the first time he was learning the thrill of full application, outside money and love: for the first time he was doing a thing in which he was not personally interested. (213)

Raju's "earnest effort" and "full application" fill him with enthusiasm and vigor to go through the ordeal. On the fourth day of his fast, he goes down to the river and prays with perfect composure. Undoubtedly, it is "a supplication to the heavens to send down rain and save humanity" (213). The rhythmic chant, his form of prayer, lulls his tired body, and numbs his weak knees. Quite exhausted, he comes up to rest for a while on a mat near the temple.

Raju's fast and prayer become an edifying scene not only to Mangala, not only to the entire vicinity, but to the entire nation as well. Journalists keep reporting through various news media about Raju's fast and his condition. Even an American, James J. Malone, film producer from California, expresses his desire to carry the scene back to his country with the help of his television camera.

On the eleventh morning of his fast, Raju, helped by Velan and others, steps into the river:

> Everyone followed in a solemn, silent pace. The eastern sky was red. Many in the camp were still sleeping. Raju could not walk, but he insisted upon pulling himself along all the same. He panted with the effort. He went down the steps of the river, halting for breath on each step, and finally reached his basin of water. He stepped into it, shut his eyes and turned towards the mountain, his lips muttering the prayer. Velan and another held him each by an arm. The morning sun was out by now; a great shaft of light illuminated the surroundings. It was difficult to hold Raju to his feet, as he had a tendency to flop down. They held him as if he were a baby. Raju opened his eyes, looked about, and said, "Velan, it's raining in the hills. I can feel it coming up under my feet, up my legs—" and with that he sagged down. (221)

With eyes fixed on the sunlit mountain, and with lips chanting the prayer for rain, Raju finally collapses in the river. As Narasimhaiah indicates, Raju merges "literally and symbolically, into the world of nature" (178). Regarding this end of the novel, Narayan says in *My Days*: "Graham Green liked the story when I narrated it to him in London. While I was hesitating whether to leave my hero dead at the end of the story, Graham was definite that he should die" (168). The death, besides indicating the end of this earthly sojourn of Raju, also indicates his death to his old self. There is also the traditional Hindu belief that "gods can be propitiated and rains can be brought about to end a severe drought if somebody sacrifices his life through fasting and prayer" (Varma, 136). Raju's final words, "'Velan, it's raining in the hills. I can feel it coming up under my feet, up my legs—'. . ." (221), leave the reader to conclude on his own—the rain is just on the hills, and it may or may not reach Mangala, yet Raju feels a merging with nature.

The poverty and violence in Mangala appear as hostile factors threatening Raju's apparent safety and security; but the very same factors bring seriousness to the life of Raju. It is uncertain whether his fast really brings rain to the village; but his efforts to subdue violence and bring peace do succeed. Once he starts his fast, crowds pour into Mangala—not for any fight or violence, but to watch the Mahatma, thereby to take part in the sacrifice. There is integration. Thus, Raju's sacrifice works out a collective transcendence. Mangala and the nearby villages, representing rural India, are illiterate; poverty drives them to violence; their religiosity may be of the folk standard; and Narayan doesn't shy away from the portrayal of these irrational people. Yet the sacred customs of revering a man of god and his sacrifice, and obeying his dictums even at the cost of surrender, is vital in these simple folks' life and tradition. Thus, Raju not only calms the people, but unites them. Transcendence in Narayan's fiction is never a solitary affair.

Balarama Gupta accuses Narayan of irresponsibility:

> Narayan's attack on his roguish protagonist appears less scathing and more covert than it would have been at the hands of Mulk Raj Anand or Bhabani Bharracharya, because he can laugh at human follies and absurdities without any great involvement or a well-defined commitment to human values. (135)

But this judgment springs from his expectation that Narayan or any novelist should write for social causes and didactic purposes. Narayan, however, accepts man in his totality—both his imperfections and his aspirations. Hence, Cynthia Vanden Driesen commends Narayan: "The primary impression (in *The Guide*) is of fallibility and vulnerability—truly an Indian version of Everyman. Yet his characters remain rounded, individual and authentic portraitures" (58).

Despite severe arguments over the characterization of Raju, the pattern of transcendence with its different phases is indisputable, even though Raju's life is exceptionally disorganized. Raju has held several positions in life—a railway shopman, a railway guide, Rosie's agent, a prisoner, and finally an ascetic *guru*. While passing from one position to the next, Raju has encountered concrete realms of transition, several of them religious, but he proves immune to any spiritual milieu or transcendence. Starting as an ordinary boy minding his father's shop at the outskirts of Malgudi, Raju, a school dropout, gathers knowledge from various sources—assorted reading of secondhand books at the stall: "I read stuff that pricked up a noble thought, a philosophy that appealed, I gazed on pictures of temples . . ."; listening to tourists, etc., he "learnt much from scrap"—and elevates his position from a small-shop owner to a tourist guide. Formerly a good business man at the railway shop, he gains recognition as a versatile tourist guide—every tourist is directed to "Railway Raju." As a tourist guide, he meets different and strange people, and guides them to strange places of interest. When people wish to see the source of Sarayu, a sacred place, Raju is unaffected by such religious sensibilities though he guides people to such spots, and eloquently provides information on them. Especially when Marco arrives at Malgudi as a tourist, Raju has to accompany Marco to the ruined temples of Malgudi. Hence, before Raju starts the tour, he educates himself on "the episodes of Ramayana carved on the stone wall in the Iswara Temple"— a religious realm, but there is no spiritual experience in him.

When he encounters and makes his acquaintance with Rosie, it is a beautiful, enchanting, and religious realm of music and dance—but it does not affect Raju. Night and day he sees Rosie entirely and religiously devoted to her sacred art even during a very tragic situation in her married life. When his little house is filled with the sweet music of Rosie's ankle bells during her long hours of practice—a new and sacred realm— though Raju enjoys her art and views her as a "pure abstraction," yet even in this religious realm, Raju makes no spiritual discovery. Instead, he turns Rosie into a commercial venture. Even in prison, which may prove a bewildering physical realm for a normal human being, Raju is neither restless nor dissatisfied. He proves himself a good teacher to the fellow prisoners—personally, his value system remains unaltered, and there is no spiritual experience.

However, after his release from prison, he literally and physically enters a strange, bewildering, and religious realm, when he takes refuge in the ruined temple on the river banks at Mangala. The villagers also identify him with one of the deities in the temple, and revere him as a God-sent prophet in the religious precinct. Raju is stunned, hence he checks whether an "apostolic beard" has appeared on his chin overnight. Even an adolescent Chandran (in Narayan's *The Bachelor of Arts*) could make a spiritual discovery in a similar situation at Koopal—but not Raju. Raju accommodates himself to this new role—"beard and beads"—feeling safe in this new identity. There are the externals of religion in Raju, but there is not even the fear of God. Raju is not internally converted.

Finally, the restlessness amidst the villages caused by the drought not only dissatisfies, but scares Raju—lest the turmoil should bring the police to the scene. Raju has to step into a totally different realm when Velan's brother distorts Raju's message, and the villagers mistake the message for a fast. Raju is meditating on the ways of escaping from this strange realm of fast and prayer—yet the villager's faith wins him over: the "earnestness" of the people "brought tears to his eyes." There is a spiritual experience, and he responds. In this phase of transcendence, Raju is bewildered, stunned, yet consents to go through the fast to the very end—he really does something very much "out of character." Raju's pleasure in "doing something in which he was not personally interested" (213) is a spiritual discovery and experience not only for himself, not only for Mangala, but for several villages. The degrees of transcendence may vary, yet there is a collective transcendence—a liberation. Transcendence is never just an "inner" experience.

Undoubtedly, the spiritual discovery of Raju is different from the spiritual experience and liberation experienced by Narayan's characters in his other novels. In all the protagonists the world of contact is widened, and their spiritual discoveries affect the world positively. But here, too, Raju's case differs. He doesn't live to see the effect of collective transcendence. Nonetheless, Raju testifies to the fact that to attempt transcendence is not the monopoly of the pure and saintly.

In all his novels, Gilra says, "the comic thematic pattern is one of illusion—realization—disillusionment, or catastrophe—self-awareness—resolution" (103). But the term "resolution" is too simplistic. Gilra makes it sound like the end of a problem or process. Catastrophe and resolution may form the components of an ideal Greek tragedy, but in Narayan's work there is no final solution. In the lives of all the protagonists in all the novels of Narayan, there is no perfect or final resolution of life's problems. We are not encouraged to think that the characters will live happily ever after. Although the dynamism of these characters at the end of the novel after their liberation is obvious, transcendence is never complete and absolute. It is, and remains, a process.

All the novels are inconclusive, to varying degrees, and this suggests that transcendence is an ongoing, perennial process and never conclusive. There is no indication of any sort at the beginning of the novels about the way the interactions between the mundane and the transcendent will work out, nor is there any conclusion at the close of the novels guaranteeing the irrevocable transcendent position of the protagonists. There is also no metaphysical certainty about the degree of transcendence—sinners can be saints, and even the most saintly have conspicuous human frailties.

In all the characters, transcendence is not a flight from the mundane; rather, the mundane gets incorporated into the transcendent. Raju's mundane thirst for knowledge, and his self-education from "scrap" help him immensely when he guides the naive villagers of Mangala. His worldly wisdom, his simple psychological insights acquired through many acquaintances, and his accommodation to others' wishes aid him to the very end. And to the very end, Raju retains his natural ability to attract crowds and advise people.

Almost all the principal characters experience loneliness and alienation, during which period the mundane-transcendent interaction is intense, and during the same time the characters contemplate and evaluate their past. Raju starts narrating his true story when he is released from prison. He is not only lonely, but is totally alienated from Malgudi and other familiar company. He shuns society, since he wishes that his past be not remembered or referred to in any way. Raju differs from other protagonists. He is never left alone; yet amidst company he has no true companionship, and hence, he is lonely.

There may not be any explicit East-West issues in *The Guide* as there are in Narayan's other novels. But one can see clearly how the urbanized Raju compromises morality even when he is cautioned by the traditional characters—his mother, and Gaffur, the taxi driver. Raju's life is one of multiple ambiguities. Yet in the end, even Raju takes seriously his sacrificial fast to found a home on earth for the villagers as well as for himself.

The characters of Narayan neither premeditate nor foresee transcendence or liberation, and the earlier parts of the novels do not indicate in any way the transcendence achieved at the end. It is not always the case that the characters accept or welcome the mundane-transcendent interactions or transcend quite willingly with pure intentions. Raju dreams little of any genuine sacrifice on his part for the sake of the village or liberation of any kind when he takes refuge in the ruined temple in the outskirts of Mangala.

One of the remarkable features of all Indian literature and fine arts is the depiction of the inner urge in human nature which impels men to seek in endless ways for something they do not fully comprehend, and religion is the discipline that helps to articulate and achieve the spiritual ascent. Narayan stresses the daily mundane concerns of middle-class Indians, and the way in which mundane concerns lead to transcendent experience. Thus, while the remarkable Indian English writers like Mulk Raj Anand discuss the "economic hero," Raja Rao the "metaphysical hero," and Rabindranath Tagore the "mystical hero," Narayan observes and accepts ordinary men and women, even complex people like Raju, in their totality and discusses the "eternal" in every man. Hence, Narayan's works very uniquely appeal directly to the heart of the readers, since he mirrors ordinary men and women in their ordinary daily events, and presents the ordinariness and tangibility of transcendence. Narayan traces the journey of his protagonists, as we see in the case of Raju, during the process of transcendence, and the mundane-transcendent interactions as a compassionate observer—thus accepting them in their totality. The immense freedom that Narayan permits his characters helps the characters to work out their own transcendence in a realistic, convincing way.

Works Cited

Driesen, Cynthia V. "The Achievement of R.K. Narayan." *Literature East and West* 21, nos.1–4 (Dec./Jan. 1977), 51–64.

Gilra, Shiv K. "The Essential Narayan." *R.K. Narayan: A Critical Spectrum*. Ed. Bhagwat S. Goyal. Meerut: Shalabh Book House, 1983, 98–106.

Gupta, G.S. Balarama. "A Sinner is a Sinner is a Sinner—A Study of Raju." *Perspectives on R.K. Narayan*. Ed. Atma Ram. Ghaziabad: Vimal Prakashan, 1981, 127–35.

Kantak, V.Y. "The Achievement of R.K. Narayan." *Indian Literature of the Past Fifty Years—1917–1967*. Ed. C.D. Narsimhaiah. Mysore: University Publications, 1970, 133–46.

Narasimhaiah, C.D. "R.K. Narayan's *The Guide.*" *Aspects of Indian Writing in English*. Ed. M.K. Naik. Delhi: Macmillan, 1979: 172–98.

Narayan, R.K. *The Guide*. London: Methuen & Co., 1958.

_____. *My Days*. New York: Viking Press, 1974.

Radhakrishnan, S. *Eastern Religions and Western Thought*. New York: Oxford University Press, 1974.

Ranganath, N. "Realism in Literature: A Critique of R.K. Narayan's *The Guide.*" *Triveni* 48, no. 3 (Oct.–Dec. 1977): 81–85.

Sivaramakrishna, M. "The Cave and the Temple: Structural Symbolism in *The Guide.*" *Osmania Journal of English Studies* 14, no.1 (1978): 71–80.

Walsh, William. *R.K. Narayan: A Critical Appreciation*. London: Heinemann, 1982.

Zaehner, R.C. *Hinduism*. London: Oxford University Press, 1966.

The Ordinary and Average as Satiric Traps: The Case of R.K. Narayan

KIRPAL SINGH

R.K. Narayan is, along with Mulk Raj Anand and Raja Rao, regarded as one of India's best writers of English fiction. His exquisite use of the language, his ability to fuse character and action, his steady perception of life, his authentic portrayal of Indians, his relentless searchings for a moral center, his utilization of Indian myths and legends, are all features of his art that have helped to make him a recognized and established man of letters. Critics of Indo-English literature seldom hesitate to assign to Narayan a high place in the field. Almost all agree that Narayan's stature as being one of the finest Indo-English novelists is assured.[1] Very rarely does one hear a detracting voice.

It is with some trepidation, therefore, that I venture to offer the following critique of Narayan's work. My response is, of necessity, impressionistic, though I have tried to be as objective as is possible for one who attempts to re-define the achievement of a well-known and widely accepted writer. For over a decade now I have lived with Narayan's novels and have constantly wondered why, in spite of their wit, vision, and charm, they have not been able to *engage* me as deeply and as disturbingly as the novels of the writers with whom Narayan shares the crown of Indo-English fiction. Why, I have asked myself repeatedly, does not Narayan's work compare favorably with a novel like Raja Rao's *The Serpent and the Rope?* Why, the questions insist, does nothing in Narayan offer quite the same challenge as Mulk Raj Anand's *Coolie?*

Let it be stated at the outset that my reservations have little to do with Narayan's craftsmanship. Indeed, like the rest of his critics, I find myself in awe of Narayan's versatility. His command of language, his grasp of style—regardless of what he told Ved Mehta[2]—his control of tone are impeccable. He knows what makes a novel good and uses this knowledge to supreme advantage. He is able to tell an interesting story in an interesting manner. He has a particular gift for characterization; and insofar as character determines a novel's quality, Narayan's novels are, all of them, quite excellent. The four novels that are considered to be his best—*The Financial Expert* (1953), *The Guide* (1958), *The Man-Eater of Malgudi* (1962), and *The Sweet-Vendor* (1967)—are, without exception, flawless. When Narayan experiments with the form—as in *The Guide*—he is most careful to ensure that the reader's interest is sustained by both plot and character. For many readers and scholars, one of the major attractions of Narayan's work is that it follows fairly traditional patterns of novelistic technique. Indeed, as is often pointed out, where the best of Raja Rao and Anand is flawed, Narayan's is not. Why then, in spite of the fact that Narayan is an infinitely better craftsman than either Rao or Anand, do I hesitate to endorse his achievement?

In a thought-provoking article entitled, "The Average as Positive," Rajeev Taranath raises the question as follows: "When we consider Narayan's novels as a totality we are faced with the problem of locating the precise area of his creative genius." Taranath goes on to state that "Narayan's achievements could be described as the creative use of the ordinary." While Taranath goes into some length to demonstrate Narayan's "creative use of the ordinary," he nevertheless points out the possible dangers of such a talent: "A bias towards the average could be interpreted as a limitation in an author—it could be a pointer to many things, a lack of intensity, a refusal to commit himself, paucity of variegated experience, even an incapacity to participate in the subtler functions of imaginative life." Taranath concludes, however, that Narayan's achievement "finally lies in the uncompromising way in which he forces the ingredients of limitation towards evolving an authenticity which satisfies."

It is precisely here, I feel, where my major reservation comes in: I do not think Narayan's authenticity *finally* satisfies. It charms, often it lulls, but it does not satisfy. And the reasons for this are to be found in the specific mode in which Narayan has chosen to write: the satiric. From the time of the publication of his first novel, *Swami and Friends* (1935) Narayan has used the satiric mode for peculiar effects. Here, for example, is an extract from his novel:

> The Headmaster listened for a while and, in an undertone, demanded an explanation. They were nearing the terminal examination and Ebenezar had still not gone beyond the Nativity. When would he reach the Crucifixion and Resurrection, and begin to revise? Ebenezar was flabbergasted. He could not think of anything to say. He made a bare escape by hinting that that particular day of the week, he usually devoted to a rambling revision. Oh, no! He was not as far behind as that. He was in the proximity of the Last Supper. (11)

Ebenezar's fanaticism, his apparent familiarity with the Bible, and his skill in evading truth, are only too-well satirized in the passage. Very clever indeed, we say, to Narayan, how clever to expose hypocrisy with such consummate skill! But our adulation does not provide any answer to the question as to whether or not such writing is truly significant. It may be replied that this is from a very early work and therefore contains juvenile sketches, but such a reply is no answer. Here is a passage from *The Painter of Signs* (1976):

> A sign-board was inevitable in modern life, a token of respectable and even noble intentions. But he felt abashed when he realized that he was perhaps picking his own loot in the general scramble of a money-mad world! He wished he could do without it, but realized too that it was like a desire for a dry spot while drifting along neck deep in a cesspool. Ultimately he would evolve a scheme for doing without money. While bicycling, his mind attained a certain passivity, and ideas bubbled up, lingered a while, burst, and vanished. (13–14)

Many years after Ebenezar, Narayan is still poking fun at his characters in the same old witty fashion: the characters, the subjects, the themes might have changed, not the subtle touch of satire! In the passage just quoted, Raman's hypocrisy is satirized as mercilessly (and as mockingly) as Ebenezar's in *Swami and Friends*.

Writers of satire have seldom been accorded the status of being "great." One thinks of Juvenal, Ben Jonson, John Dryden, Alexander Pope, Jonathan Swift: first-rate writers, yes, but not great. There is something about satire that finally alienates. We feel that somehow the writer has cheated us. The disappointment is acute when we realize that we have been cheated in the process of superb entertainment. In the hands of a consummate satirist a deliberately created *distance* between observer and observed functions to allow the observer to join in the general mockery and ridicule. Like the author, we the readers feel that we are watching human folly without ourselves being involved. We feel elated at the thought that we simply could not display that spectacle of stupidity and foolishness which we see amply portrayed in the characters that the author is satirizing. It is only much later that we realize how subtly the author has betrayed us: to think that between Gulliver and the Yahoos there isn't really much space for us is indeed a sobering and disquieting thought! And we feel angry with Swift, wish he could have had a less chagrined view of human nature.

I wish to suggest that Narayan's achievement as a novelist suffers the same fate. In fact, because Malgudi is so vividly presented to us, because the men and women who move in and out of Narayan's books are so readily identifiable, because of his "fidelity" to life, Narayan's novels become all the more excruciatingly frustrating. The masters of satire have usually tended to satirize the values and behavior of the above-average; thereby allowing us, the ordinary ones, the safety-valve on non-belonging. With Narayan, however, this safety valve is gone: here the average and the ordinary become the butts of relentless ridicule. Beneath the veneer of the so-called "comic vision" for which Narayan is so frequently praised, one detects an extreme mistrust of life, a reluctance to accord to the average and the ordinary any kind of face-saving device, a desire to put the average and the ordinary in their proper places, a need somehow to prevent the average and the ordinary from triumphing. Again and again, the average and the ordinary provide Narayan the fun he is looking for, the vicarious sense of superiority that every satirist cherishes.

Put differently, the satirist is almost never really involved with his characters, he portrays them from a distance; there is a sense of superiority. In Narayan's novels, as he has often been commented, the world of Malgudi takes on a life of its own. This life is, to all intents and purposes, supposed to be faithfully rendered; the author hardly interferes with the activities of the people who inhabit Malgudi. There is a marked objectivity about the way in which Narayan presents his Malgudi to us; the conflicts, the complications, the thousand-and-one awkward situations belong to the characters themselves. From one point of view this is to be highly praised; objectivity is, after all, a precious weapon in the hands of a gifted novelist.

And yet objectivity can betray an aloofness that prides itself. For example, we ask ourselves what is the *quality* of the life that the inhabitants of Malgudi lead? Malgudi may, for all we know, be a little India, even the whole world in microscopic terms. The one distinctive feature about this fascinating town seems to be that it is utterly without hope, without glory, without any kind of magnificence. It is supremely the world of the average and the ordinary. Even when people try to break out of the ruts they are in, they return, again and again, to the same routines, the same humdrum rounds of existence they are habituated to. The most notable illustration of this feature of the Malgudi-syndrome is Jagan, the chief character in *The Sweet-Vendor*. Jagan, obsessed with a profound sense of guilt, eventually decides that the world is too much with him and that he best ought to save himself by becoming a hermit. He goes off, bent upon hermitage, but, we are told, kept his checkbook with him! Within the context of the novel, the checkbook has played a central role, and since Jagan takes it along with him at the very end, we wonder how sincere his conversion to a new life is. Here was a chance for Narayan to save a character, but he resolutely does not.

The defense for such ambiguity is that life as we know it is mostly ambiguous, that there are rarely any clear-cut answers to the large riddles of life. And, the argument concludes, Narayan ought to be congratulated for offering us a true picture of life. The response to this is that ambiguity is not the whole of life, it is a partial slice. What upsets me is that in Narayan's work, often the ambiguity is there for the sake of ambiguity, as a kind of tease. This unease on my part is substantiated by the fact that the most powerful device which Narayan uses to impress this ambiguity upon us is the device of irony. We all know how much of a past master Narayan is in his employment of irony to depict human folly. Now as far as I know no great master of irony has ever given us a world view in which human existence is seen to be ultimately meaningful. This may sound as a gross oversimplification but its essential truth is contained within the ironic mode itself. Irony always provides a disjunction, not a conjunction, it undermines, not creates. Narayan's is an ironic vision of life and the ironic vision, I submit, is the vision of a man who has not fully come to terms with the meaning of human existence. This is also why, I feel, Narayan's irony is almost always tinged with comedy; we laugh as we discover—after all the suspense—that Vasu, the intruder portrayed in *The Man-Eater of Malgudi,* has killed himself in the process of swatting a mosquito on his skull! We laugh, yes, but it is an adulterated laugh; we laugh as we realize that somehow a grim joke has been played.

It would be different if Narayan offered us pure comedy, which he does not. Laughter in his novels very frequently comes close to tears, and tears very close to laughter. Life may well be made up of tears and laughter—as Kahlil Gibran has so movingly shown us—but it is the task of the artist, we feel, to help us to see beyond laughter and tears, to help us discover a truth which we did not know, truth which could, perhaps, illuminate our lives for us. The satirist, armed with his battery of ironies, can only expose human vanity and folly, not offer a wholesome insight into human nature. Because Narayan is such a talented and versatile writer, his work has the potential of genuine exploration of the human condition—the final criterion of greatness—but he does not seem able to realize this potential. As I see it, the problem is twofold: first, he does not allow the average and the ordinary a chance to transcend their situations, and second, he is incapacitated by his ironic vision to see beyond ridicule and ambiguity.

There are, however, two exceptions that I must briefly consider. Both *The Dark Room* (1938) and *The Guide* (1958) suggest that Narayan comes close to the possibility of allowing his characters to transcend their situations. In *The Dark Room,* Savitri, who is bullied into submission, displays some potential for growth when she at first rejects her traditional role and then accepts it with a newfound sense of humility. Though this short and touching novel abounds in irony, there are, every now and then, touches of the sort that elevate the ironist above himself: Savitri's friend Janamma gives Savitri a long lecture on the duties of a good wife and thereby stops Savitri's "dark-room withdrawals":

> Janamma went on in this strain for an hour or more, recounting instances of the patience of wives: her own grandmother who had slaved cheerfully for her husband, had three concubines at home; her aunt who was beaten every day by her husband and had never uttered a word of protest for fifty years; another friend of her mother's who was prepared to jump into a well if her husband so directed her; and so on, till Savitri gradually began to feel very foolish at the thought of her own resentment, which now seemed very insignificant. (46)

Savitri's realization is genuine character growth; even if she returns to the role assigned to her, the return is marked by an inner dignity. Towards the end, when Savitri has come home to her unfaithful and loutish husband and to the children who are genuinely happy to see her, we are given to understand that everything has returned to normal. Savitri, however, knows that an irrevocable change has taken place: "A part of me is dead" (156) she utters to herself. No matter how much Narayan's typical ironic mode tries to create a comedy of the situation, we the readers know, like Savitri, that inner awareness is superior to subservience without such awareness. It has to be admitted, however, that even here the glimmer of hope is a tenuous one: intent upon his ironic-comic view of life, Narayan does not allow himself to let go completely, is afraid to give free rein to Savitri's rebellion and assertion of herself. But this ordinary housewife at least knows, through the suffering she undergoes, that to play a role is invariably to lose a part of one's real self.

When we come to Raju in *The Guide* we are as close as is ever possible in Narayan's work to seeing the average and the ordinary triumph beyond their stations in life. It is in this novel—which I consider to be Narayan's best work—that Narayan makes at least some attempt to redeem a character caught in the endless complications imposed by life. While Narayan once again maintains his distance, I feel that here he is least detached from his characters. And for the plight of Raju one feels Narayan has genuine sympathy. For once, the ironist is unable to make a joke out of the situation—though he desperately tries, as evidenced by the farcical tone of the concluding scenes of the novel. Raju's development and growth are integral to the vision of *The Guide*. This ordinary man is able to gain insight into the position he has made for himself: "He now saw the enormity of his own creation. He had created a giant with his puny self, a throne of authority with that slab of a stone" (96). When the villagers gather round him as their hope for the rains to come and save them, Raju realizes that this time there is no turning back: that he simply cannot betray their faith: "For the first time in his life he was doing a thing in which he was not personally interested" (213). The writing is straightforward, devoid of all irony and comedy, and when Raju dies at the end as a full sacrifice, he ascends to a height to which no other Narayan character has ever been allowed to ascend. For once, there is a wholesomeness about Narayan's vision. For once, he gets out of the trap that the average and the ordinary impose on his ironic vision. For once we feel satisfied.

With the accomplishment of *The Guide* in mind we can now better understand the problem that I have been trying to point to in Narayan's work. I have been suggesting that the one overriding limitation of Narayan's achievement is that he allows his satiric and ironic manner to entrap him within the world of the average and the ordinary. Because he finds it hard to transcend his own sense of irony and detachment, his novels do not, ultimately, offer the sensitive reader the satisfaction he craves for. I have tried to demonstrate that Narayan's refusal to see life beyond its ambiguous trappings leads him to a somewhat misplaced and distorted world view. While his characters live, they live a life which is, throughout, devoid of promise. After writing *The Guide* Narayan returned to the models of his earlier novels. Is there a hidden lesson in this reversion? I believe so. I believe that in *The Guide* Narayan had relaxed his hold on his creations, allowed the human spirit to go the full way towards a spiritual triumph. In the experience of writing *The Guide* Narayan must have learned how precarious the world of art can be once the satiric and ironic modes have been set aside. Finding this rather uncomfortable, he returned to the more secure world of his ironic-comic vision.

But irony, as we all know, eventually leads a writer into a *cul-de-sac*. No matter how we argue, irony does *not* allow the emergence of the final word about human existence. As a moralist, Narayan knows that morality is not a function of irony (though the reverse might sometimes hold), nor irony the best mode for a writer. I was prompted to write this essay after the painful experience of re-reading *The Painter of Signs*, which I find terribly weak—mainly because it seems to be such a poor rehash of *The Guide*. Long deliberations on my unease with Narayan's work brought to light the inescapable fact that Narayan's is a jaundiced view of humankind couched in a glittering array of wit and humor. How this could have eluded earlier commentators on his work baffles me. Surely, the world of Malgudi must sooner or later force people to ask: Is this all

Narayan is capable of giving us? The world of the average and the ordinary without redemption? Graham Greene, who has been pivotal in spreading Narayan's fame, has often compared Narayan to Chekhov; while there is a superficial resemblance (made deep through Narayan's very skillful manipulation of language), Chekhov is infinitely larger than Narayan. When Chekhov gives us the average and the ordinary (which he seldom does) he gives them to us unadulterated. Pathos is pure pathos. Chekhov uses irony, it is true, but the key difference between the two writers is that the one uses irony for tragic ends, the other comic. Tragedy always implies transcendence; comedy stasis.

So now I am able to answer my own questions. The reasons why no work by Narayan can compare favorably with *The Serpent and the Rope* is that nothing in Narayan has the immensity of Raja Rao's novel. And nothing in Narayan offers the same challenge as *Coolie* because there is nothing in Narayan that contains that singularity of purpose and sense of commitment which we find in Mulk Raj Anand's novel. Where Narayan's novels are polished and technically far superior to those of Raja Rao and Anand, the novels of these writers are flawed. And yet, I want to submit, both *The Serpent and the Rope* and *Coolie* are greater than anything Narayan has written; they involve us more, they move us more, they reward us more. And in both these novels we enter the lives of protagonists who are not average or ordinary. Rao's Rama is as above the average and the ordinary as Anand's Munoo is under the average and the ordinary. And both these writers are not primarily satirists. Their world view is not, can never be, comic-ironic.

We know that Narayan came to writing novels from the world of journalism. It may well be that his main limitation is finally the limitation of the journalist. For all his imagination, for all his craftsmanship, the journalist is primarily and ultimately a *voyeur*, a professional onlooker, never a participant.

Notes

1. See, for example, S.C. Harrex's long chapter on Narayan in his *The Fire and the Offering: The English Language Novel of India 1935–1970*, vol. 2 (Calcutta: Writers Workshop), 11–144.

2. "I am an inattentive, quick writer who has little sense of style," Narayan said to Ved Mehta. See Ved Mehta's *John is Easy to Please* (New York: Penguin, 1974), 126.

Works Cited

Narayan, R.K. *The Dark Room*. 1938. Chicago: University of Chicago Press, 1981.
_____. *The Guide*. London: Methuen, 1958.
_____. *The Painter of Signs*. 1976. London: Penguin, 1983.
_____. *Swami and Friends*. 1935. University of Chicago Press, 1980.
Taranath, Rajeev. "The Average as Positive." *Critical Essays on Indian Writing in English*. M.K. Naik, A. Desai, and G.S. Amur, eds. Madras: Macmillan, 1977, 307–19.

Irony, Structure, and Storytelling in R. K. Narayan's The Financial Expert

SURESH RAVAL

The *Financial Expert* is R.K. Narayan's most sustained and fully realized mid-career novel in the genre of comic realism managed by a consummately skillful deployment of irony at both thematic and structural levels.[1] Irony marks the name, actions, feelings, and attitudes of the novel's protagonist, and it not only informs the narrative but in fact functions as the primary structural device of its plot. The pervasive irony, as I will demonstrate, is not intended to operate as the source of undecided meaning but rather as the source that makes for the structural coherence of the novel as well as for the authenticity of its portrayal of social and personal reality as manipulated and lived by its central character. A fascinating aspect of Narayan's art in *The Financial Expert* is that irony exposes all of its protagonist's activities and responses to criticism without in the least undermining the reader's sense of the credibility of the novel's world and its main character. A distinctive aspect of Narayan's achievement in this novel is that the conduct and response one might ordinarily characterize as trite or cliche-ridden possess a freshness of perception and gentle ironic insight for which there are no clearly recognizable models upon which he might be said to be drawing for his narrative.

The novel's central and dramatic irony is that the financial expert is in fact not an expert in anything in any honest way. He is an expert only in the negative sense that he knows the ignorance, gullibility, and need of his fellow Indian villagers and knows, too, their tendency to trust almost anyone who appears to offer help. When he starts his little venture under the tree across from Central Co-operative Land Mortgage Bank, Margayya continues in an independent manner what he had already begun while still employed by the Bank: the perversion of the ideal of thrift on which the Mortgage Bank had been founded. Instead of teaching poor villagers the virtues of thrift, he teaches them a variety of ways in which they can extract more loans from the Bank even when they don't need them. Margayya's successful manipulation of government rules for extracting loans without need or purpose is a source of amazement to the peasants who flock to him because they see him as a financial wizard. In that sense, Margayya's name is a reflection of his true identity, for his name means one who shows the way. For there is no twisting and untwisting of rules and procedures that Margayya will not attempt in order to accomplish his own goal which is to get an immediate share of money from the loans he manages to get for his customers. The perversion of the ideal of thrift, in Narayan's treatment, serves an entertaining ironic function, one that takes on other more complex forms as new situations arise in Margayya's life.

There is, for instance, a deeper irony that marks both Margayya's name and conduct when it becomes clear that he succeeds only insofar as he deals with poor and illiterate villagers in need. When he succeeds in a relatively significant way, it is because he publishes a book of salacious interest that Dr. Pal has tempted him into buying. This success depends almost entirely on the way shown, in a manner of speaking, by Dr. Pal, as his failure will depend, in one of the novel's culminating ironies, on Dr. Pal's final intervention in Margayya's business affairs. When this financial expert does make considerable money, it is not because he has worked out a business scheme that has a grain of sense to it. Aided by Dr. Pal, he amasses vast amounts of deposits at 20 percent interest, collecting 20,000 rupees a day while giving out 15,000 rupees every day in interest. The remainder of the money he simply hoards, having no idea about any productive use he might make of it. While dealing with the poor and illiterate, Margayya had the advantage of experience in the handling of petty amounts of cash. But as soon as he embarks on larger financial ventures, he has no experience to draw upon. He thinks he has become a bank—which to him is a place where people leave deposits when they don't draw loans out of it.

For Margayya, interest is the mystery that lies behind any bank's power to attract large amounts of deposits. The rhapsody celebrating interest paid on loans provides one of Narayan's brilliant depictions capturing Margayya's simple-mindedness as well as consuming greed:

> [Interest] combined in it the mystery of birth and multiplication. Otherwise how could you account for the fact that a hundred rupees in a savings bank become one hundred and twenty in course of time? It was something like the ripening of corn. Every rupee, Margayya felt, contained in it seed of another rupee and that seed in it another seed and so on and on to infinity. It was something like the firmament, endless stars and within each star an endless firmament

and within each one further endless. . . .It bordered on mystic perception. It gave him the feeling of being part of infinite existence. (130–31)

As he celebrates the mystery of interest, what banks do, how money is put to productive use, what enables a bank to generate more money and pay interest on its deposits remain a complete mystery to him. Margayya here discloses his ignorance and naivete very much like the villagers he used to impress with his manipulation of rules for acquiring loans for them.

As soon as he has hit upon a scheme based on his intuition into the mystery of interest, Margayya's behavior takes on grotesquely comic aspects. Not knowing what to do with the money he collects every day, he stuffs all available space in his house with currency notes deposited by black marketeers, and thinks he is well on the way to becoming a wealthy man. He takes great pride in acquiring wealth, for mere riches

> any hard-working fool could attain by some watchfulness, while acquiring wealth was an extraordinary specialized job. It came to persons who had on them the grace of the Goddess [Lakshmi] fully and who could use their wits. He was a specialist in money and his mind always ran on lines of scientific inquiry whenever money came in question. (152)

It is this obsession with money and his sense of the significance of money that pervade all his activities and responses. Describing to his wife his quarrel with the Secretary of the Co-operative Bank, Margayya points out: "He has every right because he has more money, authority, dress, looks—above all, more money. It's money which gives people all this. Money alone is important in this world. Everything else will come to us naturally if we have money in our purse" (24). Margayya's mind constantly circles around the idea of money: "His mind began to catalogue all the good things money had done as far as he could remember. He shuddered to think how people could ever do without it. If money was absent men came near being beasts" (31).

This obsession is at the basis of everything Margayya does and thinks, generating much of the comedy that ripples through the entire narrative. When, for example, he gets up the day after the *Puja* he has performed for forty days, he looks outside the door to see if a miraculous change of fortune had occurred for him. Distraught that his austerities had brought him nothing, he starts fantasizing about selling snuff or tooth powder, something "for which every citizen would be compelled to pay a certain small sum each day" (88). Margayya does not abandon his preoccupation with money even when he receives the false telegram from a wealthy mad fellow in Madras announcing his son Balu's death. To disperse the large crowd of sympathizers and strangers who gather at his house, his brother makes an appeal to which Margayya responds with deadly sarcasm: "How can they leave? . . . If an entrance fee be charged—" his words trail off because his impulse was to add, "We might earn lakhs" (178-79). When he balks at the thought of going to Madras, a big city which he had never visited before, to search for his son's body, his brother offers to accompany him. Margayya's immediate thought is that this man is "wangling a free journey to Madras" (181). Margayya thus reads the world in a particular way, and he tries to deal with it in terms of his reading of it. When the world seems to fly in the face of his reading, he simply redoubles his efforts to confront the world again, but he never gives up his reading of the world, nor his tactics in dealing with it.

Structurally, Margayya's meeting with the old priest, his decision to perform the *Puja* as advised by the priest, the steps he takes to perform it, and his thoughts and activities during and after the *Puja,* are crucial to the construction of the novel. This particular sequence of events and actions draws the narrative together in a closely knit organization, and the following passage has ramifications for the entire novel and is in effect an allegorical blueprint for it:

> . . .when the priest said: "Margayya! What is ailing you? You can speak out," he felt that...all barriers between himself and the world had been swept away and that he stood alone; that he alone mattered. . . .He began to talk in a grand manner. . . .He would be a man of consequence, let them beware: let the Gods beware . . . After letting him run on as long as he liked, the priest opened his mouth and said: "That means you would propitiate Goddess Lakshmi, the Goddess of Wealth. When she throws a glance and it falls on someone he becomes rich, he becomes prosperous, he is treated by the world as an eminent man, his words are treated as something of importance. All this you seem to want."

> "Yes," said Margayya, authoritatively. "Why not?" He took out of his pocket his little snuff box. . .flicked it open and took a deep pinch. The priest said: "Go on, go on, no harm in it. A devotee of Goddess Lakshmi need care for nothing, not even the fact that he is in a temple where a certain decorum is to be observed. It's only a question of self-assurance. He has so much authority in his face, looks, so much money in his purse, so many to do his bidding that he cares for nothing really in the world. It is only the protégé of Goddess Saraswathi who has to mind such things. But when Saraswathi favors a man, the other Goddess withdraws her favors.

There is always a rivalry between the two. . . . .Some persons have the good fortune to be claimed by both, some on the contrary have the misfortune to be abandoned by both. Evidently you are one of those for whom both are fighting at the moment." Margayya felt immensely powerful and important...He lifted his eyes, glanced at the brilliant stars in Heaven as if there, between the luminous walls, he would get a glimpse of the crowned Goddesses tearing at each other.

"Why should they care for me?" he asked innocently. The priest replied: "How can we question?. . .it's beyond our powers to understand." Intoxicated by this, Margayya said: "A man whom the Goddess of Wealth favors need not worry much. He can buy all the knowledge he requires. He can afford to buy all the gifts that Goddess Saraswathi holds in her palm."

The priest let out a quiet chuckle at Margayya's very reckless statement. Margayya asked: "Why do you laugh?" Already a note of authority was creeping into his voice. The priest said: "Yes, this is what every man who attains wealth thinks. You are moving along the right line. . . ." (56–58)

By making Margayya the object of rivalry between the two Goddesses, Narayan exposes in an amusing manner not so much the Hindu myth as his protagonist's absurdly self-serving, simple, and narrow-minded attitude toward religion, money, and knowledge. The thought that he should be important enough to cause such a bitter rivalry fills Margayya with the kind of self-confidence he was accustomed to while dealing with poor villagers trying to get loans from the Co-operative Mortgage Bank where he had once worked. It is this self-confidence that prompts Margayya to resolve the traditional rivalry between the two Goddesses in favor of Goddess Lakshmi when he treats knowledge as something he could simply buy with money. The priest's ironic chuckle at this presages Margayya's failure in handling his son's education and the eventual ruin that follows. The mythical rivalry between the Goddesses of Wealth and Knowledge thus constitutes a major thematic and structural component of the novel, and prepares and deepens the grounds for Margayya's overvaluing of money and disregard for his son's education. As usual he pays attention only to the statement that feeds his dreams of wealth and worldly success, and consequently neglects the more pointed statement made by the priest: "Some persons have the good fortune to be claimed by both, some on the contrary have the misfortune to be abandoned by both." This is precisely what happens to Margayya at the novel's end. If earlier he misses the prophetic note implicit in the priest's remark, at the end he experiences all its consequences in his life. The conversation with the priest is thus pivotal not only in oddly influencing and determining his course of action, but in presaging his final misfortune.

As he sits chanting the mantra to worship the Goddess, repeating it a thousand times each day for forty days, Margayya's mind is far from that immersed in devotional attitude. Without any self-consciousness about their implications for his worship, his mind carries on what are to us its comic antics. His mind wanders over the details of his wife's accommodating behavior, his acquisition of the materials needed for the *Puja*, and of course Dr. Pal and his smutty manuscript which made him feel "as though his mind would not move from the subject" (79). And he begins to visualize "his future" (80), and thinks of buying his brother's house with a handsome cash offer. "He realized that this was his major concern in life"(80). Given the motivating factors behind Margayya's undertaking of the *Puja*, it is not surprising that money should be not only his primary concern during the worship, but the reason for distraction from any truly devotional attitude. The novel's most explosive and comic irony is that Dr. Pal, his manuscript, and the *Puja* are structurally linked so that Margayya's rise to and fall from fortune occur because of the fateful arrival of Dr. Pal in his life. Irony thus operates in a deeply structural way in the sense that it determines the very process of plot construction in the novel.

By deliberately narrowing his focus on Margayya's attitudes and actions, Narayan accomplishes two things at once: to reveal in Margayya an unrestrained pursuit of money that has the appearance, in Narayan's depiction of it, of comic antics; and to express through a gentle irony toward his hero that this proclivity is fairly universal in society. In this way, Margayya becomes an emblematic literary figure bearing a variety of comic implications that function as a kind of social commentary. The remarks he makes to the young priest, to his son, to the astrologers, to Dr. Pal, to others have a constant comic tinge to them. Everything he does or pursues takes on a comic charge: his grasping, mean-minded, petty actions all appear amusing, and we laugh at him without becoming severe in our judgment of him. Narayan's interest lies not in developing Margayya as a subtle and complex character, but in producing the detailed representativeness of the protagonist in a way that lends coherence and consistency to his narrative. Thus, though the novel centers on the activities of a character, the character derives its interest from Narayan's superbly controlled subordination of character to his plot. The effortlessness of Narayan's art might obscure the meticulously detailed depictions of particular actions and situations, but it only helps to clarify the thoroughness of his commitment to the act of storytelling which he never abandons for mere rhetorical fireworks and philosophical or psychological expansiveness.

Narayan's focus on Margayya's behavior and attitude is so controlled and thorough that it captures the fixity and confinement of the protagonist's mind and personality, and consequently captures the obsessive consistency of attitude that never takes any other way of being into account. Margayya is represented as pre-eminently shrewd and calculating, but the fact that he has little grasp of what it means to live well except in terms provided by money is a constant source of ironic comedy. This ironic comedy undermines his sense of being in command of his situation. Money, far from being just a means of happiness, is the sole purpose of living for Margayya, and he is without restraint dedicated to acquiring it. This shows in Narayan's highly comic treatment of Margayya seeking engagement of his son with the daughter of a wealthy man. When the first astrologer has questions about the compatibility of the horoscopes of the would-be bride and bridegroom, Margayya simply dismisses him and hires another astrologer specifically with the injunction to read their horoscopes as compatible.

Like many of Narayan's obsessive characters, Margayya is interested more in the acquisition of what he wants than in the broader psychological or moral considerations about his ends. This constitutes for Margayya the ideal attitude toward experience, and it produces, in Narayan's view, the genial comedy of conduct in its blindness to experience and value. This is why in *The Financial Expert*, as in most of Narayan's novels, plot and character are so closely intertwined, the character determining and unfolding through the plot, and the plot showing in various ways the single dominating preoccupation of Margayya's life—money. The other characters—Dr. Pal, Margayya's wife, son, brother, the publisher—all are given the sketchiest of presentation, one that serves the purpose of giving fullness and density, albeit one dimensional, to Margayya's personality. This personality expresses itself through an extravagant disregard for the feelings, interests, and needs of other people. The peculiar and theatrical way in which characters with this kind of personality or sensibility express themselves is a clear indication that their view of things is limited, that it is uncomplicated and unqualified by any consciousness that there are possibly richer and more comprehensive and more just views and attitudes than those held by Margayya.

Because Margayya is the ever-present participant in virtually all situations that arise in the novel, the responses which exhibit his sensibility are always conspicuous and serve as the substance and the basis of the comic. This is true even when Margayya makes no direct comment on, or remarks about, what is happening. The train of thought going on in his mind is always powered by his obsession with money and is frequently incongruous with the situation in question. The result is a peculiarly original comic realism that characterizes this novel, as it does most of Narayan's other novels. The realism of the novel, the realistic portrayal of everyday situations in the life of a lower middle class Indian obsessed with making money—this tempers the overall delineation and form of the action in the novel, and it controls the quality and tempo of the narrative's plot.

Nevertheless, Margayya, though often amusing in his various actions and responses, is far from a comic hero. Like the comic hero, he differs from others because even under the most trying circumstances he is always himself. He is fundamentally different, however, from the comic hero in that what he celebrates and worships is not something others spurn or mock. In Margayya, Narayan etches stronger and more detailed lineaments of what others in his society might in fact be like and seek. This protagonist simply has the resourcefulness and resilience to pursue his interest with instinctive readiness that others do not quite possess or exhibit. It is through comic treatment that the potential or real gravity of Margayya's transgressions against his society is effectively defused. He has a sharp wit and a clever tongue, and these inevitably show themselves even in situations that call for a different kind of attitude or response.

Avaricious, unprincipled, and in some ways a fraud, Margayya outrageously violates the moral and social standards of his society, for he feeds upon the gullibility and ignorance of the people who flock to him for help. As readers we deplore Margayya's senseless pursuit of money, but find it difficult not to be drawn by his frequently inventive and energetic ability to make money and, when that fails, to dream about it. Anything that seems to go against his plans or wishes, he tries to circumvent, baffle, and conquer. This is brilliantly dramatized in the episode involving the sale of the manuscript to the publisher. Moreover, in a social world consisting of routine activities Margayya contrives not only to thwart the normal pursuits of economic and social survival, but to acquire considerable wealth and status, even if these last only for a short while.

Even when he loses all he has acquired, Margayya never loses his firm grasp on himself. This is a great source of comic relief for the reader, and helps explain, to some extent, Narayan's narrative stance. Narayan's detachment, and our own, springs from the fact that though Margayya wins our interest by his obstinate resilience, he cannot be a bearer of values we hold or cherish. We do laugh at situations in which he finds himself or from which he extricates himself, and even if we do not quite regard those situations as ours, the obsessions that define and inform all of Margayya's conduct are existentially those that we see as typical of modern society anywhere. Margayya is comic not primarily because he is laughed at but because he celebrates money to the virtual exclusion of everything else and because all his actions spring from his craving for money. This craving for money is not driven by any desire for pleasure or happiness which money might make possible. Acquisition of money amounts to possession of status for him, and hence is the sole pleasure he seeks in life. The comic resonance of the novel thus arises from such a tenacity of his will to money that defeat can never entirely undermine or destroy. Margayya is the modern champion of mammon emerging at the cross-section of rural society and modernity in India, and he remains tantalizingly, amusingly alive in our minds because, as the most tenacious expression of a will to money, he is a powerful bearer of the complacent philistinism of any epoch in society.

Narayan has no interest in this novel, as in most of his other novels, in probing the complexities of the self and its relations to the community. On that score, he remains firmly entrenched in Indian values, and confines his literary attention to the surface of everyday individual and social existence. And he does this with a measure of detachment and indulgence. Consequently, the crises that occur in this novel, as in his other novels, never develop into tragic moments. Nor are the melodramatic elements of a given crisis treated in a manner antithetical to their overall light-hearted but authentic portrayal of individual and social life. Thus consistently overbearing in his attitude toward his wife, the peasants who came for loans, the teachers and officials at the school where his son studies, the astrologers who examine Balu's horoscope in relation to his would-be wife's horoscope—all these are aspects of Margayya's personality that are not intended to lend complexity, depth, or subtlety to his character. They rather imply a plausible working out of his personality which is engaged only by certain things in a fixed and determinate manner. For Margayya can never comprehend the absurdity of his obsession with money, and indeed feels himself to be defiantly free to pursue anything that appears to provide fulfillment of his goal. If he does not feel defeated it is because he never loses faith in himself, in his ability to make money, and in the value of money. This is the reason why neither Margayya as a character nor the unfolding of the novel's plot needs a dimension of introspective self-examination. Everything happens on surface in the novel's world and in its protagonist's life, and even when it appears to be serious, as during the *Puja*, or critical, as during the (false) telegram about Balu's death, the ripple of genial light comedy never ceases to mark the narrative.

The unobtrusive, detached attitude of the narrator enables the narrative to immerse itself in the actualities of Margayya's life as they form around his obsession with money. But this is not to say that the novel is realistic in the mechanical sense of acquiring some sort of one-to-one correspondence with historical actuality. As Narayan says in the Introduction to the novel, he had of course heard about a financial expert who served as a prototypical figure for his own invention.[3] Once Narayan had the idea of this character in mind, he invented a series of actions that he could then plot to work out the central implications of that idea. And he certainly employs a host of beliefs prevalent in India about poor and illiterate villagers seeking to receive financial help from so-called experts whose primary goal is to exploit the ignorance and gullibility of their clients.

Narayan's detachment as a writer stems form his immersion in the details of everyday life in the context of his story and its main characters. And this accounts for his avoidance of all obtrusive, larger philosophical or social perspectives by which a writer might express or dramatize a commitment.[4] This attitude produces the "realism" of Narayan's art, creating the illusion that what Narayan has portrayed has indeed an authentic objective counterpart in Indian social reality. William Walsh has perceptively argued that Narayan's instinctive knowledge and grasp of Indian culture, its values and feelings, is delicately captured in the everyday texture of life as he portrays it in his novels. "These things are present and influential," Walsh observes, "not as dogma or metaphysics but as part of a whole mode of perception and a habit of reaction" (16). The religious and cultural inheritance of India, which underlie Narayan's imagination and his sense of reality are at the basis of his detachment as a novelist. This inheritance invests the comic dimension of his portrayals of individual and social life with tolerance and even sympathy. Hence the freshness of perception that marks his portrayals of situations and characters that otherwise seem quite ordinary and trite.

Notes

1. R.K. Narayan, *The Financial Expert* (New York: Time-Life Books, 1966), first published in 1953. All page references in my essay are to this edition of *The Financial Expert*.

2. Narayan's versions of two of India's greatest epics attest to this: see *The Ramayana* (London: Chatto and Windus, 1973), and *The Mahabharata* (London: Heinemann, 1978).

3. See Narayan's discussion of this in his Introduction to the 1966 edition of *The Financial Expert*, xxiii–xviii.

4. Thus Narayan has said: "I write a story or a sketch primarily because it is my habit and profession and I enjoy doing it. I'm not out to enlighten the world or improve it. But the academic man views a book only as raw material for a thesis or seminar paper, hunts for hidden meanings, social implications, 'commitments' and 'concerns' or the 'Nation's ethos.'" Cf. R.K. Narayan, *A Writer's Nightmare: Selected Essays 1958–88* (New Delhi: Penguin Books, 1988), 200.

Works Cited

Narayan, R.K. *The Financial Expert*. 1953. New York: Time-Life Books, 1966.

Walsh, William. *R.K. Narayan: A Critical Appreciation*. London: Heinemann, 1982.

Eternal, Insatiable Appetite:
The Irony of R. K. Narayan's Baited Hero

GEOFFREY KAIN

V. S. Naipaul has remarked that "Narayan's novels are . . . religious books . . . and intensely Hindu" (13). While I am not convinced that this observation applies equally to each of Narayan's novels, it usefully alerts the reader to the centrality of Hindu traditionalism in Narayan's work, especially as that traditionalism is challenged by characters who entertain more "modern," more overtly individualistic values. Interestingly, a number of Narayan's prominent characters work to resist traditional religious and familial duties or expectations (dharma), then inadvertently or (seemingly) fortuitously fall into roles that exemplify the very values or lifestyles they reject. Of these tales I would regard *Waiting for the Mahatma* (1955), *The Guide* (1958), and *A Tiger for Malgudi* (1982) as sequential developments of essentially the same theme. The fundamental force directing the unfolding of the plot in each case is appetite and, ironically, the central character in each of the novels is ultimately driven by appetite (self-absorption) to a transcendence of appetite, from an urge to have and control to a position of being claimed and controlled. And perhaps most significant in this smoothly depicted transition, or reversal, is that the central character in each of the novels—Sriram in *Waiting for the Mahatma*, Raju in *The Guide*, and Raja in *A Tiger for Malgudi*—is finally "claimed" or changed by what may be best described as some agent of the socio-religious tradition; the sacred makes its claim on the profane (or bestial, as is the case in *Tiger*) in such a way as to suggest that these self-absorbed, appetite-directed characters may in fact have been baited, urged unwittingly toward the immanent divine.

Waiting for the Mahatma introduces a narrative pattern that is clearly similar to that of *The Guide* and *A Tiger for Malgudi*, but it doesn't go quite so far as either of the two later novels in depicting the spiritual transformation of the central character; it might be regarded, therefore, as the earlier suggestion for these later possibilities. But the elements central to this thematic construct are all present in *Mahatma*: the spiritually disin-terested character who encounters someone (or something) who inflames his desire or appetite, who then pursues that object or desire, and in the process comes under the influence of an agent who clearly embodies socio-religious traditionalism.

The spiritually slumbering character in this case is Sriram, who one day encounters a young woman, Bharati, who is collecting money to support the continuing travels of Ghandi—about to arrive in Malgudi. As soon as he sees her, Sriram's "throat went dry" and he "had a wild hope that the girl would let him touch her hand" (19). He becomes instantly obsessed with her and attends Gandhi's meeting only so that he can again see Bharati:

> He assumed a tone of bluster which carried him through the various obstacles and brought him to the first row below the dais . . . . He found himself beside the enclosure where the women were assem-bled. . . . Sriram sat unashamedly staring at the gathering. (25)

He persists in his perusal of the women until he recalls Gandhi's sugges-tion that

> all women are your sisters and mothers. Never look at them with thoughts of lust. If you are troubled by such thoughts, this is the remedy: walk with your head down looking at the ground during the day, and with your eyes up, looking at the stars at night. (25)

Already Gandhi's influence is intimated, but it is not to be realized for some time. In fact, when Gandhi speaks to the crowd about their feel-ings toward their nation and toward the British, Sriram interprets his remarks more personally, according to the true object of his interest:

> ". . . be sure that you have in your heart love and not bitterness." Sri-ram told himself looking at the vision beside the microphone, "Def-initely it's not bitterness. I love her." (28)

Sriram becomes so intent on having the young woman that he is in danger of losing his self-control. As they sit on the edge of the river at night, during one of their first conversations,

> Sriram felt like taking the girl in his arms, but he resisted the idea. He feared that if he touched her she might push him into the river. . . . Her proximity pricked his blood and set it coursing. "There is no one about. What can she do? he reflected. "Let her try and push me into the river, and she will know with whom she is dealing," and the next moment he blamed himself for his own crude thoughts. (51)

Sriram manages to retain self-control, but his potent attraction to Bharati draws him (and then keeps him) within the influence of the Mahatma. As an active figure in the "Quit India" campaign and as an adherent to the principles of a regenerated Hindu traditionalism, Sriram eventually transcends his simple self-indulgence and channels his energies into far less selfish pursuits, enduring imprisonment and pain during his commitment to the Gandhian campaign.

When Sriram and Bharati rejoin after several years, they decide to approach Gandhi for permission to marry. Gandhi is fasting and he asks Sriram in an offhand way, "Do you know how well a fast can purify?" Sriram answers, "I will fast if you order me to"; and Bharati adds, "If it is decided, I'll be prepared to go through a fast myself" (239). Gandhi agrees to their marriage after Sriram admits that for five years he has thought of "nothing else" (240). As events indicate, however, and as Sriram's offer to fast underscores, his disciplined work under Gandhi's influence, the calculated delay in fulfilling his desire, has served—as a fast in its own way—to alter, to purify his feelings for Bharati, and to effect in him a commitment to far more than the "slender beauty" with which he became so immediately obsessed upon first encountering her.

In *The Guide* Narayan offers a deeper, more complex, more playfully ironic treatment of the baited hero theme than he does in *Waiting for the Mahatma*. Much of the novel's interest for us lies in the curious yet believable way in which the central character, Raju, comes ever closer to the snare (or embrace) of the transcendent while seeming to drift further and further away from it. The more lustful, greedy, self-centered, and manipulative he becomes, the closer he approaches that point where he cannot escape the cleansing transformation of self, the overcoming of his thirst for sensual and egotistical gratification. And as Raju arrives at and finally settles into his role as sadhu, we are invited to ask ourselves, as Raju must ask himself, "Who could have foreseen that *this* man would arrive in *this* situation by such an unlikely path?" The ironic direction of events is suggestive (to me) of the Oedipus myth except, almost as the inversion of the Oedipus myth, we imagine that the gods observing (and involved in) the events in *The Guide* laugh in the end not maliciously or sardonically, but gleefully. *The Guide* becomes a celebration of the unexpected, the unforeseeable. "Raju serves as a conduit of the possibilities of affirmation" (Raichura, 115).

Yet, as we survey the events of the plot we find a seamless series of events that appear anything but haphazard or directed by chance or whim; just as Raju says, playing the role of the holy man, providing the villagers a traditional message they would like or expect to hear: "What must happen must happen; no power on earth or in heaven can change its course, just as no one can change the course of that river" (18). At this point, Raju does not believe what he says, yet this traditional belief becomes the central theme of the text, the principle to which Raju must ultimately surrender, self-directed though he would like to consider himself.

Raju begins his trek to self-control by obeying his own nature, by acting according to impulse. As he tends his father's small shop along the railway, Raju is frequently approached by traveling strangers seeking information about the surrounding area. In hindsight, Raju reflects that

> it is written on the brow of some that they shall not be left alone. I am one such, I think. Although I never looked for acquaintances, they somehow came looking for me. Men who had just arrived always stopped at my shop . . . and . . . asked, "How far is . . .?" or . . . "Are there many historical spots?" . . . I never said, "I don't know." Not in my nature, I suppose. If I had the inclination to say "I don't know . . .," my life would have taken a different turn. (47)

But as it is, Raju is apparently *unable* to answer in any other way, and this compulsion to behave as though informed, to tell others what they want to hear, leads him to enter into—and help create—the stream of events that leads him ultimately (and apparently inevitably) to his final role.

Raju's pride in his growing reputation as a guide rests in his ability to quickly perceive and then capitalize on the needs or interests of individuals. He describes this as something like a predatory instinct: "Even as the train steamed in at the outer signal, I could scent a customer. . . . If I felt the pull of good business, I drifted in the direction of the coming train" (51). And when Rosie arrives at Malgudi station, Raju is immediately drawn to her: "She was not very glamorous, if that is what you expect, but she did have a figure . . . beautifully fashioned . . . ." (56). Raju is quickly determined to satisfy Rosie's interest in seeing a king cobra, odd as her immediately-expressed request seemed at first, hoping to win her favor—which, before long, he does.

Because Rosie is so grateful for Raju's sympathizing with her determination to dance and providing her with the opportunity (long denied by her husband, "Marco") to cultivate her art, Raju is able to regularly satisfy his hunger for physical love. Without true appreciation for the sacred implications of the Bharat Natyam, Raju enters willingly into an extended trance-like state, enthralled by the erotic beauty of Rosie's dancing. His appetite for sex annihilates his previous thirst for business and leaves him idle but satisfied. However, soon his sensuous idyll is disturbed by the pressing need for money.

Raju's rapid escalation to renown as Rosie/Nalini's business manager (guide) further deepens his self-absorption. His hunger now becomes for a greater accumulation of riches, as well as for increasing attention and admiration from people of influence. When Rosie informs Raju that she is tired of the never-ending performances, that her enjoyment is quickly waning, Raju is not sympathetic:

> I though it was a dangerous line of thought. It seemed absurd that we should earn less than the maximum we could manage. My philosophy was that while it lasted the maximum money had to be squeezed out. We needed all the money in the world. If I were less prosperous who would care for me? Where would be the smiles which greeted me now wherever I turned, and the respectful agreement shown to my remarks when I said something to the man in the next chair? It filled me with dread that I should be expected to do with less. (173)

Raju's desire for control and recognition grows from his days as Railway Raju to his period as the extravagant manager of Nalini. His pride rests—as it did during his less spectacularly successful days as Railway Raju—on his own belief in himself as an operator, a manipulator, a controller of people and situations:

> At that time I was puffed up with the thought of how I had made Rosie. I am now disposed to think that even Marco could not have suppressed her permanently . . . . at the time there was no limit to my self-congratulation. When I watched her in a large hall with a thousand eyes focused on her, I had no doubt that people were telling themselves and each other, "There he is, the man but for whom—" And I imagined all this adulation lapping around my ears like wavelets. . . . I liked the way the president of the occasion sat next to me. . . .I shook my head, laughed with restraint, and said something in reply; leaving the watching audience at our back to guess the import of our exchanges. (162)

Raju's delusion of control and self-importance goes so far as to leave him puzzled and angry—later, in prison—that Rosie is able to continue her career without his involvement:

> It filled me with gall that she should go on without me. Who sat now on that middle sofa? How could the performance start without my signal with the small finger? How could she know when to stop? . . . I chuckled to myself at the thought of how she must have been missing her trains after every performance. (204)

Raju's hunger for money and his insistent urge to keep Rosie under control and almost perpetually involved in performing/money-making— and entirely away from any contact with Marco, even through the mail—leads to his critical mistake of forging her signature on the note of conveyance delivered from Marco. Raju's possessiveness, his exploitative thirst for expanding wealth and status have taken him to this pass, and have also affected his vision of everyone around him. He suspects even his heretofore trusted servant, Mani, of treachery:

> Awful cunning! He had worked for me for months and months without my noticing anything against him, but now he and everyone around appeared sinister, diabolical, and cunning. (186)

Raju's reversal of character begins, to some extent, in prison, but his spiritual transformation comes much later and by agencies other than regimentation and seclusion from mainstream society. Significantly, the meaningful change comes within the context of, and under the influence of, vehicles and vessels of Hindu traditionalism. Raju transcends the demands of his physical self while hiding within the walls of an ancient, abandoned shrine, and under the direction (albeit naive) of a faithful, devout peasant, Velan. As in *Waiting for the Mahatma*, the traditional is essentially synonymous with the sacred and it becomes the means for effecting spiritual regeneration.

When Raju arrives at the abandoned temple, shortly after his release from prison, his chief concern is that he not be recognized. He stays on at the temple for as long as he does because food comes to him without his having to expend much energy for it—he can simply rely on his successful method of playing whatever role and saying whatever words his newest benefactor might expect of him. His central focus while residing at the shrine becomes food, and as in the past his appetite determines his immediate course of action (or, in this case, inaction):

> He had to decide on his future today. He should either go back to the town of his birth, bear the giggles and stares for a few days, or go somewhere else. Where could he go? He had not trained himself to make a living out of hard work. Food was coming to him unasked now. If he went away somewhere else certainly nobody was going to take the trouble to bring him food in return for just waiting for it. The only other place where it could happen was the prison. Where could he go now? Nowhere. . . . He realized that he had no alternative: he must play the role that Velan had given him. (28)

Raju's new "imprisonment" in this place and in this role leaves him frequently surprised not only at the unfolding of events, but at his own response to them. He becomes a spectator of himself:

> Raju spoke to the young boys on godliness, cleanliness, spoke on Ramayana, the characters in the epics; he addressed them on all

kinds of things. He was hypnotized by his own voice; he felt himself growing in stature. . . . .No one was more impressed with the grandeur of the whole thing than Raju himself. (40)

As he continues to play out his role, Raju's entrapment becomes increasingly well defined: "Raju felt cornered: 'I have to play the part expected of me; there is no escape'" (43).

Velan's half-wit brother finally secures Raju's immobility when he misinterprets Raju's message for the feuding villagers. Raju's natural commitment to role-playing allows him to be swept further along toward his final position of self-denial and self-control when he accepts, reluctantly, that he has "offered" to fast until the rain comes and ends the drought that is driving everyone to desperation. The villagers delude themselves by believing that "out of his love for us he is undertaking it. . . . .Only great souls. . .take upon themselves tasks such as this—"(89). Raju's thoughts, however, center on escape—but, just as he had earlier, Raju sees that he cannot move. The manipulator has been manipulated; and this web is of his own making. With the fast before him Raju recognizes the import of the situation, and the first stirrings of transformation begin:

> He felt that he had worked himself into a position from which he could not get out. He could not betray his surprise. He felt that after all, the time had come for him to be serious—to attach value to his own words. . . . He got down from the pedestal; that was the first step to take. The seat had acquired a glamour, and as long as he occupied it people would not listen to him as to an ordinary mortal. He now saw the enormity of his own creation. (95)

Hoping to escape his role, Raju confesses his past to Velan and clarifies by what path he came to arrive at the shrine. Velan sees nothing unusual in this, and his faith in Raju remains unshaken. Raju becomes frustrated and irritated over his lack of control over his own life, and he sees that this simple peasant has him in his grasp: "Raju almost glared at him. This single man was responsible for his present plight" (211). And as he continues to exercise self-denial, "his awareness of his surroundings was gradually lessening in a sort of inverse proportion" (212).

Like Rosie who danced before the image of Nataraja (embodying the principle of control over the vital forces of nature), Raju, as he moves deeper into the experience of the fast, becomes a sort of carnival side show. Narayan offers a comic yet disturbing depiction of the scene; now sincere in his endeavor to perhaps exert some influence over the forces of nature by controlling the demands of his own nature, Raju sits absorbed in his focused self-control while "the hum of humanity around was increasing" (212). Eventually, the business-minded capitalize on him as he had capitalized on Rosie's performance. Special buses bring spectators to the "event," new shops emerge spontaneously, hawkers sell balloons, sweets, and whistles, and an American film and television producer capitalizes on the spectacle. Cables, lights, cameras—Malone, the producer, interviews Raju, asking how he likes it here. Raju offers a very intriguing, ambiguous answer: "I am only doing what I have to do; that's all. My likes and dislikes do not count" (217).

However one reads the novel's conclusion—that is, whether it actually does begin to rain, and what the implications may be whether it rains or not—it is Raju's claim that he is only doing what he must that is of most importance. Essentially he says what he has said before, that "what must happen must happen" and that he "must play the role assigned" him. This is his dharma and he accepts it; he has arrived at this juncture seemingly through self-direction and individual, independent scheming—the "modern" mode of life. Yet his increasingly greedy pursuit of self-gratification leads him to a place where the simple man of faith (the embodiment of traditionalism in this novel) exercises control over him which, in turn, finally effects Raju's control over himself.

In keeping with my reading of *Mahatma, The Guide,* and *A Tiger for Malgudi,* I believe we are meant to see the results of Raju's enforced, brief asceticism as a victory for the forces of Hindu traditionalism, a reminder of the regenerative possibilities inherent in the persisting native socio-religious fabric. As Britta Olinder remarks:

> In *The Guide,* the question of holiness is at the very centre. . . . When Narayan reaches the point of deepest mysticism he is also most graphically concrete and realistic. . . . There is a complete fusion between realistic description and insight into the mystical powers in human life. (18)

Raju's spiritual transformation is inadvertently arrived at through his response—even his dedication—to the practical affairs of everyday life.

In *A Tiger for Malgudi,* Narayan takes the traditional theme of one's struggle for self-control into the realm of what might best be regarded as extended fable or folktale. As he points out in the introduction to the novel, he came upon his theme while reading a newspaper account about a hermit and his companion tiger who arrived at Allahabad during the Kumbh Mela festival. There is a rich body of lore in South and Southeast Asia that centers on the tiger as familiar, the central element of the tales typically being either that the tiger-companion is not a "real" tiger but something or someone else that temporarily assumes the form of a tiger, or—as is the case here—that the "true familiar . . . [has] a psychic alliance or affinity with a certain person" (Wessing, 64). Such a tradition no doubt recommended itself to Narayan and, beyond that, this specific incident of man-tiger companionship offered to the author another potential narrative structure through which to explore the transformation of self from sensually absorbed to spiritually aware. While *Mahatma* and *The Guide* entertain this same philosophical orientation, *A Tiger for Malgudi* allows Narayan to investigate the struggle for control over the senses by entering into the experience of the man-eater. The man-eater motif serves the author beyond his interest in self-ascendancy, however, as it also allows him to achieve his essential meaning through irony in establishing again the sacred appetite manifest in experience that calls the consciousness of the world toward its own self, effecting awareness in the changing individual as it does so. Brahma can be imagined as man-eater. As Master says at one point to Raja, "You are quite right in thinking of your God as a superb tiger" (158).

Long before he comes under the Master's control, when he is still a single, wild beast, his inflated pride in being a controller, a manipulator, reminds us somewhat of Raju's hunger for recognition and appreciation:

> When I passed by, rabbits scurried off, and if a jackal happened to be in my path, he put his ears back, lowered his tail, rolled his eyes in humility, and cried softly: "Here is our Lord and Master. Keep his path clear . . . " Such attention pleased me, and seemed to add to my stature. (14)

The series of events that leads him to transcendence begins when he first encounters a force equal to, or perhaps greater than, himself. His fierce battle with the female tiger ends in his recognizing that he had "never encountered anyone so strong" (19) and in their mutual submission to one another.

Raja recognizes the jungle as a world of predators, "a devilish place" (21), and it is not long before his family is killed by hunters. Both anguish for his family and hatred for the men lure Raja to the village, where he is of course finally trapped—after a long period of stealthily filching the villagers' animals.

It is not so significant that the tiger is trapped after being baited by a lamb, but it is most significant that the captor is Captain, director of the Grand Malgudi Circus. Using reward and punishment (giving and denying food), Captain, the animal tamer, gains control of the tiger. Raja realizes that only if he performs as Captain wishes (running around and around in circles) will he be provided for:

> Life was not so bad after all. Captain was not such a monster after all. I began to admire him—a sort of worshipful attitude was developing in me. I had thought in the jungle that I was supreme. Now

that was gone. I was a defeated king, and Captain was the unquestioned suzerain. (53)

Captain is masterful in his ability to contain even the most ferocious of appetites, yet he lacks the crucial understanding that violence is not the means to maintain this control. As Raja reflects:

> . . . he had a wrong philosophy of depending upon the whip and his terrible voice, not realizing that I could be made to go through all those meaningless motions even without all that violence just by being told what to do. (97)

Raja is barely held at bay, persistently aware that "the agony of self-control was worse than the raging hunger" (74). Even though Raja is seemingly tamed and under Captain's control ("Raja is my tiger"), Captain's wife sees the persistence of the beast's wild hunger: ". . . if you relax even for a split second he'll, God knows what he will do . . . . The way he glares!" (79).

When Captain resorts to the emblem of artificial control, the electric prod, Raja's resentment grows, and he finally rejects this controlling agency: "It was surprising that such a flimsy creature, no better than a membrane stretched over some thin framework, with so little stuff inside, should have held me in fear so long" (115). In batting away the hated mechanical prod, Raja also tears off the Captain's head. The controlling agent gone, pure appetite is unleashed, and chaos and fear ensue on the streets of Malgudi.

At this point enters the agent of traditional spirituality—the "Mahatma," the "Velan" of this novel; his function is the same in that he begins to subdue the appetite of the central character in favor of that character's spiritual awakening, yet his method is unlike either agent in the other two novels. While Sriram is affected by the "presence," the teaching, and the awesome reputation of the Mahatma, and Raju is grudgingly urged toward a position of awareness by Velan's naive faith in him, Raja comes under the Master's power suddenly, surprisingly, quite unbelievably—were this not a religious fable. We willingly accept this sudden and lightly comic "take charge" position of the Master for what it is: an almost anticipated element within a tale whose means is metaphorical rather than wholly realistic, and whose import is a repeated expression of the theme of *Mahatma* and *The Guide*, in another guise.

When the Master enters the headmaster's room in the school, where Raja lies waiting underneath the headmaster's desk, his influence over Raja is immediate. Like Raju in *The Guide*, Raja senses that he "has no choice" but must act according to the will of this new intervening agent:

I saw him enter. I just heard him say, "Understand that you are not a tiger . . . I am your friend . . ." How I was beginning to understand his speech is a mystery. He was exercising some strange power over me. (144)

Master tells Raja the he will "have to change" (145), that he will have to abandon his aggressiveness; like Raju, Raja "was feeling uncomfortable with some change coming inside me. I was beginning to understand" (146). And, like Raju, this sense of becoming cornered or ensnared leads him at first to thoughts of escape. He

> wanted. . . to get away from the whole situation, back to my familiar life; . . . ever since the unfortunate day I stepped into that village in the forest to the present moment I was being hemmed in. (146)

Alphonse, the would-be tiger slayer, ironically succumbs to self-indulgence, falling into a drunken sleep outside the school building; Master, the self-controlled, walks past him with the now-obedient tiger at his side. The townspeople are amazed, and immediately rumors begin to circulate that the hermit "must have come from the Himalayas" where there are said to be many "extraordinary souls who . . . can control anything by their yogic powers" (151).

Echoing Gandhi, Master tells Raja that "the eye is the starting point of all mischief . . . so don't look at anything except the path" (155). Then, as they settle (for a time) together in the Mempi Hills, Master initiates Raja's spiritual instruction, introducing the concept of God:

> In *Bhagavad Gita* He reveals himself in a mighty terrifying form which pervades the whole universe . . . . Remember also He is within every one of us and we derive our strength from Him . . . (158)

Master ties this last idea to the issue of appetite and admits that "God has decided for you a difficult diet. I can help your mind and soul, but I cannot affect your body or its functions" (157). Nevertheless, Raja comes to be "seized with remorse" after killing, and would then try "to attain some kind of purification by reducing the frequency of seeking for food" (159). Eventually, Raja "preferred to go without food" (173)—and it is at this point that Master and tiger separate, to achieve release "from all bondage" (174). Master commits Raja to a zoo where, he says, Raja can make others happy.

It is important to note that the Master himself has had to "control the beast within" to arrive at his current status. When his wife (whom he suddenly left years before) seeks him out in the Hills and implores him to return, we discover that she remembers him for his "inordinate demands for food and my perpetual anxiety to see you satisfied, and my total surrender to you night or day when passion seized you" (170). Given the pattern of *Mahatma, The Guide,* and Raja's experience in this novel, we are inclined to wonder where the Master's appetite led him so that he might encounter some agency which would effect his spiritual transformation.

About the Master's hazy past and the events of the novel beginning with the sudden appearance of the Master, David Atkinson in his "Tradition and Transformation in R. K. Narayan's *A Tiger for Malgudi*," raises several questions:

> While to some the closure of the novel might seem contrived and weak, it is possible to see Narayan consciously placing the novel against an ironic backdrop which brings into question its religious and philosophic underpinnings. (12)

Because the Master is presented as a "shadowy and unconvincing figure" and becomes "when his wife appears, . . . a very contradictory one," Atkinson questions "to what degree Narayan is committed to the Hindu world view that *A Tiger for Malgudi* seems so clearly to espouse" (12). To this I would reply that the "system" of committed asceticism may not always achieve its professed results, and while Narayan reveals in his work the presence of sham holy men, I have little reason to question Narayan's commitment to the regenerative capacity of Hindu traditionalism. Despite the clarity and simplicity of Narayan's depiction of these tenets (which troubles Atkinson), when we consider these several novels together, the seeming simplicity becomes subordinated to the author's attraction to the implicit irony in the narrative framework. We encounter a character who by pursuing the inclinations of his appetite arrives at a transcendence of appetite, who by working to corner that which will gratify his appetite is in turn ensnared, who by seeking to control is then controlled—and because of this external control arrives at self-control and heightened spirituality. And in each of the novels discussed here, the agent enforcing this control works as a vehicle for socio-religious tradition.

Regarding Narayan's insistence on the enduring value and pervasive power of the traditional, Satyanarain Singh remarks that:

> Malgudi to Narayan symbolizes the essential inviolability of old world values leading to life's eternal verities above and beyond the humdrum rat race for ephemeral pleasure and a mad struggle for acquisitive goods. (105)

In many of Narayan's works, "the seeker has to cultivate disinterestedness from carnal desires and material pursuits and resign himself to the higher truth of realizing his true identity" (Singh, 105–6). Singh sees in this persistent theme, the return to religious traditionalism, a deficient social concern: "What constricts Narayan's vision . . . is the emphasis on individual redemption without at the same time developing a social conscience" (108). Yet, while it is true in the three novels I have considered in this discussion that individual awakening, self-control, and self-knowledge are indeed the focus, it is clear that in each case this change in the self is not self-willed, not consciously pursued—at the expense of anything. It is, ironically, *through* pursuit of desire, through immersion in the "rat race for ephemeral pleasure" that the spiritual recognition occurs in these narratives. And in that twist of events lies the beauty of surprise, the "comic" irony (as expressed in these instances) that Narayan is known for.

When I consider the almost sequential relationship of *Waiting for the Mahatma*, *The Guide*, and *A Tiger for Malgudi*, I am reminded of what might serve as an icon for the "triad" of novels: a tempera and water color painting from about 1820, which is held in the Victoria and Albert Museum, depicting Vasishta, one of the ten great sages born of Brahma; he wears his hair in the ascetic's chignon and sits, composed, cross-legged on the skin of a tiger. I have to wonder who and what led him to that seat.

Works Cited

Atkinson, David W. "Tradition and Transformation in R. K. Narayan's *A Tiger for Malgudi*." *International Fiction Review* 14, no. 1 (1987): 8–14.
Naipaul, V. S. *India: A Wounded Civilization*. New York: Vintage Books, 1977.
Narayan, R. K. *The Guide*. 1958. New York: Penguin Books, 1980.
_____. *A Tiger for Malgudi*. New York: Viking Press, 1983.
_____. *Waiting for the Mahatma*. East Lansing: Michigan State University Press, 1955.
Olinder, Britta. "Reality and Myth in R. K. Narayan's Novels." *The Literary Criterion* 20, no. 2 (1985): 8–22.
Raichura, Suresh. "R. K. Narayan: *The Guide*." *Major Indian Novels: An Evaluation.* Atlantic Highlands, New Jersey: Humanities, 1986: 104–34.
Singh, Satyanarain. "A Note on the World View of R.K. Narayan." *Indian Literature* 24, no. 1 (Jan.–Feb. 1981): 104–9.
Wessing, Robert. *The Soul of Ambiguity: The Tiger in Southeast Asia*. Northern Illinois University: Center for Southeast Asian Studies, 1986.
Woodcock, George. "The Maker of Malgudi: Notes on R. K. Narayan." *The Tamarack Review* 73 (1978): 82–95.

Daisy Paints Her Signs Otherwise

SHANTHA KRISHNASWAMY

Starting with the premise that different readings can be differently useful, though not all may be equally acceptable, and that there is no single right reading for any complex literary text, I am attempting through this paper to decode certain interesting signs found in *The Painter of Signs* by R.K. Narayan.[1] These are signs that I consider relevant because their untangling or decoding gives rise to a process of interrogation that makes us aware not only of what has been done in the field but also of what is to be done next or what can be done differently and daringly.

When I began this paper I realized I was facing something unprecedented, something dangerous in Daisy, the chief female protagonist in *The Painter of Signs*. This protagonist is one of a kind in Indian fiction, both classical and contemporary. This type of a protagonist has not been created by any other Indian writer, and certainly not by R.K. Narayan again, not even in his latest fictive offering, *The World of Nagaraj*. The conventional Indian female protagonist tends to be weaned from parental tutelage to be ushered into a well-worn life as a bridge, there to await the only crowning achievement of her life—the begetting of sons. Modern innovations like amniocentesis assist her in this selective birth process. Despite a feeble protest or two, mostly through barely audible whispers, she awaits her end placidly, like the proverbial cow under the Indian sun. Anyway who cares about a girl, a wife, an old mother? Bah! They are born to water the neighbor's gardens.

Daisy bursts into this milieu, daring to be somebody different. She uses her education not to further the interest of the symbolic order, the patriarchy, but to subvert it and deconstruct it deliberately. She not only looks down upon the conventional choices allotted to Indian women as wives and mothers, but she also sets herself up as an arch devil, proselytizing converts to her cause of birth control, with the missionary zeal of an intrepid warrior. Daisy is a dangerous, disruptive, and fanatical nun wedded to her goal, out to destroy the Malgudian order of things. In her story we see how what was once a wholly patriarchal culture begins to evolve, fragmentarily, sometimes haltingly, sometimes convulsively, but always irreversibly, into a "masculinist feminist culture" (if we can label it so), a culture whose style and structure will no longer be patriarchal nor will they be explicitly feminist in the Western sense of the term. Daisy posts her signs, signs indicating this new order, this new language that she devises, the language of the other. Daisy has to speak otherwise in order to be heard, in order to forge ahead. It is enervating and sometimes unnerving to confront the rapid social changes that are ushered in by Daisy, changes that bring about a diminution of man's authority and a corresponding accretion of woman's responsibility.

Daisy is the other who chooses to opt out of the symbolic order on her own terms, yet managing to keep her wits and her integrity about her. She illustrates how gender and class lie at the center of the nexus between power and discourse and how it is necessary to transform a society divided by these issues in order to deepen and enrich human lives.

The very name Daisy is nondenominational. One is tempted to ask: Daisy who? What religion does she belong to? What is her caste? Where are her guardians, her parents, brothers, husband, sons? Daisy maintains such a confrontational demeanor that no one dares ask her these questions though they matter very much in the Malgudian context. Her lover, Raman, is discomfited about her lack of antecedents. To his aunt he mumbles something about a flower native to England in a feeble attempt to clarify this non-Malgudian name. His aunt, however, is aghast at this volcanic eruption of female independence in her hometown, her Malgudi.

Daisy arrives as the family planning officer; she does not partake of the quiet but desperate lifestyles of her sisters in Malgudi; nor is she apathetic to the point of laying all the blame on her karma, a way of living that Raman's old aunt would have understood and approved of. She is brimful of inspirational ideology and relevant statistics and enough psycological acumen to net any stray semen that may venture out like a tremulous Woody Allen. She not only exposes the sexist biases in the society but also puts forth new choices—no wifehood, no motherhood—to a moribund society that has, over a long period of time, salved its conscience by taking umbrage under the concept of bhogam or bhogopakaranam. This is to be construed as bliss in domestic life during the stage of the householder. I would loosely translate this as jouissance; the nearest approximation to it (minus the Hindu and Brahminical trappings) has perhaps been formulated by Roland Barthes.

This concept has been used to assuage ruffled feminist tempers or any glimmerings of it; it is the riposte that sexual enjoyment (in the Hindu context) has always been a cooperative and enjoyable aspect of life, in consonance with the prescriptions of the scriptures, that sexual bliss is part of the larger bliss of life and as such something to be celebrated and not to be indulged in furtively or guiltily (here the erotic sculptures of Kajuraho, the hymns or ashtaphathis of Jayadeva and the Kama Sutra will be trotted out in proud display), and that what is taken amiss as male dominance has been only one of the inevitable states of mind, of Lila or Maya, that the human goes through in his journey through life or it is only an accident of history. We also have the convenient examples of foreign invasions like those of the Moghuls and the Huns and the Tartars and others to bolster the argument. The Hindu concept of bhogopakaranam, according to this thesis, has never been intentionally sexist in origin. Daisy explodes all this myth of equality, of neutrality, and of inevitability.

The lady with a nameless name in the Indian context does not rest as a token of trendiness. She is an unabashed iconoclast, out to break all past salvos shoring up male hegemony. Very little of her pre-Malgudian life is given to the reader. She is usually a brisk person, busy with the activities for the day. But she does let slip a few anecdotes from her past, anecdotes with their interstices of inherent significance. She shares a few rare and meditative moments, sitting with her lover, Raman, the local painter of signboards, on the banks of the Sarayu that runs behind Raman's house (178–79). She recalls how as a young girl, barely out of her teens, she disliked intensely the collective living in an extended Hindu joint family system. She had realized even then that femininity as a social construct placed an unequal and frustrating yoke upon her. She describes how she was interviewed or inspected by a prospective bridegroom and his parents. On the surface it is a hilarious scene; however, there is the underlying pathos of a spirited and intelligent girl being bound by the scourge whips of convention. In narrating this single episode from her girlhood, Daisy—she may have been Gauri or Lakshmi or Parvathi at that stage in her life—illustrates how the Indian woman acquires identity through repression. When she objected to her family's matchmaking, saying she would rather work than get married, she was objecting to the conjunction of her identity with her anatomy. The Hindu woman has been the site of a constant silent political struggle. On the one hand she, like all human beings, seeks an identity of her own and on the other hand, the society pushes her into marriage and motherhood, promising the highest state of bliss in domesticity, all the while repressing and marginalizing her.

Daisy refuses to assist in the meek transference of the goals of hierarchy from one generation to another. She turns the tables on the system, the male order. When the proposed bridegroom and his family await the usual shy girl with downcast eyes, ready to do obeisance in their august presence, in strides our Daisy, with masculine gestures and pose, and starts conducting the interview amidst the rustle of her brocade sari and the clatter of borrowed jewelery around her person. When she is asked a question, she answers briskly and puts forth five questions of her own. She demolishes the reputation of the bridegroom's party in five minutes and shows him up to the world as stupid, vacuous and bumbling poseur, living off his ancestral landholdings. But reality comes crowding in. Bridegrooms are rare commodities and when one is available, parents treat him as a precious jewel. Daisy, castigated for damaging the image of the family (Who would now come forward for an alliance? What about the other girls in the family? How to live down the shame?), runs away from home, is rescued by missionaries who bring her up, send her to college, and infuse her with the spirit of service to society.

When Raman, the eligible bachelor about town falls in love with her, he does not know what to make of her, for she is a puzzle to him. They seem to be made for each other—he is sensitive, handsome, and endowed with a sense of humor that lets him keep a running dialogue with himself in the process of finding a meaning in his life. All the significance he seeks seems to be centered in Daisy. He is willing to be an unconventional husband—he is willing to change his style of living; he throws overboard everything that smacks of antiquarianism; he sees his only relative, his old aunt, off to Benares, with regret no doubt, but also with keen anticipation of Daisy's arrival in his home; he is willing to sign away any issue resulting from his affair with Daisy, at her behest, just like King Santhanu of *Mahabharatha*.

Daisy, on her part, bold and mannish though she usually is, seems to bring forth the softer and finer aspects of her character in Raman's company. There is the hint of her blossoming physically too as a result of her relationship with Raman. The two recall the idyllic love of Shakuntala and Dushyantha in the few instances when they get together. But Daisy is not the classical coy maiden; she is rational and ever conscious of the goals she has set for herself. Population control and urgency of rural family planning measures crowd out the brief romantic interlude. At story's end she breaks off from domesticity and love; she states wistfully and at the same time firmly, "Married life is not for me. I have thought it over. It frightens me. I am not cut out for the life you imagine. I can't live except alone. It won't work" (178–79). The novel is an unsettling tale about love, about man-woman relationships in Malgudi, in India and, by extension, in Asia.

The application of French feminist theories to Daisy opens up interesting lines of inquiry. Arguing along the lines of Julia Kristeva, Daisy seems to have breached the marginality and positionality of being woman.[2] What seems to be intriguing in Daisy's character may then be argued to be the dissolving properties of all entities with fluid parameters for frontiers. The text, in keeping with this, initiates a seemingly playful series of binary oppositions that make the presence of the dark, the female, felt constantly. The Kristevan semioteke is not only the mysterious primordial world from beyond time responsible for the generation of hallucinations, voices, psychoses, madness, and other fluid phenomena, but also the dark seductive continent, the source of female ingenuity and endurance; this is Daisy's natal terrain.

The granite harshness, the stony permanence of the Malgudian landscape, is given a shakeup when Daisy asserts her claim to equality along with the man in her milieu. It is ironic that Raman finds it difficult to go along with her all the way in her professed way of living. Leaving aside the sexual part of life for an instant, we read about Daisy accommodating any type of food, any type of bed, any shelter anywhere, anytime. It is Raman whose taste buds have been cultivated by the assiduous cooking and care of brahminical living who finds equality not completely to his taste. When Daisy stakes her claim to equality, she gets to be more equal than he!

Daisy then seems to proceed to a place on the second rung of the three-tiered scale envisioned by Kristeva for woman—the rung where woman, going beyond demanding equality or equal access to the symbolic order, advocates radical feminism and totally rejects the male order in the name of difference and specificity. If so, Daisy seems to be heading inevitably toward an inverted form of sexism. She seems to wear the pants all the time and Raman is reduced to a misshapen mass of weak-kneed flesh in her company. This introduces the comic vein in the story, but no right-thinking woman (or man, for that matter) would be happy reducing the other to a jelly. The implication here is that Daisy's way out of biologism deconstructs the female out of existence and that she cannot hope to escape donning the mantle of chauvinism. Chauvinism is something to be regretted, something to be shunned, regardless of whether it is male or female.

Daisy has, of course, refused to tow the path of compromise and silent suffering because she knows such a course of conduct would reinforce the very symbolic order she sets out to eschew. She refuses to be silent and passive because experience has taught her that meekness is rewarded only with violence in a predatory society. How is she, then, to create a space for herself outside the linear time of history and politics without being perceived as a counter ideologist, a sexist in reverse? How is she to exist inserting herself into the symbolic order without embracing the masculine model for femininity? Is her liberation to lead her only to lonely, barren exultations?

The problems encountered by Western feminists like Kristeva are detailed in the text along with a few others peculiar to the Malgudian context. On the one hand, the construction of revolutionary counterculture does not ensure a harmonious relationship between the sexes because it merely ensures a change of power without the necessary and accompanying change in the nature of power. As long as we base human relationships on the nexus between politics and power, somebody or some party is bound to suffer. Then there is the problem of the idealization of female experience. Either it comes through to the surface as the experience of a unique, out-of-the-ordinary being (either goddess or whore), or else it is bottled up, only to burst forth occasionally in the form of psychosis.

Terry Eagleton has remarked that "what a society cannot accomplish historically, it nurtures in the realm of myth" (93). Mythologizing, however, merely consolidates male power, and mythmaking is a false and insulting resolution of the feminist dilemma. Woman as goddess (the Western equivalent would be the madonna) or whore is an equally essentialistic concept. It may result in an identity, raw and bold but still questionable, still out of bounds for many. And Kristeva adds, "What can identity, even sexual identity, mean in a new theoretical and scientific space where the very notion of identity is challenged?" (214–15). This troubled and troubling area of grey existence is allotted to the woman who refuses to be mythologized and at the same time refuses equally to be desexed because of her positionality as an extreme radical.

Coming to the Malgudian context, Daisy seems to be neither man nor woman. She cohabits freely with Raman but she refuses to move into his house as a live-in partner. She refuses to sanctify their relationship, even by the rites of a Gandharva marriage, which Raman wants to ease his conscience. She is not bothered by the narrow, sanctimonious strictures of the people around her while Raman is tortured by them every waking moment of his life. As for Daisy's concept of motherhood, one can write a separate paper on that topic. It is sufficient for our purposes to note here that Daisy considers motherhood as a severe limitation both on the personal and on the national levels. She is the personification of birth control. According to her, every mother is destined to a demented, debilitating jouissance. She opts for a childless existence, ordering Raman to give up for adoption any child they may, by accident, conceive. Every act of deviation, every sign she posts, is a further twist of the dagger into the Malgudian society that measures a woman mainly by her fecundity, her capacity to bear sons.

Once again in Kristevan terms, Daisy seems to symbolize the woman's struggle against the implacable difference, the violence, that is ever prevalent in affirming personal and sexual identity. By taking a brave stance, Daisy ironically seems to lose all grace in her being. She not only desexes herself, but in the process, deconstructs herself into a miasma of despair and oblivion by disintegrating the very nucleus of her being. One wonders whether this struggle is worth so much of sacrifice? The irony lies in the fact that Daisy does not prefer this bleak Lady Macbethian type of existence.

One cannot disagree with Kristeva when she argues for the founding of a special space where individual and sexual difference can be allowed free play, where both man and woman would accept sexual difference as the founding moment of civilization, where feminist anarchy and male chauvinism will be avoided, where men will not become scapegoats and women will not become sacrificial victims. Such a space will release at once the individuality and the multiplicity of each person's possible identities. Unfortunately, we do not find this space in *The Painter of Signs*.

The resolution of the novel is sacrificial in the sense that Raman is the ready and willing scapegoat and Daisy goes her lonely way, deprived of all jouissance, all prospect of domestic bliss (bhogopakaranam).[3] The sacrificial nature of their respective struggles for identification and meaning result only in intense frustration and failure and they both fall into what Kristeva calls the "metaphysical trap" where the binary oppositions remain operative. Daisy's solution of being indifferent to the structure of male-female power relations does not provide a solution to the ordinary Indian woman's dilemma, or if it does, in a manner of speaking, it is too coercive and too bleak, shorn of all vestiges of earthly happiness, and she is too impersonal to be followed as a role model. Daisy is not able to provide a practicable frame of reference to cut across the layers of convention, tradition and myth.

The novel does not open up the Kristevan space for the Indian woman. Nor does it provide peace and domestic harmony for the Indian man. Raman is left high and dry, muttering about the prospects of a reunion in the next life while Daisy resumes her family planning activities in other towns, in other hamlets. The gulf between the two is not bridged, the essence of female sexuality and identity do not have their equivalence in the other sex and the two are impoverished.

Interesting as the French feminist theories are, they do not account for the peculiar variations that arise out of differences in race, religion, class, and culture. Daisy finds her problem of being woman compounded by the Malgudian milieu. Here the Western notion of space as emptiness, a clean, uncluttered void, is not valid. In Malgudi, as in other Asian milieus, space is always peopled with spirit. Space is the dynamic interaction not only between subject and object (or, between object and object to maintain the tenor of equality), but also the interaction between surrounding and interpenetrating space. This in turn posits the question of cohabitation, adjustment, and fine tuning. It is a sort of tightrope walking because at any moment there is the danger of the hard-won equilibrium descending into the pit of domination and servitude, apathy and karma. There is clearly a need for further explication, a discourse in depth about this imagined space of Kristeva.[4]

Daisy's attempts to create a special space outside linear time and history, outside the Malgudian context, do not bear fruition. She realizes the system hampers her, rebel though she is, and she finds her wings clipped. As for Raman, though he tries to undertake a long journey into the semiotic night, he is feeble and man after all, judging by his frequent lapses into nostalgic and impotent reveries of a once male-ordered, smooth-sprung world where he could assume the innate insignificance of the women in his life. He is conscious of being marginalized by Daisy, of being emasculated, submerged as he is in his love for her. Daisy is also aware of this and her way of easing the pressure on both of them is the path of self-abnegation.

What we are offered is a tragic negation beneath the surface humor. Daisy is given the choice of being either the goddess wife or the demon whore; in either case she would not be the free woman she wants to be. She would end up with the flawed identity of a fetish, mythologized without the comforts of the supernatural blanket that wraps epic heroines like Sita and Savithri. When she refuses to be a pawn in the protracted play of power interests in Malgudi, she loses her share in jouissance.

Daisy is not a rabid, fire-breathing feminist; nor is she a manic depressive, haunted by female psychosis. She is not one who chooses not to be. She is a normal, healthy, and highly intelligent girl who wants her share of happiness on earth. She opts out of the symbolic order to fulfill her goal of birth control; when her biological drives tempt her back, she finds she cannot reenter the power game at all without being stripped from full subjecthood, without being instantly falsified, by the extant rules of discourse. She is driven into a bleak, missionary existence, out on the margins of the Malgudian world.

One may then ask: What is the point of it all? Every feminist reading of a text is, in a sense, a revolutionary reading. Daisy's text, though ending on a bleak note, is still a volcanic text, glowing of the red fire rocks below. She has set a whole process of reassessment in motion; Malgudi in the post-Daisy era will be, hopefully—will have to be—different. As Daisy is part of the deeper and broader discursive formations in Malgudi, and as she is part of an ancient living culture, rereading her alerts us to far-reaching institutional implications. Fifty years ago R.K. Narayan wrote *The Dark Room* in which the protagonist, Savithri, finds herself at the losing end of the power game, tries to be independent, gives up the struggle after two days, and is brought mercilessly back to her husband's iron-fisted tether. But Daisy ventures out bravely beyond Savithri's space. It is an act of courage, not only on her part but also on the part of the novelist, given the granite harshness of Brahmin orthodoxy in the Malgudian context.

Notes

1. A plurality of readings is generated not only by feminist inquiry but also by other lines of critical inquiry. See Robert Scholes, *Structuralism in Literature* (New Haven: Yale University Press, 1974), 144–45.

2. Julia Kristeva, "Woman's Time," in *The Feminine Reader*, eds., C. Belsey and J. Moore (London: Macmillan Co., 1989), 197–217. I am deeply indebted to Julia Kristeva for the ideological underpinnings of this paper.

3. Julia Kristeva says, "Anthropology has shown that the social order is sacrificial, but sacrifice orders violence, binds it, tames it." See Julia Kristeva, "Woman's Time," 209. Daisy's choice of exclusion from domestic bliss (bhogopakaranam), and her exclusion from mainstream Malgudian life, should not make us forget the radical nature of her chosen lifestyle, and her bold demystification of the bonds of marriage and family.

4. Kristeva, while appropriating the concept of monumental and/or cyclical temporality for "feminine space," does grant that this is not incompatible with "masculine" values. See J. Kristeva, "Woman's Time," "About Chinese Women," in *The Kristeva Reader* ed. Toril Moi (Oxford: Basil/Blackwell, 1987).

The belief that all forms of life and behavioral traits are cyclical and repetitive is dominant in the realms of Asian philosophy and religion and this belief automatically eschews notions of linearity and finality as far as birth and death processes and temporality are concerned. The Hindu "superstition" that particular man and woman are bound together in matrimony for seven successive reincarnated lives is concomitant to this belief. I am, however, not appropriating this terrain of thought for the purposes of this paper, as I have avowed at the outset my intention to focus on the psychoanalytical feminist theories from France. The Indians, like the English, are wary of dealing with psychoanalysis, though for different reasons.

Works Cited

Eagleton, Terry. *The Rape of Clarissa*. Oxford: Basil Blackwell, 1985.
Kristeva, Julia. "Woman's Time." *The Feminine Reader*. Eds. C. Belsey and J. Moore. London: Macmilliam Co., 1989: 197–217.
Narayan, R.K. *The Painter of Signs*. Mysore, India: Indian Thought Publication, 1977.
_____. *The World of Nagaraj*. London: William Heinemann, 1990.

The Painter of Signs: *Breaking the Frontier*

SADHANA ALLISON PURANIK

The frontier does not immediately come to mind when one thinks of R.K. Narayan's novels. The small town of Malgudi, in which all are set, is as established a place as one could imagine. With each novel, Malgudi's map gains greater specificity, and by the time Narayan published *The Painter of Signs* in 1976, there were ten novels and more than a forty-year literary history through which to see it. The town's carefully drawn parameters, illustrated in a map published with the collection of short stories, *Malgudi Days*, enclose a space which has been described by critics as highly localized and particular, as a microcosm of India, and of the world. By setting those parameters, however, Narayan also distinguishes the town from its surroundings, which constitute unfamiliar territory for both his characters and his readers. Once we see that he constructs the borders, the river, and the villages and countryside around Malgudi as frontiers, we get a clear view of how he uses a novelistic convention to examine the relationship between marginality and individuality "within [the] broad climate of inherited culture" (Narayan, *Malgudi Days*, 7) that characterizes Malgudi.

All of Narayan's novels are concerned with questions of individuality and tradition, but *The Painter of Signs* most fully demonstrates his use of Malgudi's borders and surroundings as frontiers. In this book, the town always constitutes the "center" and "civilization" in relation to the frontier. The countryside and the outlying villages represent the beginning of the rest of India, and even the world beyond it. The river bank is a different kind of frontier, when seen in relation to Raman's house rather than to the town as a whole. While the river is a frontier in the more literal sense of being a border, the countryside is a frontier zone, in that it shares characteristics with the popularly delineated image of the frontier in fiction.

Fictional portrayals of the frontiers in India have conditioned us to associate such areas with certain types of experiences. Kipling's portrayal of northern frontiers, particularly the Northwest Frontier, spring to mind when we think of the Indian subcontinent. In a nutshell, though, his short story "Georgie Porgie" is a clear example of his treatment of such areas. The frontier in question is Upper Burma, but, as Burma was actually administered as a province of India until 1937, and Kipling's attitudes to the two countries are similar throughout his work, the story can be seen as typical of his treatment of parallel areas in India. By setting up "home," or England, against the frontier, which was 'still smoldering and would blaze when least expected,' (Kipling, "Georgie Porgie," 278) Kipling quickly establishes an area that would seem remote to his readers (of any nationality) in its way of life as in its distance. In this lawless area, Georgie's life with the Burmese woman, which would be judged immoral by English standards, is seen to be somehow fitting. Although he paints Georgie humorously, Kipling clearly sees his character as the type who is fit to handle the challenge of the area:

> Among the forerunners of Civilization was Georgie Porgie, reckoned by all who knew him a strong man. He held an appointment in Lower Burma when the order came to break the Frontier . . . . When he went to Upper Burma he had no special regard for God or Man, but he knew how to make himself respected. . . (Kipling, "Georgie Porgie," 277–278)

Kipling's association of the frontier with physically strong and strong-willed men is standard, as is his perception of the area as lawless and remote.

"Georgie Porgie" makes another lasting literary impression; that is, its association of the Frontier with sexual exploitation or, seen from another angle, sexual freedom. By contrasting his hero's unconventional relationship with "Georgina" with his conventional attachment to an English-woman, Kipling places Georgie, as an individual, between cultures. While he remains "marginal," Georgie can never be fully a part of one or the other cultural tradition. In order to maintain, or even regain, his Englishness, he must reject his Burmese "wife." The short story underlines one of the basic assumptions of *Kim*, and other tales: a "marginal" character, existing between cultures, can never be truly integrated into one culture.

In *A Passage to India*, a novel widely considered to be a liberal and tolerant alternative to Kipling's presentations of India, Forster makes the same assumption. This point is best illustrated by the scene at the end of the novel. Forster chooses the Mau jungles, distanced from the clutter of the rest of India, to isolate Aziz and Fielding as individuals. The landscape, "park-like as England," still "[does] not cease being queer" (Forster, 311). The description situates each man far from his respective culture, making the theater for their final meeting seem as remote and unfamiliar as a Kipling frontier. It is here that we witness a scene drawn with greater clarity than any other in the novel, as the clear sky and landscape underline the final meeting between the two men who can, at last, see their relationship and separate destinies without obstructions.

There is a struggle throughout the novel for clear images, which may be physically describable, but which are nevertheless surrounded by a Conradian sense of the "unknowable." The caves, for instance, may have "bland and bald. . .precipices," but these connect them not to any present reality, but to a primordial scene, "before man, with his itch for the seemly, had been born" (Forster, 158). Throughout the novel, such language obscures interpretation, until the final, vivid scene. The two characters, standing on the cultural border represented by the Mau jungle, begin to understand the marginal spaces they inhabit. The two best-known English writers dealing with the Indian scene, then, strongly associate the Frontier with qualities of western individualism, whether based on self-reliance, self-realization, or personal freedom. This association goes hand in hand with the exclusion of such individuals from Indian life, as the marginal position between cultures and a central position within one culture are mutually exclusive.

Narayan suggests that these attitudes may not be entirely appropriate to India when he writes, "Even great writers such as Kipling and E.M. Forster, when they wrote about India, exhibited only a limited understanding, inevitable owing to their racial and other circumstances" (Narayan, "Raj," 31). His project, he continues, is to paint one piece of the Indian jigsaw from, of course, an Indian perspective. He thus consciously perceives his work as an Indian alternative to the English view of his country; however, because he is writing in the tradition of the English novel, he walks a fine line between the two.

The Painter of Signs demonstrates his skill as a tight-rope walker, which is particularly evident in his adaption of the frontier convention. He redefines the position of marginality, creating the possibility of a person being both marginal and central at the same time. By playing on our knowledge of the frontier, which is so clearly associated with empire, to describe an insular local environment like Malgudi, Narayan appropriates a convention based on British-Indian experience to frame a particular problem of Mrs. Gandhi's India: that is, the clash between western notions of individuality and traditional modes of life.

Daisy is the personification of that clash in *The Painter of Signs*, and she is also a symbol of the severity of the conventional view that will not allow a person to occupy a marginal position and still somehow remain rooted in his or her traditional culture. She displays the crusading attitude of the missionary when she summons the signboard painter to help her to spread her message ("We are two; let ours be two; limit your family") through the countryside (47). In their conversation she reveals something like Georgie Porgie's spirit of individualism, but sheltered under communal values:

> Daisy said, "I have now come to ask if you are prepared to do a little work outside in some of the villages. We have an intensive campaign in the rural ares."
>
> "What would you expect me to do?"
>
> "I am going on a tour of the surrounding villages for an initial survey, and to look out for places where we can write our message on the walls permanently. . . ."

When he laughs at her proposed message, she responds with righteous anger:

> She had grown slightly red in the face. It seemed as if her faith had been abused. Such missionary zeal! . . .As far as he was concerned, it was purely professional—his duty being to inscribe whatever he was ordered—and he could not share anyone's passion for the cause. (46–47)

Narayan obviously shares Raman's view of Daisy as an over-zealous missionary, carrying "civilized" values out of the town into the remote Indian countryside. Like Georgie, she has "no special regard for God or Man but [knows] how to make [herself] respected." Kipling's description is particularly fitting, for Daisy not only rejects the Hindu gods of her childhood, but also the Christian God who was part of her later missionary upbringing. She replaces these gods with a notion of civilization that is borrowed mainly from the missionaries, but which includes some elements of Hindu asceticism. The irony of her position is clear as soon as she reaches the villages; she is intent on "civilizing" people who already live within a highly structured and unchanging social framework.

We get an idea of the tension between her values and those of the villagers as she is leaving. In her clinical manner, she tells the children, "Don't suck your thumb. . . .Stand erect, don't slouch . . ." (64); she is a born mentor, born to lead. But the villagers think, "'The doctor is leaving,'" almost with relief. They would not have to feel apologetic any more for being fathers and mothers (65). This tension shows that, although Daisy approaches rural India like a frontiersman, the frontier principle of pioneering in an unworked area falls apart in the tradition-bound villages of

India. Her well-meaning idealism is perverted, in this setting, into dehumanizing idealism.

Much of the humor of Narayan's depiction of Daisy, and its underlying political force, can be gleaned from an understanding of some key points in Indian history contemporaneous with the writing of the novel. The population explosion that India had been experiencing reached a crisis in the early 1970s with frightening statistics about the numbers of India's ever-increasing masses (Walsh 193). That decade also saw the institution of Mrs. Gandhi's State of Emergency, which lasted from 1975 to 1977. The Prime Minister's authoritative attitude, coupled with the blatant disregard for civil rights during that period, made her highly unpopular and eventually led to her fall from power in 1977. In his chronology of the development of Indian literature in English, William Walsh relates that in 1976, the "target of 7.5 million vasectomies [was] reached" (194). This, he says, was also one element of her electoral defeat. The currency of the population question and controversy surrounding it undoubtedly plays some part in the depiction of Daisy as a crusading zealot with a genuine cause that becomes dehumanizing. Her crisp and authoritative manner further links her to India's period of emergency and the woman behind it. As her attitude to the countryside shows, Daisy's character is based on the western model of the individual—often found on fictional frontiers—who values action and strength. Her independent position belies the sprawling Indian family system of which Raman's life with his aunt is a last vestige. By linking Daisy with Mrs. Gandhi's India, Narayan implicitly criticizes the attitude of cultural extremism apparent in the government's domestic policies.

The countryside, that frontier zone between Malgudi and the world, is the place where the two ruling ideologies of Raman's life meet in hand-to-hand combat. Away from the town's institutions and its gossip, he suddenly finds himself in a position to test both his rationalist ideas and his faintly Gandhian principles which, incongruously, exist side by side. At the beginning of the novel, Raman understands "rationalism" as some sort of system of western efficiency different from the superstitious ways in which his fellow Malgudians traditionally do things:

> All day long he was engaged in arguing with his old aunt who advised him to do this or that according to the stars. He was determined to establish the Age of Reason in the world. "I want a rational explanation for everything," he cried. "Otherwise my mind refuses to accept any statement." He was bursting with self-declarations. "I'm a rationalist, and I don't do anything unless I see some logic in it." (PS, 8)

His Gandhian ideas take the form of a desperate effort to control his sexual desires by remembering some of that great man's advice. This sexual
element figures largely in the two incidents that best illustrate how
Narayan plays off some established perceptions of the frontier, and how
he uses that space to test his hero's "progressive" and "traditional" views.
The first is his encounter with the temple priest, and the second is his
unsuccessful attempt to satisfy his sexual desire for Daisy.

The temple incident condenses several elements of Raman's personality into one very funny and revealing scene. He approaches the old priest
to try to extract permission to paint a family planning slogan on the face
of the cave temple. Ostensibly, he is interested in this project because he
wants to impress or please Daisy, who has taken on the mantle of local
birth police. Raman's mission is immediately humorous because the site
is famous for its reputed power to cure infertility. The situation suggests
sex, suppressed in Raman's proposed sign as well as, one imagines, in the
dark recesses of the cave. (The cave/sex link has emerged, like the related
link between the frontier and individualism, as a convention in literature
set in India. Its wide-ranging implications invite detailed analysis not
possible within the confines of this study.) His tactless suggestion that
this might be the secret to the cave's powers signals his mounting sexual
frustration. He is, however, driven to offend the old man, a definite
taboo for any God-fearing Hindu, by the sense, developed over weeks
spent touring villages, that he is in an area with laws and standards different from those at home. In the spirit of the frontier, he assumes that
different laws mean no laws, and therefore he oversteps his limits at the
temple.

The scene provides one of the best examples of Narayan's narrative
technique of supplementing his protagonists' speeches with their
unvoiced thoughts, which are often more to the point and much funnier.
Raman's short conversation with the priest proves that there is more at
stake in his visit to the cave than simply impressing Daisy. Painting the
sign on the temple represents to him a conquest over traditional religion-
bound ideas. Because he cannot voice this blasphemous thought to the
old man, the narrator transmits this message to the reader: "Still he
[Raman] could not tell him [the priest] that his aim in life was to establish
the Age of Reason, and he could think of no boons to ask of a goddess"
(63). Reason conflicts with religion and, in a typical Narayan maneuvre,
neither prevails. Instead, Raman asks the Goddess to give him Daisy.
The request signals his failure to impress her with his modern ideas and,
as we learn later, his failure to conquer her love in a traditional way.

Like Daisy, Raman sets out to paint his signs of progress all over the
countryside; but he justifies his actions not with her missionary ideals,

but with a curious blend of capitalist economic concerns and the deep-seated Hindu notion of *dharma*. We recall Raman's earlier remark that "it was purely professional, his duty being to inscribe whatever was ordered." His interpretation of "professionalism" is evident in the opening scene with the lawyer, but his real attitude to his work lies in an observation that he makes early in the first chapter, when he muses, "a signboard was inevitable in modern life—a token of respectable and even noble intentions" (14). Inherent in these economic, aesthetic, and social aspects of his work is the notion that painting signs is his "duty." In the earlier quotation, "duty" could be interpreted simply as part of his perception of professionalism but, against Daisy's rampant missionary rhetoric, it looks more like a retreat into the safety of old and familiar language.

When Raman faces the priest, all these influences on his work and his character come into play. In the cave, we witness a war between his desire for rationalism and individualism and his urge to bow down to the priest, be humble and subservient, and gain merit by fulfilling part of his moral obligation. This tension gives a mocking and sarcastic edge to Raman's declarations, "When one meets a great soul and hears his talk, one attains merit. . . ." (61) and "No one dare argue with you" (62). But Raman's skepticism fails him as he leaves the temple "shame-faced" (64). He is ashamed because he has asked permission to paint Daisy's blasphemous message on the temple walls, and he does not have the courage of his convictions that she possesses, to reject outright such potent religious symbols as the cave goddess and her priest. He is also ashamed of his tactless insinuation about the priest's method of curing barrenness. His insistence that he wants "a rational explanation for everything" has finally put him in the position of having to test that hitherto casual declaration. The cross-cultural balancing that makes Raman seem marginal in Malgudi is tested here, and neither Western nor Indian philosophies prove fit to conquer the frontier that the cave represents. Narayan forces Raman to remain out of place in this environment, as the temple priest continues to hold his fortified position as keeper of the ancient traditions.

Richard Cronin connects this priest with another spokesperson for tradition—Raman's aunt. He makes this connection in order to demonstrate the extent of Narayan's sympathy with traditional religious life. While Cronin acknowledges that "the spokesperson for the religious point of view is a cantankerous, boastful, and thoroughly unattractive old priest. . .," he concludes that "Narayan's distance from the priest's style does not mark any serious disagreement with his point of view" (68). The conclusion would be justified if Narayan were consistent in his representations of tradition and religion. Cronin observes that the author ridicules the priest, but does not point out that he also limits that man's influence to one remote area—a cave in the middle of nowhere in relation to Malgudi. Narayan consolidates the character's isolation by refusing to allow any fresh ideas to enter his circumscribed mind. At the same time, he repudiates Raman for dragging his relatively cosmopolitan ideas into the priest's domain. By constructing the area as a frontier, and then playing this double game with it, Narayan uses a literary convention to destabilize both establishment and antiestablishment positions.

The enigma of Narayan's outlook is that this radical overturning of convention exists side by side with what Cronin recognizes as his love of traditional elements of Indian life and art. The portrayal of the old aunt spinning her rambling yarns and espousing her belief in God's will is closely and delicately observed, so that when her nephew's involvement with Daisy drives Aunt out of the house, the reader sympathizes with her predicament. But Narayan does not condemn Aunt, his "mouthpiece of traditional wisdom" (Cronin 68), to the kind of isolation in which he places the obstinate temple priest. He sends her instead on a holy pilgrimage, and packs her off with all the respect due to one who chooses to end her life so honorably. The enigmatic energy of Narayan's viewpoint apparent in this comparison suggests not the "deep-rooted conservatism" and "comprehensive hostility to radical change" that Cronin and so many others see in Narayan (72), but rather an uneasy marginality.

After the cave temple, the second incident that shakes Raman's foundations occurs in a border area—on the trunk road that connects Malgudi with the villages. A long history of sexual repression precedes Raman's attempted rape of Daisy in a bullock cart stopped by the side of that road. Earlier in the narrative, he is aroused by the sight of a woman's bare thigh, visible as she washes clothes in the river. When he meets Daisy soon after, he is instantly attracted to her, but tries to quell his sexual desire by remembering Gandhi's words: "'Walk with your eyes fixed on your toes during the day, and on the stars at night'" (35). It does not work, neither do the distorting sunglasses that he buys in order to see Daisy as disfigured and warped. She simply takes them off his face, and he is forced to look at her. Another method of distancing Daisy, and thus controlling his temptations, is to imagine her a siren—a temptress from the old legends. She is depicted as a heavenly creature—flower-scented and of mysterious origins. Both armed and disarmed by his self-created image of her, and by the equally mythical sounding Gandhi-ism, Raman undertakes the journey to the villages with his would-be lover. As the days and weeks pass in her company, and her scientific rhetoric and abrupt manner force him to see her as a real person, he finds himself "standing on the borders of myth and modernity" (Bhabha).

As we have seen in the cave-temple, Raman's experience in the villages charges him with something of Daisy's frontier-brand individualism, which clashes with his perceptions of rationalism and Hinduism. As the couple make their way back to Malgudi, on their last night away from town and from their everyday lives, Raman makes a final effort to conquer tradition, Daisy, and the frontier. His struggle with his conscience reveals a carefully traced movement from myth to rationalism to opportunism, and finally, and ironically, to Daisy's idea of individualism, which leads to self-righteous dominance. He is lying underneath the cart, and she is sleeping in it above him when he starts to think:

> His whole being was convulsed with waves of desire now. He said to himself, I adore her, but this silly tension that's rising within me must be quelled. I should, perhaps, meditate on the Third Eye of Shiva, by opening which he reduced the God of Love to ashes, and perhaps achieved what we nowadays call sublimation. He brooded and projected himself ahead. He would just slip in and hold her down if she resisted. (74)

He follows up these thoughts with a rational, albeit limited, consideration of the consequences if he were to rape her. She would get pregnant, he assumes, but decides that it would be a good thing, because then he would have her under complete control. After thinking it through, he decides to go ahead with his plan:

> He felt one was wasting one's opportunities lying on hard ground. . . . He hesitated for a moment whether to call her in a soft whisper and then proceed or—it seemed irrelevant to go through all such formality; this was no time for hesitation. This was a God-given moment meant for action. . . . (75)

Raman thus progressively convinces himself that his assault would be justified, but to do so he has to shift his standards from his hybrid Indian/Western philosophies to those of the frontier. Like all of Narayan's heroes, he still must behave in a way which he can consider moral, so he twists the situation to make himself the recipient of "a God-given moment." This final justification, based on divine providence rather than reason, cancels the preceding, somewhat rational, thought process, and invalidates his image of himself as a rationalist. Like Georgie Porgie, he simply disregards the moral codes and even the laws of home in order to "break the frontier."

Narayan quite clearly does not condone this attitude, and his depiction of Raman's failure and the morning after negates his hero's machismo and reasserts the laws of Malgudi. He wakes up "appalled by the potentialities that lay buried within him. No reference, no reference, he told himself" (77). The ivory tower of Raman's "rationalism" has now collapsed. By undermining his authority, Narayan also deposes the romantic vision of sexual dominance borrowed from the West. We recall how Raman

> debated within himself whether to dash up, seize her, and behave like Rudolph Valentino in *The Sheik*, which he had seen as a student. Women liked an aggressive lover—so said the novelists. (74)

Of course, Narayan does not suggest that such inanities are the products of only western societies. The morning's conversation between Raman and the cart driver is based on strictly local preconceptions of marital relationships, as Raman has told the driver that he and Daisy are married. The lengths to which Raman goes to prove to the driver that he can dominate a woman make both men seem utterly ridiculous.

Daisy's threats to report her would-be assailant to the police torments him for weeks. Her threat is the culmination of her refusal to be victimized by men, or by the traditional structures that propel Raman to discover his "appall[ing]. . .potentialities." Narayan displays his ambivalence toward his heroine by sensitively rendering her recognition of the dangerous possibilities of Raman stirring under the cart, and then poking fun at her earnestness by having her spend the night in a tree. The following morning, Raman is ridiculous, but Daisy is perhaps too self-righteous as she wields the legal system like a weapon. Although Narayan ends by repudiating Daisy, she triumphs in this scene, as her weapon finds its mark.

It would be simplistic to say that by this affirmation of law and order Narayan simply draws his hero back into the fold of society. While on one hand Narayan may affirm order and the rule of law, he convincingly rejects certain laws and orders. In the cart scene, Raman is utterly transparent. By allowing us to witness the hero's thought process in the context of his earlier life, Narayan focuses our attention on the dangerous possibilities of sexual repression engendered by the orthodox morality of the town. Raman's philosophy having failed the test of the frontier, he returns to Malgudi confused and disoriented. A process follows in which he tries to reconcile the reality outside Malgudi with that inside. This new challenge occurs on a smaller frontier, the river bank, which is a border area between the home and the town, rather than the town and the world. By focusing on his home life, we see how he begins to inhabit his marginal space in a way that will "direct and define reality rather than"— as the temple incident and the trunk road incident have done—"denature it" (Bhabha).

All of Narayan's novels explore how people change according to whether they are inside or outside the home. In his most recent novel, *The World of Nagaraj*, the hero experiences "supreme contentment" when he sits on the *pyol*, or porch, outside his house watching the activity of Kabir street, but inside the house he is a "prisoner of domesticity" (Nagaraj, 5). Another memorable example is the grandmother in *Waiting for the Mahatma*, who "seemed to shrink under an open sky—she who dominated the landscape under the roof of Number 14 lost her stature completely in the open" (11). Like Granny, Aunt in *The Painter of Signs* commands respect in her own home, and she personifies the layers of history and tradition deep in the foundation of the structure. Raman, like Sriram in the earlier story, must press for his own space, and when he finally gains it, it is at the cost of Aunt, and thus at the cost of all the traditions on which his life has been built.

Daisy's presence in the house is always intrusive, and effects a change in Raman's life symbolized by the Hindu gods being locked in a cupboard. Her lack of sympathy with this feeling of loss at his aunt's absence reinforces Daisy's image as the bureaucratic, clinical, and rather militant face of Emergency India. Narayan tells us that "a home, in Daisy's view, was only a retreat from sun and rain, and for sleeping, washing, and depositing one's trunk" (130). Raman, on the other hand, feels compelled to assert his right to live as he pleases in his own home, with Daisy, and in an untraditional manner: "He was deeply rooted in these surroundings, and he was obliged to no one in being there" (126). His real connection to his home is felt when he considers moving to a more stylish part of town:

> But his self-esteem asserted itself and he said to himself, Why should I change my locality or the town—where I have lived since my childhood? Let others go out if they don't like to see me go up and down on my own business, living my own life. The more he thought of his home, the more he began to love it—there was no other spot in the whole town—such a coveted spot by the river, with the breeze blowing. Why should I leave this place? (115)

While he is "deeply rooted" in his home and his town, he feels the need to justify his lifestyle to himself. His defensiveness emphasizes how stifling he finds the atmosphere of bourgeois conservatism in Malgudi, but his love for his home supersedes this criticism.

Recalling that the house is at the end of Ellaman Street, with our "topographical knowledge. . .absorbed unawares" ("Well Met," 254) from other Malgudi novels, we might surmise that it is by the river. In any case, Narayan tells us that it is, and in doing so evokes a whole range of river associations. To name a few from some of his earlier novels, Savitri tries to drown herself on its far bank in *The Dark Room*; the Untouchables' Village, where Gandhi stays, occupies its banks in *Waiting for the Mahatma*; and, it is where Raju learns sincerity and achieves spiritual freedom in *The Guide*. In all of these instances, as in *The Painter of Signs*, the Sarayu represents one of the boundaries of Malgudi. At that boundary, great events take place; people are transformed; and people push themselves to their absolute limits. These associations run deep; we have only to recall the river bank of Kipling's *Head of the District* and to remember the significance of the Jumna and the Ganges in Indian lore to trace some of the Sarayu's many sources.

For Raman, the river is the frontier between his home, with its complex web of relationships, and Malgudi, with both its conservatism and its familiarity. The river and its banks provide him with the perfect edge, the edge of a river at the edge of town, for breaking down barriers between himself and Daisy:

> The stars shone, the darkness was welcome, cool breeze, cold water lapping at their feet, the voices and sounds of the living town far away and muffled. . . .The air had become charged with rich possibilities. (98)

The river steps become the theater for the interplay between Daisy's account of her adamant refusal to take part in the traditional joint-family life, and Raman's thoughts about his "philosophy of life" on which he has gained some perspective since his disastrous trip with her weeks earlier. He "wanted to say many things to her which would express his innermost feelings, with all the intensity, muddle and turbulence" (99). His feelings for her are mixed with a desire to justify his occupation to her. His thoughts on the subject have developed since his musings in the first chapter, and we now find him reflecting that a "signboard painter... concentrated in his hands the entire business and aspirations of a whole community" (99). (The obvious, and as we shall later see, important, exception to this observation is, of course, the Boardless Hotel.) She, however, has become inspired to tell her life's story, which is characterized by her evaluation of the basic quality that makes Indian life so joyful, and so painful. "All individuality," she says, "was lost in this mass existence" (102). This early rejection of her joint-family leads to a larger distrust of any family ties, including the western nuclear family. Her individualism thus determines her future isolation, while Raman's individualism determines his future integration. The meeting at the river steps ends in frustration for Raman, as he becomes aware of the complexities in scaling Daisy's mountain of independence, which he had originally sought to blast through.

The novel ends with her leaving town to continue her mission, and Raman returning to "that solid, real world of sublime souls who minded their own business" (143). That final statement is ironic because we cannot forget that the world of the Boardless Hotel, which Raman seemingly champions, is also the world of "hostile, peering crowds" which he has lamented as inhabiting "this conservative town unused to modern life" (115). The Boardless, which, as its name indicates, has no signboard, is also the one place where his justification of his occupation falls apart. But in seeking to adjust his life to his loneliness Raman feels the need to reimmerse himself in Malgudi life. At the same time, he remains a painter of signs—commercial signs, signs of modernity, or, as he sees it, signs of the times. He understands himself to be married to Daisy, by way of an ancient Hindu custom, but in a modern-day role reversal, he stays at home, waiting for her improbable return. The story closes with Raman still marginal, but also one of the masses of Malgudi. This final paradox echoes the symbolism of the river, which is both a border and an integral part of the town.

Raman's character is more interesting than Daisy's because Narayan sets him up, as Homi Bhabha notes, to be "the most marginal man in Malgudi." Bhabha's choice of words aptly describes Raman in two ways. First, it suggests the unlikely combination of his preferred image of himself as a rationalist, and his rootedness in Hindu political and philosophical ideas, such as *dharma*, loosely translated as duty or moral obligation. Second, the term "marginal" situates him outside the mainstream of Malgudi life. Narayan backs up this position by making Raman live in "the last house in Ellaman Street" (7). This is, in fact, part of the first sentence of the novel—an indication that marginality is an absolutely basic fact of the signboard painter's life. Events continuously force Raman to remake his marginality, the nature of which, by the end of the novel, has evolved from an unconscious balancing of philosophies to a fuller awareness of what it means to integrate his marginal ideas with those accepted in Malgudi.

The book's four-part structure supports the process of Raman's integration, and reflects Narayan's presentation of him as both a marginal presence and one of the Malgudi masses. It also helps to delineate the key settings of the two middle chapters as frontiers. In those sections, Raman feels unconnected with Malgudi life and alienated from his neighbors. The structure encloses his period of alienation within larger periods of integration, and is thus consistent with his final situation. The process by which he reaches this odd balance is traced through the four chapters of the novel. His philosophies regarding sexual behavior and professional conduct are revealed in the first chapter and challenged in the second, during his tour through Malgudi's frontier lands—the surrounding villages and countryside. The third chapter follows with a reassessment of his life and priorities based on his misadventures during that tour, the pivotal scene taking place on the river bank. The last chapter sees Raman living his life on his own terms, and the final, ironic ending results in the integration between marginality and centrality.

Bhabha is quick to point out that Narayan is not a "'marginal' writer in any conventional sense," but invites the label because he strives to portray accurately "the individual, or society, that stands on the borders of myth and modernity, where the unseen does not denature reality but directs and defines it." The "unseen" may be God, or it may be an abstract philosophical system, but the above quotation draws attention to a process that develops throughout the novel. We follow Raman through the process of finding a space in which his eclectic ideas of philosophy and religion can have meaning within a local framework of inherited attitudes and customs. Bhabha recognizes that one of Narayan's accomplishments is his success in inscribing, or giving value to, the marginal space that Raman occupies, so that it can be integrated into the pattern of Indian life.

Narayan's focus on frontiers reflects the struggle, which can be seen in varying degrees throughout his work, to integrate the marginal man or woman into society. That struggle is more fully played out in *The Painter of Signs* than in any of his other novels. Raman, the author of signboards, occupies the marginal space with which Narayan, the author of books, is so preoccupied. The title "puns and plays" with notions of signification (Bhabha), and therefore invites us to ask what the author-figure in the text, Raman, signifies. Narayan clearly destabilizes and restabilizes the position of author within the novel, and he tests his hero's authority on the frontier. In light of the essay, in which he argues that in fiction there must be Indian alternatives to British views of India, we can look at *The Painter of Signs* as the testing ground for the authority of Narayan's contributions to the Indian/British dialogue. In other words, his struggle to integrate a cosmopolitan yet peculiarly local figure like Raman into Indian society, his repudiation of Daisy and the temple priest, and his fond farewell to Aunt, are all part of this effort to place one distinctly Indian understanding of life in the field of the novel, and *The Painter of Signs* tests the validity of his convictions. The novel genre is Narayan's frontier between Britain and India, and the writer himself stands out as an example of the Indian paradox he outlines—the condition of simultaneously occupying the margins and the center of Indian life.

Works Cited

Bhabha, Homi K. "A Brahmin in the Bazaar." Review of *The Painter of Signs*. *Times Literary Supplement* 8 April 1977, 421.

Cronin, Richard. *Imagining India*. London: Macmillan, 1989.

Forster, E.M. *A Passage to India*. 1924. London: Penguin, 1989.

Kipling, Rudyard. "Georgie Porgie." *Life's Handicap*. Ed. A.O.J. Cockshut. Oxford: Oxford University Press, 1987: 277–85

Narayan, R.K. "After the Raj." *A Storyteller's World*. London: Penguin, 1989.

_____. *Malgudi Days*. London: Penguin, 1984.

_____. *The Painter of Signs*. 1976. London: Penguin, 1982.

_____. *Waiting for the Mahatma*. 1955. London: Mandarin, 1990.

_____. *The World of Nagaraj*. New York: Viking Press, 1990.

Times Literary Supplement. "Well Met in Malgudi." 9 May 1958, 254.

Walsh, William. *Indian Literature in English*. London: Longman, 1990.

Plot and Character in R. K. Narayan's The Man-Eater of Malgudi: A Reassessment*

FAKRUL ALAM

At the heart of R. K. Narayan's *The Man-Eater of Malgudi* (1961) is the relationship between the narrator, Nataraj, a wily but warm-hearted printer of the town of Malgudi, and Vasu, an eccentric taxidermist who forces himself into Nataraj's attic and uses it to house himself and practice his profession. Commentators of the novel do not hesitate to identify Nataraj as the protagonist and Vasu as the antagonist of the novel. Most of them prefer to read the events of the narrative as a confrontation between the two characters, with Vasu, in the words of George Woodcock, cast in "the role of the malign titan Ravanna" pitted in a "great fight between good and evil forces" against Nataraj and his friends (Woodcock, 21). According to this way of looking at their characters and the plot, the sociable, tolerant, passive Nataraj is unsettled for a while by the egotistical, destructive, unforbearing Vasu till the latter self-destructs, as demons are supposed to do, albeit in comic fashion, killing himself while trying to squash a mosquito that has landed on his forehead.

A few commentators, however, have not failed to observe that the Nataraj-Vasu relationship is somewhat complicated by the deeply conventional printer's admiration for the truculent taxidermist. Far from being continually repelled by Vasu, Nataraj is at times attracted by aspects of the outsider's personality, which is very different from that of himself and his townspeople. Noting Nataraj's fascination for Vasu and repeated overtures to his difficult tenant, Meenakshi Mukherjee concludes that "evil is not merely stronger but also more attractive than goodness" (Mukherjee, 155). In "*A Proper Detachment: The Novels of R. K. Narayan*," Shirley Chew also detects the "sneaking attraction" that Nataraj has for Vasu (72). But while both Mukherjee and Chew fail to integrate their observations into their readings of the novel, M. M. Mahood offers a political interpretation of what she describes as a "love-hate relationship" (100). According to Mahood, Nataraj's "colonial

* Originally printed in *Ariel* 19, no. 3 (July 1988): 77-92.

mentality" makes him desire the domineering outsider's unconventional approach to life. Vasu, in her opinion, represents the modern alternative to traditional India, and after being allured by this option for a while, Nataraj rejects it and the "alien political philosophies and economic aims" they represent (101, 106, 113).

Although Mahood's attempt to use the Vasu-Nataraj relationship as a basis for a reading of the novel is laudable, she has not treated the relationship with the concentration that it deserves because of her preoccupation with political hares. For, as this essay will try to demonstrate, Mahood has skirted the psychological aspects of the relationship, bypassed its storm center, and misread the false calm that descends on Malgudi after Vasu's death. It will be the contention of this paper that Mahood, as well as the other critics mentioned above, has been less than fair in judging Vasu and Nataraj, has failed to trace the involutions of their relationship, and has ignored the identity transference that takes place in the course of the narrative. To prove these assertions, it is necessary, first, to reappraise the two leading characters and reassess the nature of the events that befall Nataraj after his meeting with Vasu, and then use these revaluations to represent the plot of the novel.

To take the character of Nataraj first, it is difficult to deny him a certain amount of charm and virtue. In many respects he is friendly, meek, helpful, and passive. He is a good citizen interested in the welfare of the community at large for whose benefit he is willing to forego even the profits he makes from his press. No better example of Nataraj's altruism can be seen than in his sustained attempt to organize a festival to commemorate the publication of the epic written by his friend, the monosyllabic poet. For this event he stops working and tries to arouse the whole town and channel its resources on his friend's behalf and for the cause of culture. Nataraj also shows his good side in his dedication to the cause of the temple elephant when its life is threatened by Vasu.

But Nataraj has more to him than charm and virtue. He is also cunning, aggressive, ambitious, and not free from self-interest. As the narrator, it is obviously in his own interest to make himself appear as attractive as possible, but he is not always what he pretends to be.

The opening pages of the narrative prepare us for the complexity of Nataraj's stance. Although he appears to be altruistic in opening up his parlor to any casual visitor, he is aware that "while they rested there, people got ideas for bill forms, visiting cards, or wedding invitations which they asked me to print" (2). In the interest of his own business, he does not hesitate to pass off as his own the neighboring press's prize possession, an original Heidelberg machine. Shrewdly, he has managed to win over the citizens of Malgudi by his seeming disinterestedness.

Content to let everyone imagine him to be ready for big tasks on the strength of the Star's machine, Nataraj was "so free with the next-door establishment that no one knew whether I owned it or whether the Star owned me" (3).

In his personal relationships, Nataraj has a tendency to dissimulate. Outwardly, he wants himself to be seen as inoffensive or friendly. Inwardly, however, he can be skeptical, resentful, or impatient with his fellow citizens. On his way back from his daily walk to the river, for example, he meets the "adjournment lawyer"—so called because of his skills at delaying legal proceedings—with mock horror: "I am undone: Mr. Adjournment will get me now" (5). Outwardly, however, he says or does nothing, content to be the butt of the lawyer's wit. Later, in a delightfully comic scene, when the lawyer speaks sentimentally of the expenses incurred in raising a family, Nataraj cannot help thinking: "and you have to manage all this by seeking endless adjournments." Outwardly, though, he sympathizes with the disagreeable man: "'Yes life today is most expensive'" (58).

Not that Nataraj is always so passive with the people of this community. For instance, with K.J., a customer whose order of fruit-juice labels he has not been able to deliver in time, he is quite aggressive. Although K.J. comes thundering in to demand an explanation, Nataraj so successfully cows him and makes him look "so ignorant, wrong and presumptuous" that the fruit-juice seller can only remain dumb (140). Indeed, so relentless is Nataraj in his offensive that in the end he manages to extract from this profiteer a promise to offer free drinks at the festival. At home, Nataraj alternates between being the husband who is eager to please his wife and child, and the tyrannical man who must be appeased. As his wife puts it on one occasion when he is acting impetuous: "But now I have your breakfast on the fire, and I know how you will dance for it and make us dance who serve you, the moment you come out of the bathroom" (167).

If Nataraj is a more complex character than previous critics have made him out to be, so is Vasu. He, too, should not be seen in black-and-white terms. Indeed, far from being obviously demonic, Vasu has his good qualities. The negative aspects of Vasu's character can be conceded readily—he is brutal, self-centered, menacing; he has no respect for tradition, religion, or the law; he sets himself up against nature; he loves to bully the weak; and he will do anything to achieve the goals he has set for himself. But Vasu is all these and also spontaneous in his responses, spirited in his attitude towards life, good-humored, and endearingly nonsensical in his way of looking at others. Among his other admirable characteristics, one notices that he is a patriot, an artist, or at the least a hard-working craftsman who recognizes merit and achievement in others. Also, despite his immense strength and violent profession, he tries his best to control himself and remain non-violent in the face of provocations.

Vasu's spontaneity is evident in his initial commitment to Nataraj. Without knowing anything about the printer, Vasu embraces him as a friend. Evidence of his spiritedness and patriotism can be seen in the sketch of his life that he offers to Nataraj: he had joined the civil disobedience movement aimed at ending British rule and had been incarcerated for his nationalistic views and activities (so much for Mahood's view of Vasu as the type of the neocolonialist!).

Not only is Vasu spirited, he is ready to admire people who are lively. He likes Nataraj, for instance, because of his quick responses to his provocative comments. Passing pedestrians, whom Vasu habitually intimidates when driving, get a word of praise when they swear back at him. As he confides to Nataraj on one such occasion, "That is how I like to see my countrymen. They must show better spirit'" (133). As a doer, a man of action who detests small talk, he may hate the poet and the journalist for gossiping away their time in Nataraj's parlor, but, by the same token, he is ready to applaud them when he hears that the poet has just completed his *magnum opus*, the epic on the life of Krishna, and the journalist has made arrangements for starting a newssheet in Malgudi.

Vasu's admiration for the poet's achievement reminds the reader that he is a kind of artist himself. Indeed, he has chosen taxidermy as a profession precisely because it has an aesthetic side. As he puts it while praising his master: "'That is what Suleiman taught me; he was an artist, as good as a sculptor, or a surgeon, so delicate and precise!'" (62). It is as an artist, a creator, that he sets himself up as a rival to God/nature. From this perspective, he can take immense pride in his creations, for example, in the pair of eyes of the stuffed eagle which had seemed to Nataraj to be natural: "So you are taken in! You poor fool! Those eyes were given it by me, not by God. That's why I call my work an art!"(63). As an artist, Vasu's masterpiece, of course, is the stuffed tiger cub that he creates, something that evokes a divided response in Nataraj; fascinating him with its obvious beauty, but repelling him because it reminds him of the destructive aspects of Vasu's craft.

But if there is a violent side to Vasu's profession, and if he has the physique of a demon, he exerts great control over his immense physical strength when dealing with people. Thus when Vasu and the journalist seem to be coming to blows, the strong man assures the anxious Nataraj that he never hits anyone unless hit first. Nataraj, in fact, comes to admire this aspect of Vasu's character. As he reflects later: "Considering his enormous strength, it was surprising that he did not do more damage to his surroundings" (47). It is only when the town police inspector tries to slap him that Vasu, instinctively fighting back, dislocates the policeman's wrist, reminding Nataraj of the tremendous control he exerts over his strength in everyday life.

Although Vasu's unpredictable behavior and aggressive tactics cause the Malgudi folks to stay away from him out of fear or bewilderment, it is significant that the two people who come to know him best, his mistress Rangi and his reluctant host Nataraj, can see his attractive as well as his repulsive side. Thus Rangi, despite her determination to stop him from shooting the elephant and disrupting the festival organized to celebrate the poet's achievement, and despite her confession that her lover often tried to make her jealous by bringing home other women, admits, "He cares for me very much" (160). Far from being repelled by his abrasive methods, Rangi, as Nataraj phrases it, is "obsessed with the grandeur and invincibility of the man" (205).

Previous critics of the novel have therefore been less than fair in their evaluation of Vasu and Nataraj, for Nataraj is not all goodness and Vasu has some desirable qualities. Recognition of this fact leads to the second stage of this revaluation of the characters and their relationship and this reconstitution of the plot of the novel. In this stage, the focus will be on the way in which Vasu obviously discomfits Nataraj as well as the manner in which his admiration of some of Vasu's traits begins to influence his own behavior.

That Vasu can easily discomfit Nataraj is obvious in their very first meeting. Then the printer alternates between fascinated attention, abashment, indignation, uncertainty, and aggression, as he tries to adjust to this strange visitor to his press. This pattern and these emotions are repeated later, when Vasu picks him up from his press, drives him to a neighboring town and, hot on a trail, abandons him to fend as best as he can in an alien environment with nothing more than an empty pocket, a growling stomach, and his native wits. On occasions like this, a note of fear, of something like paranoia, possesses Nataraj as he fantasizes of being abducted by Vasu to a tiger cave and held for a ransom. Often, Nataraj is simply bewildered by Vasu, as when the taxidermist, offended by the printer's timid attempt to make him leave his attic, serves him with a summons from the rent controller, demanding explanation for his unlawful bid to evict a tenant, although Vasu has signed no agreement and paid no rent. And in the climax of the story, Vasu obviously manages to perplex Nataraj and his Malgudi allies for a long time by refusing to deny that he meant to shoot the temple elephant and disrupt the festival.

If fear is one of the major emotions evoked by Vasu in Nataraj, admiration, paradoxically enough, is another. There is, for instance, an element of admiration in Nataraj when he begins to see Vasu's gruffness as merely a stance: "I understood the situation now; every other sentence was likely to provide provocation. I began to feel intrigued by the man. I didn't want to lose him" (14). When he comes to know him even better, Nataraj learns to appreciate Vasu's professionalism, despite the brutality associated with taxidermy: "I admired him for his capacity for work, for all the dreadful things he was able to accomplish single-handed" (93). Even in a difficult period of their relationship, when Nataraj is brooding on the summons Vasu has engineered against him, he finds something to praise in this most unpredictable tenant: "Amidst all his impossible qualities, he had just one virtue; he never tried to come to my part of the house" (85). A note of admiration can also be detected in Nataraj's reflections on Vasu's relationship with Rangi:

> She went about her business with such assurance, walking in and out of a place like a postman. My mind was seething with speculations. Did Vasu bring her in his jeep at the darkest hour? Not likely. What a man he must be who could turn his mistress out in cold blood when morning came! (109)

Indeed, so attracted is Nataraj to Vasu that despite himself, despite what his conscience, his friends, acquaintances, and his wife tell him, he persists in harboring this disturbing presence, or at the least, enigmatically refuses to drive him out. In the beginning, Nataraj's feelings about having Vasu as a tenant are somewhat mixed—a complex of apprehension and anticipation: ". . .it was like having a middle-aged man-eater in your office and home, with the same uncertainties, possibilities, and potentialities" (30). But as Vasu makes a "charnel house" of his attic, and exhibits other offensive tendencies, Nataraj finds himself asking the obvious question: "Why couldn't I ask him to get out?" Try as he might, however, he cannot account for his reluctance to dislodge Vasu; it was something that was "impossible to explain" (66). Other people found no reason for him to be so considerate. His wife, for instance, "said simply, sweetly . . .'Ask him to go, that's all'" (69). Neighbors remind him that he has only himself to blame for his predicament. When Nataraj, trying to account for the summons from the rent controller, informs the lawyer that he is letting Vasu stay as a friend who does not have to pay him rent, the lawyer points out: "If I were a judge, I would not believe you. Why should you let him live with you?" (81). The old man whose grandson's dog was so heartlessly shot also asks the obvious questions: "What's your connection with him? Is he related to you? Is he your friend? . . .Who is this man? Why should you harbour him?" (91). And near the end of the narrative, at a time when public opinion is pointing a finger at Nataraj as the murderer of his tenant, his assistant Sastri, acquiescing in the dominant interpretation of the cause of Vasu's death, reminds his boss yet again, "On the very first day he came here you should have turned him out. You didn't" (225).

Not only does Nataraj put up with Vasu despite the latter's provocative actions, but he also tries to shield his tenant from the accusing eyes of Malgudi's people. Faced with the indignant grandfather who wants to confront the man who has shot his grandson's dog, for example, Nataraj anxiously hopes "that the old man should be bundled off before someone or other should offer to point Vasu out to him" (92). When the warden of Mempi forest, concerned at the number of wild animals killed in his reserve forest, wants to know about Vasu's activities, Nataraj does his best to feign ignorance and evade implicating the taxidermist, even refusing pointblank to cooperate with this representative of the law. When Sastri, full of righteous indignation, reports the presence of immoral women in the attic, Nataraj, instead of joining in condemnation, sidesteps the issue by thinking of some customers wanting to do business (107).

Even when Vasu's hostility toward him becomes obvious, and the strong man seems to be doing his best to unsettle him with one aggressive act after another, Nataraj does not stop craving for Vasu's attention. On the contrary, as the relationship between them enters the stormy stage, Nataraj finds himself regretting Vasu's "rough company" (93), and abjectly hoping for a reconciliation. "I was longing for a word with Vasu. I stood like a child at the treadle, hoping he would look at me and nod and that all would be well again" (94). Although Sastri uses his religious learning to predict Vasu's destruction and a Vasu-free attic, Nataraj chooses to ignore his assistant's predictions, hoping instead that "we would part on speaking terms" (97). All along, the printer seems to be holding out hopes for a reconciliation with his tormentor. Thus when Vasu, with typical unpredictability and indifference to what has happened between them in the immediate past, summons Nataraj to his jeep, the printer has "an impulse to drop whatever . . .[he] was doing, rush up to him and seize the chance to make friends with the monster again" (102). Although his pride wins over his instincts on this occasion, later, in a similar situation, Nataraj decides to respond to Vasu's summons to go to his jeep, since "it was better than being continuously ignored" (132).

However, Nataraj is not content merely to tolerate, harbor, defend, or admire Vasu; he also occasionally acts like him or perceives their two situations as not dissimilar. For example, Nataraj sees himself as not too different from Vasu in the work that they do. Although their professions appear to have nothing in common, and although the printer has his assistant to help him while the taxidermist works alone, Nataraj cannot help thinking that their businesses are somewhat similar. Such a conclusion is surprising, and Nataraj checks himself on this occasion thus: "I do not know why I should ever have compared myself with him, but there it was. I was getting into an abnormal frame of mind" (68). Later, when the relationship between the two has become strained, and Vasu appears to be aloof, indifferent, or even hostile, Nataraj once again perceives himself to be reacting like his strange tenant: "I was, I suppose, getting into a state of abnormal watchfulness myself" (92). But it is especially during his efforts to organize the festival, when he is in a hyperactive state, that Nataraj starts to behave like Vasu. On this occasion, after he rebukes the poet for thinking while they were busy printing, he realizes somewhat guiltily that he had "sounded like Vasu," and immediately assumes a softer tone (154). Later, as he reflects bitterly on his wife's suspicions about his relationship with Rangi, suspicions which were planted in her mind when the temple-dancer prostitute called on her husband, Nataraj finds himself approaching the situation from Vasu's point of view: "When Rangi spoke to me on an important matter, the thing for a rational being to do was to ask what exactly it was all about and approach things in a scientific frame of mind. . . .No wonder Vasu was bitter against the world for its lack of scientific approach" (215).

In fact, Nataraj's responses to Rangi consistently bring out the Vasu-side of his character. From the moment Sastri reports to him that "loose women" like Rangi were frequenting Vasu's quarter, Nataraj finds himself fascinated by the notion of such women visiting his attic. So when Sastri comes to him in a state of panic about the failure to meet a customer-imposed deadline, Nataraj confesses: "My mind was busy following the fleshy image of Rangi and perhaps I resented the intrusion" (110). Like a voyeur, he spies on Vasu's love-life through a pinhole in a bamboo curtain, making sure, however, that other eyes should not follow the strong man's affairs. There seems to him to be "an irresistible physical attraction" around Rangi (157). The "monogamous chastity" he had so unquestioningly practiced in a "whole lifetime" seems to be threatened by the "halo" that she, no less than Vasu, has around her (159). Totally aroused, and eager to be seduced, Nataraj even dares public opinion in trying to attract Rangi's attention while she is dancing in the festival parade. When Rangi comes to him later to tell him how determined Vasu was to shoot the elephant and thwart the festival proceedings, and to say that she would go back to Vasu despite his terrifying mood, Nataraj, "with a grand show of confidence and aggression" (205), asks her not to go to her lover, unwilling to let her be further enchanted with Vasu's prowess.

Indeed, for a man who has been described as timid, tolerant, and passive, Nataraj shows a great deal of confidence in himself and aggressiveness in the later part of the narrative. Moreover, he seems to grow more and more active and forceful as Vasu appears to be more and more hemmed in by the forces of law and order and by public opinion, which Nataraj has tried in some ways to mobilize against him to prevent him from disrupting the festival. This shift in roles becomes noticeable at the moment when Nataraj takes it on himself to organize the festival, and at a time when increased surveillance of the Mempi forest and a collective indignation at Vasu's anti-social stance constrict his predatory activities. Then, Nataraj finds himself harboring almost violent impulses such as "flinging a tumbler of cold water" over the poet's head or "shouting in his ears" (153) as they try to rush a copy of the epic into print before festival day. Frenetically, he attempts to involve the town in the festival proceedings, trusting no one but himself to do all the organizational work. In this state of mind, Vasu's stature is reduced in his eyes until "the man-eater" of his anxiety-ridden past becomes no more than "an irrelevant thought" (181). The external world appears unimportant as Nataraj observes the start of the festival, which he has set into motion. Unused to such hypertension, however, Nataraj gives a mighty scream and then collapses, causing a bystander to observe that he was a man "possessed" (183). Significantly though, his domineering mood does not completely desert him when he returns to his senses. Then, finding himself surrounded by Malgudi's notables, he feels better when he realizes that he "had an odd commanding position. People were prepared to do anything I suggested" (184).

Perceiving that Nataraj is the instigator of the campaign against him, Vasu throws a challenge to the printer and, for the last time, defies conventional society by humiliating the police officer who comes to threaten him. Significantly, Nataraj decides to take up the challenge offered by Vasu and proceeds to climb up to the attic in a bid to neutralize the man-eater of Malgudi. As he is on his way up, Nataraj considers, among other things, stunning Vasu from behind to render him harmless, but decides in the end to try other, non-violent, methods to stop him. Once in the attic, however, Nataraj, oblivious of the fact that the Vasu stretched out on the easy chair before him is dead, dashes for the hunter's gun, seizes it, and decides to stand guard until the procession passes his establishment. This he does, leaving only when the parade has passed out of view and when, comically, the alarm bell set by Vasu goes off, making him "dash for the landing out of Vasu's reach" (218).

What is one to make of one's recognition that both Nataraj and Vasu are complex characters, and one's perception that Nataraj is fascinated by Vasu and starts acting like him, ultimately trying to even contain him? The answer to this question can be found in the concept that psychoanalysts know as *identification*. Freud has described the concept thus:

The basis of the process is what we call identification, that is to say that one ego becomes like another, which results in the first ego behaving itself in certain respects in the same way as the second; it imitates it, and as it were takes it into itself. This identification has not been inappropriately compared with the oral cannibalistic incorporation of another person. (86)

There is of course more to the concept than that, as this account by Charles Brenner brings out:

. . .identification plays its part in ego development on more than one score. It is first of all an inherent part of one's relationship to a highly cathected object. . . .In addition we have noted the tendency to identify with an admired though hated object, which Anna Freud called "identification with the aggressor." Finally, there is the last mentioned factor that the loss of a highly cathected object leads to a greater or lesser degree of identification with the lost object. However, regardless of the way in which identification takes place, the *result* is always that the ego has become enriched thereby, whether for better or for worse. (48–49)

Equipped with these insights into human relationships, one can draw on the preceding revaluation of the major characters and events of *The Man-Eater of Malgudi* to represent its plot: it is a narrative of identification; and it is plotted to show how the narrator-protagonist is aroused by an aggressive figure with whom he increasingly identifies until, having incorporated many features of this more instinctive, more primitive being, he can dispose of him symbolically by putting himself into a position where he can stand guard and contemplate the destruction of this other self.

Nataraj, the man who in the beginning of the narrative is the embodiment of timidity and passivity, as can be seen in his opening confession that "he could not explain himself to sordid people" who were critical of his business sense (1), is gradually aroused by his contact with the spontaneous, spirited, and enigmatic Vasu. Even in their initial encounter, Nataraj realizes that they were fated to meet and interact: "I began to feel intrigued by the man. I didn't want to lose him. Even if I wanted to, I had no means of getting rid of him. He had sought me out and I'd have to have him until he decided to leave" (14–15). Significantly, in this first meeting Vasu manages to bring out Nataraj's other, dormant side, as the printer responds to the taxidermist by being aggressive and pugnacious, and by confessing that he too could enjoy "the thrill of provoking" another person (17). And by the time they have their second encounter, Nataraj is ready to confess that "somehow this man's presence roused in me a sort of pugnacity" (19).

That Vasu's presence was subtly transforming Nataraj into another person becomes obvious when he comments on the forest warden's manuscript of selected epigrammatic sentiments and moralizings: "It was meant to elevate young minds no doubt, but I'd have resented being told every hour of the day what I should do, say, or think. It would be boring to be steadfastly good night and day" (33). In the middle part of the narrative, Vasu manages to bewilder Nataraj by his erratic behavior, but, as has been indicated above, even here Nataraj finds himself admiring Vasu, and continues to shield him from the world's censure. Now, as he unconsciously tracks Vasu, he gets "into a state of abnormal watchfulness" (92). Soon, he starts to identify himself with the aggressor.

Nataraj, of course, is not aware except in some dim way that in some aspects of his thought and behavior he is becoming like, or imitating Vasu; but once the work on the festival begins, this becomes clearly apparent even to himself. Now Nataraj suddenly seizes the initiative and displays reservoirs of energy that no one would previously suspect him of containing. He also longs for Vasu's woman, and sounds and acts like the strong man. The two next appear set on a confrontation course: Vasu with his plans to shoot the elephant and Nataraj with his determination to make the festival a success. Ultimately, Nataraj wins; the festival is a triumph, and in intention, if not in actuality, he manages to render Vasu inoperative by the kind of instinctive, aggressive gesture that only the taxidermist was capable of. Or perhaps Vasu, having realized that Nataraj had awakened to a new and more formidable self, decides to leave by self-destructing.

After the discovery of Vasu's death, Nataraj goes through a period of depression, "a clinical condition in whose psychopathology unconscious identification with a lost object regularly plays an important role" (Brenner, 48). Nataraj is especially depressed as he thinks of the once-powerful man's helplessness after life has passed him by: "I was depressed to think that a man who had twisted iron rods and burst three-inch panel doors with his fist was going to do nothing more than lie still and wait for the doctor to cut him and examine his insides to find out what had caused his death" (226). Nataraj then discovers that the townspeople, including his wife and son, were suspecting him of Vasu's murder, and looking at him with either awe or apprehension, feelings which the man-eater had previously aroused in them. However, their suspicions dismay him only for a time until it occurs to him that it was not improbable that he himself has destroyed the threat to Malgudi's settled ways: "Perhaps while he slept I had rammed the butt of the gun into his skull, who could say?" (235). After all, "It had been an evening of strange lapses." Recognition of his capacity for destruction, and the fear and unease that he was so unwittingly generating in Malgudi, now makes him even more Vasu-like: "A touch of aggression was creeping into my speech nowadays. My line of thinking was, 'So be it. If I have rid the world of Vasu, I have achieved something'" (237). This mood alternates, however, with one of self-pity: he cannot help lament the loss of his reputation and his alienation from his fellow citizens, and blames Vasu for this state of affairs.

Rangi's confession that she was a witness to the taxidermist's self-destruction manages to clear things up and removes Nataraj from approbation associated with murder. But Sastri, who breaks the news to his boss, cannot help being frightened somewhat by the sight of Nataraj holding Vasu's stuffed tiger cub in his hand while listening to his account. In a sense, once the strong man's function of arousing the timid printer is over, he can disappear from the narrative. But the tiger cub—the ultimate symbol of Vasu's aggression as well as his creative powers—which Nataraj had inexplicably stolen from Vasu's possessions after his death and which he now seems destined to possess for the rest of his life as his inheritance—indicates once more that to a certain extent, Nataraj has become the image of the dead man. The Malgudi folks can return to their old ways, but in a subtle and profound way, Nataraj has been changed. One notes, thus, the confident, mock-servile tone that Nataraj assumes in talking to Sastri in the last paragraph of the book: "'When you are gone for lunch it [the coloring ink] will be drying, and ready for a second printing when you return. Yes Sastri, I am at your service!' I said" (242). This contrasts tellingly with the craven, whimpering voice that can be heard in the second chapter: "What about my lunch? Sastri did not care whether I had time for food or not . . . he was a tyrant when it came to printing labels, but there was no way of protesting. He would brush everything aside" (11). The inescapable conclusion: it is a new, self-assured protagonist that has emerged in the course of the narrative once Nataraj's relationship with Vasu has run its course.

It is not enough to say then, as Woodcock does, that The Man-Eater of Malgudi is simply about "the great fight between good and evil forces" (Woodcock, 21). This reading has tried to indicate that there is a more complex pattern in the novel than that—a pattern based on identification as well as displacement. Recognition of this pattern should lead to an appreciation of just how intricately plotted Narayan's work is and how fascinating his characters are. Thus, although this essay disagrees with William Walsh's interpretation of plot and character—for Walsh, too, reads the novel as a story of good and evil and places Nataraj squarely on the side of good and categorizes Vasu as a demon—it should reinforce his general assessment of "the complex tone of Narayan's serious comedies" as something based on "the rebirth of the self and the process and condition of its pregnancy and education" (Walsh, 168). Similarly, though it has differed from Woodcock's reading, it should buttress his defence of the Indian novelist as "a very urbane and subtle man" against V. S. Naipaul's patronizing description of him as "'an instinctive, unstudied writer'" (Woodcock, 12). It is to be hoped that this reading of Narayan's *The Man-Eater of Malgudi* as a narrative of one self's identification with another will reaffirm this novelist's complexity, urbanity, and subtlety, and will place this work in the tradition of such classic studies of identification as Dostoevski's *The Double* and Conrad's "The Secret Sharer."

Works Cited

Brenner, Charles. *An Elementary Textbook of Psychoanalysis.* New York: Anchor, 1957.
Chew, Shirley. "A Proper Detachment: The Novels of R. K. Narayan." *Readings in Commonwealth Literature.* William Walsh, ed. Oxford: Clarendon, 1973: 58–74.
Freud, Sigmund. *New Introductory Lectures on Psycho-Analysis.* Trans. W. J. H. Sprott. London: Hogarth, 1933.
Mahood, M. M. *The Colonial Encounter: A Reading of Six Novels.* London: Collings, 1977.
Mukherjee, Meenakshi. *The TwiceBorn Fiction: Themes and Techniques of the Indian Novel in English.* New Delhi: Heinemann, 1971.
Narayan, R. K. *The Man-Eater of Malgudi.* London: Heinemann, 1961.
Walsh, William. *R. K. Narayan: A Critical Appreciation.* London: Heinemann, 1982.
Woodcock, George. "Two Great Commonwealth Novelists: R. K. Narayan and V. S. Naipaul." *Sewanee Review* 87 (Winter 1979): 1–28.

Kali as Man-Eater and as Goddess: Myth-Making in R. K. Narayan's The Man-Eater of Malgudi

ROSANNE KANHAI-BRUNTON

The process of decolonization has produced texts that attempt to heal the wounds of domination by invoking the precolonial society, by recording colonization, and by speculating on decolonization. Postcolonial writing can be reclamation, compensation and/or reconstruction. The body of R. K. Narayan's writing, however, displays not nostalgia of the past, nor predictions for the future, but an affirmation that Hinduism can incorporate even the trauma of colonialism. Many of his novels are set in the fictional village, Malgudi, which, located in the south of India, maintains an Indian consciousness although its structure is very much dominated by the British bureaucracy. It must be kept in mind that while the presence of the British Raj was overt in many of the major cities of India, much of rural India remained culturally intact, the British presence manifesting itself in bureaucratic issues but the Indian consciousness assimilating British manners in such a way that there was a type of colonization in reverse. British institutions became Indianized to the point of absurdity—a significant comment on the capacity of the Hindu consciousness for absorption and reductionism.

One such institution in Narayan's *The Man-Eater of Malgudi* is the teashop. Situated on the edge of the Mempi forest, it services passengers of buses and lorries that stop on their way up the mountainside. The high manners of taking tea the British way, the delicacy and sophistication associated with the elitism of the British, are brought to comedy by Nataraj's description:

> Presently his customers began to arrive—mostly coolies carrying pick-axes, crow-bars and spades on their way to that mysterious project beyond the hills. Caravans of bullock carts carrying firewood and timber stopped by. Loudspeaker music blared forth from the

> tent-cinema, where they were testing their sound again and again—
> part of some horribly mutilated Elvis Presley tune, Indianized by the
> film producer. I sat there and no one noticed me: arms stretched
> right over my head for glasses of tea; sometimes brown tea trickled
> over the side of the glass tumbler and fell on my clothes. (38)

The "mysterious project beyond the hills" is the building of a holy shrine at "the confluence of the mountains and the plains" (36) and the teashop occupies the location of encounter between the mysticism that the shrine symbolizes and the civilized life of Malgudi. A common motif in Hindu mythology is the forest as the place where the forces of good (actualized as gods and heroes) and evil (actualized as demons and criminals) confront each other. As Malgudi, with its ordered streets and British-imposed hierarchy is a microcosm of ordered civilization, in the same way, the forest, with its tangle of vegetation and wild animals, represents the chaos of the cosmos. Stopping at the teashop becomes a ritual, a rite of passage necessary for moving from one location to the next. The juxtaposing of pickaxes and crowbars with Elvis Presley tunes, and the mention of tea trickling over Nataraj's clothes all signify the ambivalence of colonization and of counter-colonization as the people strive for decolonization. The bus itself perches on the border of both worlds, defying every norm of punctuality and efficiency in a haphazardness that is totally un-British. Narayan makes skillful use of humor to describe the relaxed incoherence of Indianizing: the absurd overcrowding of the bus, the pomposity of the conductor and, most of all, the forced nonchalance of The Circle. The effect of Narayan's comic tone is to illustrate the capacity of human society to be creative even in the face of a horror such as colonialism. He undercuts the power of the British reign by treating it as if it were another adversity with which Indian society has come to terms in a very human way.

In a broader sense, however, this inclusivity is coherent with the concept of oneness that is at the basis of Hindu mythology and philosophy. Narayan's affiliation with Hindu religious systems is indisputable. Not only does he produce his own versions of the *Ramayana* and the *Mahabharata*, very often his texts uphold Hindu virtues, in particular those of humility, non-aggression, and acceptance. These qualities make sense only within a framework that negates Western-oriented linearity and Darwinism. By privileging oneness, Narayan affirms a cosmic system that appreciates inclusion and cyclicity. In *Man-Eater*, this representation of oneness takes the form of Kali, represented fictionally in the character of Rangi.

Kali is sometimes described as the consort of Shiva and therefore as the goddess of destruction. Even in this capacity, she is perhaps the most ambivalent and therefore the most powerful of deities, since destruction is inevitably bound up with creation. According to Hindu mythology, the universe is seen as always in flux—creation, preservation, and destruction being manifest outside the limits of past, present, or future. Therefore, creation leads inevitably to destruction, and destruction itself carries the inspiration of creation. There is one Absolute Reality that has three aspects: Brahma (creation), Vishnu (preservation), and Shiva (destruction). These godheads have female energies: Sarasvati, Lakshmi, and Devi or Kali, respectively. Kali, therefore, combines the element of death with that of the female. Sexuality as in procreation, and its variations, as in seduction and lust, figure prominently in her persona. She is often portrayed with a rigid tongue sticking out, or with snakes for hair, or with a full array of vampire-like teeth—the treacherous vagina that can create or devour life.

Studies that delve into earlier manifestations of the Kali figure suggest, however, that she is in fact the Absolute Reality—a female energy from which the male godheads spring—and that the more recent identification of her as the female counterpart of Shiva is an attempt to reappropriate female power to the male gods. The *Women's Encyclopedia of Myths and Secrets* describes her as:

> The basic archetypal image of the birth-and-death Mother, simultaneously womb and tomb, giver of life and devourer of her children . . . Tantric worshippers of Kali thought it essential to face her Curse, the terror of death, as willingly as they accepted Blessings from her beautiful, nurturing, maternal aspect. For them, wisdom meant learning that no coin has only one side: as death can't exist without life, so also life can't exist without death . . . Kali stood for existence, which meant Becoming because all her world was an external flux from which all things rose and disappeared again, in endless cycles. (488–89)

Narayan's version of Kali, told in his *Gods, Demons, and Others*, refers to her as Devi, "the highest form of beauty and energy, [she] battles with and destroys the demon Mahisha, who symbolizes the unmitigated brute" (47). She is described as emanating from the face of each of the gods. "From Brahma's face a blood-red one, from Shiva a dazzling whiteness, from Vishnu a dark one. All these combined to form an effulgent female personality, the three colors sparkling as through a prism. The Devi, as she was called, had eighteen arms" (*Gods,* 54). Mahisha responded to the Devi's beauty by trying to seduce her but she hurled her weapons at him and, raising a bowl of wine ceremoniously to her lips, she severed his head with a discus and celebrated his end (*Gods,* 62). Praise to the Devi took the form of a celebration of the mother:

The gods burst into a prayer, beginning, "Great Mother, through your grace the Trinity carries on the functions of Creation, Protection, and Dissolution. You are all pervasive, and everything in creation is part of you. Wild beasts, poisonous trees, and asuras are also your creation. Even to them you afford a victory of the moment, and then punish, vanquish, and help them evolve into beings. Saints who realize your subtle, secret presence attain unshakable peace and understanding, through meditation." (*Gods,* 62–63)

Myths of the Hindus and Buddhists also describes Kali as "a phase of the mother-divinity who for so many worshippers is nearer and dearer than the far-off and impersonal Shiva" (330). From the varying versions we can see similarities: that Devi/Kali is associated with the Mother in her capacity as generator and consumer of life; that she is sexually desirable with an attraction that can be fatal; that her focus is to fight evil and bring about good; that she combines the elements of the tri-godhead. Kali is about everything, about unity without separation into disparate parts, about the collapse of binaries and the negation of linearity.

Thus it is not surprising that Narayan, with his emphasis on sublimation through unity, should choose Kali to be the all-pervasive anima of his novel. Narayan sets up the schisms in the human consciousness by exploring the characters of Nataraj and Vasu. He relates their limitations to the acceptance of values affirmed in Western thought—materialism, aggression, and arrogance. Then he offers Rangi as the figure that will mitigate differences, destroy evil, and restore equilibrium at a higher level.

Rangi appears in the third chapter of the text and by this time the characters of Nataraj, the protagonist, and Vasu, the antagonist, are established. Functioning within Hindu mythology, Nataraj comes closest to a representation of Vishnu, the Preserver. *The Wonder That Was India* describes Vishnu as:

The source of the universe and of all things. . . .He sleeps in the primeval ocean and in his sleep a lotus grows from his stomach, and from the lotus is born the demiurge Brahma, who creates the world. Once the world is created Vishnu awakes, to reign in the highest heavens. . .Vishnu is generally thought of as being wholly benevolent. . . .The god works continuously for the benefit of the world, and with this in mind he has from time to time incarnated himself, either wholly or partially. (303–4)

Nataraj's version of his Vishnu aspect is, however, corrupted by the Western value of materialism (this is not to say that materialism does not thrive in India but that the relationship between India and the West is

one that is forged through and on behalf of Western materialism. Thus
Narayan can use Westernization as a motif of materialism). Thus Nataraj
is seen as very preoccupied with: the house in which he lives, the articles
of furniture, the money he earns from his clients, and the raising of funds
for the temple celebration. So engrossed is he that he often forgets the
purpose of his activities, and, in so doing, he preserves the matter to the
neglect of the spirit. Nataraj's attempt at preservation also takes the form
of imposing rigid structure to his daily life. In his little printing shop,
carefully separated from his home by a green curtain, he pins down the
elusiveness of the word, his work extending from juice labels to the
Mahabharata itself. He takes pride in recounting his rituals of ablutions
every morning even as he constructs an exclusive place for himself by a
spot he chooses at the river, as well as by the carefully controlled conversations he has with people of varying ranks. In addition to his carefully constructed social life, the encounter with Rangi reveals Nataraj's
repressions regarding his sex life. Affiliated with Lakshmi, goddess of
wealth and also of the home and the hearth, Nataraj's wife represents
the stability of marriage, which causes Nataraj to suppress the adventure
of sex that Rangi represents. Again, Nataraj interprets preservation as
repression as he short circuits the Kali aspect of life in his inability to see
that chaos is necessary for creativity. His life both as printer and as
householder is a sterile one—oppositional and complementary to Vasu's,
which is destructive though unrepressed.

A psychoanalytic analysis suggests that the attic above his shop,
which he allows Vasu to occupy, is the uncharted area of his unconscious. Nataraj's fascination with Vasu's strength, his venture as far as
the outskirts of the Mempi forest, his consternation when Vasu avoids
him, and finally his attempt to confront the armed Vasu, all attest to
attraction and repulsion between the two men.

If Nataraj reflects Vishnu, his wife reflects Lakshmi, and Rangi reflects
Kali, the obvious parallel to Vasu is Shiva. Sifting through myths of
Shiva, the dominating elements are his connections with the erotic, with
death and destruction, and the inter-connectedness of all of these. "The
Supremacy of Shiva," related in *Myths of the Hindus*, "tells of Shiva's illustration of the supremacy of the lingam (phallus)." Interrupting a jostle for
superiority between Vishnu and Brahma, Shiva conjures up "a glorious
shining lingam, a fiery pillar, like a hundred universe-consuming fires,
without beginning, middle, or end, indescribable," (286) thus forcing the
gods to witness the power of the phallus and establishing its worship in
the three worlds of creation, preservation, and destruction. It is also significant that although Shiva "dwelt in royal state, worshipped by gods
and rishis; . . . more often he spent his time wandering about the hill like

a beggar, his body smeared with ashes, and with Sati [his wife, incarnation of Kali] wearing ragged robes; sometimes also he was seen in the cremation grounds, surrounded by dancing imps and taking part in horrid rites" (Coomaraswamy, 288). Shiva is associated with the "horrible and the erotic" especially because of the manner of his courtship of Sati. He appears waving a yellow skull from which the flesh still hung:

> reviling himself before her, he means it ostensibly as a deterrent to her love for him, but there is in all the wine and wildness, which he seems to censure, the Dionysian quality of life that strengthens her love even as he speaks of horrible things . . . all the qualities that he describes, inappropriate as they may be for a conventional bridegroom, are not only symbols of his greatness but also symbols of great erotic appeal. The snakes, the bloody elephant skin, the third eye in his forehead—all may transcend their conventional and literal repulsiveness and exert a magical erotic power. (O'Flaherty, 236)

Vasu bears too many characteristics of Shiva to be ignored. He courts Rangi amidst the paraphernalia of killing, skinning, and defleshing, just as he repels but attracts the town of Malgudi with his Dionysian life. His obsession with killing the temple elephant also rings a bell. Snakes do not figure prominently around Vasu, probably because they have been appropriated by Rangi herself, who, as the death scene later reveals, also controls the third eye. The problem is that Vasu is not Shiva, not any more than Nataraj is Vishnu. Both have developed a sense of arrogance that makes them forget the cosmic order in which they exist. Nataraj is able to accept his humanity in the temple when he cries out to Vishnu but Vasu cannot because he is, in actuality, a rakshasa.

Sastri's definition of a rakshasa is: "a demoniac creature who possessed enormous strength, strange powers, and genius, but recognized no sorts of restraints of man or god" (*Man-Eater,* 72). Says Sastri, "Every demon appears in the world with a special boon of indestructibility. Yet the universe has survived all the rakshasas that were ever born. Every demon carries within him, unknown to himself, a tiny seed of self-destruction, and goes up in thin air at the most unexpected moment" (173–74). However, it is not revealed until the very end of the novel, that the rakshasa will indeed be vanquished so we, together with Nataraj, must experience the various conflicts. The figure of Rangi/Kali pulls the layers of conflict together.

Kali/Rangi first appears in her capacity as sex goddess and seducer. We see, hear, and smell her through Nataraj's eyes:

> I heard the sound of bangles and there she was—Rangi, stepping between the hyena and the mongoose and making for the door. She was dark, squat, seductive, overloaded with jewelery; the flowers in

her hair were crushed, and her clothes rumpled; she had big round arms and legs and wore a pink sari. . . .I felt curious to know what she would look like in the evenings—perhaps she would powder her face, the talcum floating uneasily over her ebonite skin. Anyway, whatever might be the hour, every inch proclaimed her what she was—a perfect female animal. (81–82)

Indeed she is the essence of sensuality and of profusion—the crushed flowers, the bangles, the pink sari, and the jewelery complementing her voluptuous body. The ebonite skin refers to Kali's identity as the "dark goddess"—for she evokes the taboos of sexuality and of death.

Ironically, Rangi steps easily between the stuffed hyena and mongoose; both exist in a living death that does not belong in the natural universe. An account of Kali worship in Calcutta reveals her relationship with animal sacrifices:

To the Goddess is due the lifeblood of all creatures—since it is she who has bestowed it—and that is why the beasts must be slaughtered in her temple; that is why temple and slaughterhouse are one.

This rite is performed amid gruesome filth; in the mud compounded of blood and earth, the heads of animals are heaped up like trophies before the statue of the Goddess, while those sacrificing return home for a family banquet of the bodies of their animals. (Walker, 493)

Disequilibrium in Malgudi occurs because Vasu, as taxidermist, usurps Kali's power over the animals, and also because Nataraj and the villagers of Malgudi have to come to terms with the filthy aspects of existence. Nataraj is repulsed by the stench of flesh that invades his shop, by the skins he sees soaking in alum, by the decaying flesh and raw hide scattered around the room. Vasu's response is to point out the hygienic conditions under which the work is taking place and that human flesh rots as well. What is monstrous is that Vasu is killing animals without the rituals and due respect that belongs to Kali worship, and therefore, she herself must appear to right the situation. The villagers of Malgudi seem to have forgotten the power of the Goddess and the cosmic implications of wanton killing. Instead in very British terms they think of how "the tanning and curing of skins should be prohibited in a residential area as it gave rise to bad odour and unsanitary conditions" (65). Not surprisingly, the Indianized British bureaucracy is incompetent. The sanitary inspector quotes laws, sends off endorsements, and advises legal manipulation, but never acknowledges the real situation. It is up to Rangi to destroy the evil.

Kali's double role as goddess and sex symbol is best displayed during the celebration. The ambivalence of Rangi as village prostitute and as temple dancer is explainable within Hindu culture and contradicts the norms of Westernized morality. Significantly, Rangi claims virtue in her own terms, "Sir, I am only a public dancer, following what is my dharma. I may be a sinner to you, but I do nothing worse than what some so-called family women are doing. I observe our rules. Whatever I may do, I don't take opium" (*Man-Eater*, 115). Rangi is an independent woman, in contrast to Nataraj's wife who, as homemaker, must structure her activities around her family's. Rangi seems to be a contemporary version of a temple prostitute for she must earn a living by secular activities. A. L. Basham explains temple prostitution in his *The Wonder That Was India*:

> The god in his temple was treated like an earthly king; he had his wives, his ministers and attendants, and all the paraphernalia of a court—including his attendant prostitutes. . . . They attended on the god's person, danced and sang before him, and, like the servants of an earthly king, were at the disposal of the courtiers whom he favored, in this case the male worshippers who paid their fee to the temple. . . .Temple prostitution was most common in the South, where it survived until early times. The wild fertility cults of the early Tamils involved orgiastic dancing, and their literature shows that prostitution was common among them. (186–87)

And indeed, Malgudi calls upon Rangi to dance before the golden images of Krishna and Radha at the highlight of the celebration. The celebration sees a reign of chaos, of confusion, and plenty, as common prostitute and holy dancer assume the same personality. It is the reign of Kali, and two men are on the margins of it: Nataraj and Vasu. Vasu's alienation is the more obvious one for he sets himself up at a vantage point, prepared to shoot the holy elephant. Nataraj, on the other hand, seems to be at the center but he is emotionally and spiritually on the outside where he thinks he can have control. As the whole village works itself into a fervor of excitement, Nataraj occupies himself with details, order, and control. He calculates the number of chrysanthemums, oleanders, bamboos, banana fibers, jasmine buds, etc, etc. He makes all the arrangements for performers, for the serving of meals, for the procession route, for the accommodation of people, etc, etc. All along we have seen his despicable preoccupation with money—his bargaining with clients, his intense accountability. He condemns Vasu for his greed but in his own petty way reinscribes the same values. As Vasu annihilates animals by stuffing them, Nataraj sterilizes the *Mahabharata* by putting it into print. Narayan cannot help but point out the humor—the printers have run out of K's and R's for Krishna and Radha and must substitute stars. Now Nataraj marvels at the throng of unrestrained humanity:

> I had lived a circumscribed life and never thought that our town contained such a variety of humanity—bearded, clean-shaven, untidy, tidy; women elegant, ravishing, tub-shaped and coarse; and the children, thousands of them, dressed, undressed, matted-hair, chasing each other between the legs of adults, screaming with joy and trying to press forward and grab the fruit offerings kept for the Gods. (131)

We see Narayan at his best here, exulting in the plenitude and diversity of the Indian crowd, free of the constraints of British structure, showing its vibrancy in the Kali celebration that unites all levels of humanity. It is in this setting, aided by "the sight of the God, the sound of music, the rhythm of cymbals and the scent of jasmine and incense" that Nataraj allows himself to become a Hindu again; to give up the control that his occupation as printer has engendered; to cry out to Vishnu to save the elephant and the innocent men and women who are pulling the chariot. Rangi stops in her dance; the woman is stunned, the goddess has triumphed, and Nataraj begins the evolution to a higher state of equilibrium.

Kali-as-Rangi's role in the death of Vasu needs to be explicated for it considers various ways of dealing with evil forces. The first is the British bureaucracy—actualized in the figures of Muthu, Sen, the journalist, the veterinarian, and the superintendent of police. Typical of western-type behavior they confront Vasu with direct investigation about his intentions to shoot the elephant and disrupt the procession, but he easily dodges them by retreating into a philosophical discourse that skirts the issue. He knows British law and is able to manipulate it for his own protection by quoting it, by getting necessary licenses, and by threatening to get a lawyer. The failure of "the authorities" to deter Vasu marks the failure of the institutionalized system to cope with the reality of the sacred elephant, the crowds, and the rakshasa about to cause havoc.

The next strategy is that of nonviolence. Indeed nonviolence is what Nataraj has been practicing all the time, usually out of fear, not courage. Many a time he has stifled the sharp words coming out of his mouth about Vasu's behavior because he has been afraid of his physical strength. He even subvocalizes his desire for Rangi but is afraid to articulate it to his wife—again out of cowardice. Now he is pushed into a situation where he must examine the motives for his non-violence and he does so by invoking the Mahatma: "Nonviolence would be the safest policy with him. Mahatma Gandhi was right in asking people to carry on their fight of nonviolence; the chances of getting hurt were much less" (155). Again Nataraj corrupts the ideal, misinterpreting the Mahatma. Thus even his attempt at bravery is brought to ridicule—at the moment when the procession is coming into view, he is startled by an alarm clock going off, jumps, drops the gun, and makes a dash for the landing out of Vasu's reach.

It is Rangi, mediator of the mythological forces in the Hindu cosmos that presides over Vasu's death. She had brought him food, in addition to and representative of the sex she usually brings, and she is now able to turn the man-eater's power on him. The swatting of the mosquitoes on his forehead is a grotesque inversion of Shiva's third eye. The significance of the third eye is explained in *Siva: The Erotic Ascetic*:

> The third eye is a natural symbol for extraordinary or magical vision, and as such it appears throughout world folklore. In India, it is the attribute of the great Indian magician, the yogi. This is its primary connotation as an attribute of Siva, an ascetic and anti-erotic force which is used to burn Kama [lust]. (249)

The third eye is also associated with the grotesque for, "a third eye in the middle of the forehead produces a reaction of horror and aversion as a mere physical deformity" (248). At other times the third eye is seen as the potential to transform so the focus can change from eroticism to benevolence. In all cases, however, "the fire of the third eye and the absence of the eye (darkness) produce two equivalent extremes: doomsday" (249). Vasu's physicality has been described in such extreme terms that it is easy for us to see him as a monstrosity. Missing, however, is any strain of benevolence, and, as the mosquitoes, presided over by Rangi, splatter into a bloody mess on Vasu's forehead, Kali has her revenge.

Narayan is not the first to invoke Kali as an affirmation of Indian nationalism. Aislie T. Embree's account of Muslim-Hindu conflicts that were part of the independence movement explains:

> The casting of Muslims in the role of villains probably did not rise as much from anti-Muslim feelings as from the frustrations of a generation resentful of foreign domination and conscious of its own weakness. An important aspect of the movement was an undertone of religious mysticism, an exaltation of selfless devotion to Kali, the mother-goddess whose cult was widely popular in Bengal. Kali is a representation of the dark, vital forces of nature, the slayer of demons whose cult involved blood sacrifices and whose worship demanded passionate commitment. The identification of this mother-goddess figure with India, the motherland, was an easy step. (38)

Now, as India decolonizes, the challenge of relating aspects of Hindu culture to a contemporary situation becomes more complicated. Surely

Narayan does not suggest a Kali-type scenario. The function of Sastri, as Hindu sage and holy man, brings other options into focus. We see from early on that the relationship between Sastri and Nataraj is ambiguous; the roles of employer and employee are reversed. Sastri is also without the pretensions and anxieties that plague Nataraj and the end of the novel sees Nataraj declaring himself to be at Sastri's service. In addition, Sastri is the first to spot Rangi and first to identify Vasu as a rakshasa; he seems more receptive to the cosmic order according to Hindu mythology. Curiously, Sastri is absent when the destruction does come, curiously he is the one to whom Rangi tells her story. At the same time, Narayan adds enough of a comic tone to the first person narrative in the text to make it obvious that the voice of the protagonist is not that of the author. Instead the author is behind the curtain, doing the actual printing—a correlation to Narayan's own writing. Sastri's voice is that of Narayan—the printer/writer who knows the story and is confident that the cycle of creation, preservation, and destruction will run its course and that equilibrium will be re-established. To go the way of Kali would be to indulge in the type of violence that has bloodied Indian politics. Even as this paper is being written, the assassination of Rajiv Gandhi is still fresh in our memories. Is the alternative the nonviolence of the written word? The confidence of the writer to disrupt and then restore order? Is it up to the postcolonial writer, therefore, to negotiate a nationalism that values the Hindu capacity for creativity without the blood sacrifices Kali demands? How that can be done is the life's work of R. K. Narayan.

Works Cited

Basham, A. L. *The Wonder That Was India*. Calcutta: Fontana Books, 1981.

Coomaraswamy, Ananda K. and Sister Nivedita. *Myths of the Hindus and Buddhists*. New York: Dover Publications, 1967.

Embree, Aislie T. *India's Search for National Identity*. Delhi: Chanakya Publications, 1980.

_____. *The Hindu Tradition*. New York: Vintage Books, 1972.

Narayan, R. K. *Gods, Demons, and Others*. 1964. New Delhi: Vision Books, 1987.

_____. *The Man-Eater of Malgudi*. New York: Penguin Books, 1983.

O'Flaherty, Wendy Doniger. *Siva: The Erotic Ascetic*. Oxford: Oxford University Press, 1973.

Walker, Barbara G. *The Women's Encyclopedia of Myths and Secrets*. San Francisco: Harper & Row, 1983.

The Holy Man in R. K. Narayan's Novels

GANESWAR MISHRA

The holy man is a part of traditional Indian society and represents, in a way, the ancient Indian values and wisdom. He has fascinated the Indian mind, in all ages, whether called *rishi, sanyasi, sadhu,* or *swami.* In classical works like the *Ramayana,* sages (*rishis*) are shown as taking part in state affairs by acting as advisers to the king, and teaching young Brahmins and princes about the *shastras* and the art of administration. They are described as ascetic, wise, endowed with supernatural powers, and susceptible to wrath and jealousy. In puranic literature, the image of the holy man mostly conforms to that of the classical works. In folktales, interestingly, one quite often encounters characters of fraudulent holy men.

Though each religious community has its own holy men—the Muslims have their *mulla,* the Sikhs have their *bhai,* and Christians have their "priest"—the place of the holy man in Hindu society and the attitude of the Hindu toward the holy man have comparatively greater significance. According to the Hindu view of the world, every man, in the last of the four stages of his life, is supposed to lead the life of a holy man (*sanyasa*). Thus, according to the Hindu view of life, there is no line of demarcation between the holy man and the man of the world. Professor Edward Shils records that many Westernized Indians, in their interviews, told him of their desire to "go into the forest" in the last phase of their lives (64). The holy man is not only respected by society, he in a way symbolizes the cherished hope of many Hindus who want to live like him. Obviously, few Hindus ever take to *sanyasa,* but their ambition to do so influences their character and personality in certain ways.

The holy man embodies the Hindu idea of renunciation, asceticism, and detachment. He is not attached to anything mundane or worldly: wealth, fame, family, or friends. He is aware that this world is nothing but an illusion (*maya*). He is the ideal human being who is sometimes referred to as *jivanmukta* (free from life or bondage) and *sthita-prajna* (who has attained serenity in wisdom). In Hindu imagination greatness in any form is viewed as spiritual greatness, and politicians and poets are sometimes viewed as holy men.

All forms of Hindu literature, classical and puranic, emphasize asceticism as a supreme virtue, and it is an important motif in Indian art and literature. Ancient Sanskrit works like the *Ramayana*, the *Mahabharata* and the *Upanishads* contain innumerable allegories in which human beings and demons attain miraculous powers from Brahma, the Supreme God, by practicing ascetic measures. Many of the ancient kings and sages were supposed to achieve their greatness by renouncing worldly pleasures and taking to severe austerities. In *Gods, Demons, and Others*, R. K. Narayan retells such a story of asceticism. It is about the king Yayati who entered into heaven, in physical body, by leading the life of an ascetic:

> He ate the roots of plants and leaves; he overcame all desires and all moods and emotions, and his purity of mind helped him please the spirits of his ancestors as well as the gods. He lived on water alone for thirty years, completely controlling and suppressing his thoughts and words. One whole year he nourished himself by swallowing air and nothing else; he stood on one leg and meditated, surrounding himself on all four sides with fire and the blazing sun above. (45)

The life of Yayati, in a way, sets the ideal that every holy man should follow. Since the ideal is seldom practiced, Indian authors often find it convenient to suggest, in the character of the holy man, the gulf between the religious ideal and the common norm, the anachronism of ancient beliefs, and the corrupt nature of religious institutions. But it is not rare for holy men to be presented as noble and wise, in line with ancient sages. In Bankim Chandra Chatterjee's *Anand Math* (1882) we find holy men, who play an important role in the story, portrayed in this vein.

Religious motives being fundamental to the Hindu way of life and the Hindu social structure, we often find family men in society following, consciously or unconsciously, the ideal of the holy man. The act of sex, for instance, is forbidden for the holy man, and a householder living with his wife is sometimes guided by the idea that sex is a sin. Such complex situations provide the Indian novelist rich material for probing human minds and behavior. An important aspect of character portrayal in Indian fiction, after Gandhi's emergence as political leader, has been to present Gandhi and freedom fighters as holy men. Like Rama, Sita, and Bharata, Gandhi, in Indian literature, seems now an archetypal character. He is portrayed as an ascetic, champion of the creed of nonviolence, a friend of the poor and devoted to God; and an ideal man is often shown as conforming to this image of Gandhi.

In R. K. Narayan's novels, the holy man (or the *sadhu* or the *sanyasi* as he prefers to call him) appears frequently, though we rarely find him playing a significant role in Malgudi society. Apart from *The Guide* (1958), in no Narayan novel is the holy man the central character. Nonetheless, the holy man is an important aspect of Narayan's character portrayal, and Narayan's treatment of this very Indian character can explain something of his method of characterization.

It is not easy to determine whether Narayan repeatedly introduces the holy men to make the work interesting for his Western audience, or if it is a coincidence that Narayan is fascinated by a character who also arouses so much interest in the West. Indeed, with his Brahminic background and roots in Indian tradition and culture, it would be surprising if Narayan overlooked a character like the holy man who represents, however imperfectly, the lore and wisdom of ancient India. In his interview with Ved Mehta he is reported as saying that he perhaps could not write without "Krishna, Ganesa, Hanuman, astrologers, pundits, temples, and devadasis" and "to be a good writer anywhere, you must have roots— both in religion and in family" (141, 148).

Unlike Mulk Raj Anand who introduces the holy man in several of his novels as belonging to the class of oppressors, Narayan shows him as an ordinary member of society, as noble or fraudulent as the rest of it. Mostly, Narayan depicts the holy man in domestic and social situations, both as wise and foolish, comic and pathetic. He provides few details about his daily rituals and background (except in *The Guide* where the monologue of Raju reveals so much of his past life), but makes his distinct presence felt by the few sentences he [the holy man] utters or the few acts he performs. We have an interesting episode about a holy man in *The Bachelor of Arts* (1937), the first novel in which Narayan introduces such a character:

> Next day Chandran was out of bed at four, and with his father, went hunting in the garden. Nothing happened for about ten minutes. Then a slight noise was heard near the gate. Father was behind the rose bush, and Chandran had pressed himself close to the compound wall. A figure heaved itself on to the portion of the wall next to the gate, and jumped into the garden. The stranger looked about for a fraction of a second and went towards the jasmine creeper in a businesslike way.
>
> Hardly had he plucked half a dozen flowers when father and son threw themselves on him with war cries. It was quite a surprise for Chandran to see his father so violent. They dragged the thief into the house, held him down, and shouted to mother to wake up and light the lamp.

The light showed the thief to be a middle-aged man, bare bodied, with matted hair, wearing only a loincloth. The loincloth was ochre-coloured, indicating that he was a *sanyasi*, an ascetic. Father relaxed his hold on noticing this.

Mother screamed, "Oh, hold him, hold him." She was shaking with excitement. "Take him away and give him to the police."

Chandran said to the thief, "You wear the garb of a *sanyasi*, and yet you do this sort of thing!"

"Is he a sanyasi?" Mother asked, and noticed the colour of the thief's loincloth. "Ah, leave him alone, let him go." She was seized with fear now. The curse of a holy man might fall on the family. "You can go, sir," she said respectfully.

Chandran was cynical. "What, Mother, you are frightened by every long hair and ochre dress you see. If you are really a holy man, why should you do this?"

"What have I done?" asked the thief. (42–43)

Narayan treats the entire episode in a comic vein, but there is a tinge of sadness about it. The encounter between the holy man and the semi-Westernized family of the New Extension of Malgudi is in a way an encounter between ancient and modern India. The modern has reverence for the ancient, the ancient cannot ignore the modern, but they hardly understand each other. The holy man of the episode—and we have no reason to assume that he is a fraud—perhaps believes in values in which private property does not mean anything. Being one who has renounced all worldly belongings and attachments, he is supposed to have free access to every household and it is the sacred duty of society to look after him. It is perfectly justifiable, in the context of his beliefs, for him to enter a private garden to collect flowers for worship. He can be viewed as bestowing divine blessings on the owner of the garden by using his flowers for a religious purpose.

Chandran and his parents obviously fail to understand the holy man's views. If Chandran's mother wants the holy man to be allowed to go, it is not because she understands him, but because she is afraid of his curse. Chandran's father, in spite of his Western education, does not oppose his wife. The situation is typically Indian. The wife is traditional and superstitious; the husband, though Westernized, does not oppose his wife. In Indian fiction, we do not come across many themes of conflict between husband and wife, in middle-class families, in matters of faith and religion. The law protecting private property, and the holy man with his belief in his right of access to others' houses and gardens, exist side by side in Malgudi, an epitome of modern India, without coming into confrontation.

The flower-stealing episode acquires new significance when Chandran, who was once cynical and unsympathetic towards the holy man, himself wears the ochre-coloured robe, shaves his head, and becomes a holy man. His new way of life is not different from that of the holy man whom once he attacked with "war cries." The situation is rather ambivalent. Narayan perhaps suggests that the presence of the holy man in Malgudi is not as anachronistic as it may appear on the surface. Every Indian, however Westernized, has in him something of a holy man's attitude to life: viewing worldly things as an illusion (*maya*) and seeking peace in renouncing private belongings. Chandran might have failed to turn into a holy man, but in his attitude he has a strong affinity with the holy man whom he caught as a trespasser in his garden.

In *The Guide*, the story starts when Velan, a peasant, mistakes Raju, just released from jail, for a holy man; and by a strange development of events, Raju has to assume this mistaken identity for the rest of his life and end up as a martyr to the cause of bringing rain to the drought-stricken land. Raju is among Narayan's most memorable characters; and by narrating the story with movements forward and backward in time, he portrays the full life story of Raju, who, before assuming the role of the holy man, was a tourist guide, lover, dance proprietor, and convict.

In his treatment of the character of Raju as holy man, Narayan reminds one of Pirandello's theme of illusion and reality. Raju, in whose past life there was nothing to suggest his religious bent of mind, decides to assume the role of a holy man because that would mean a free supply of food from villagers:

> He had to decide on his future today. He should either go back to the town of his birth, bear the giggles and stares for a few days or go somewhere else. Where could he go? He had not trained himself to make a living out of hard work. Food was coming to him unasked now. If he went away somewhere else certainly nobody was going to take the trouble to bring him food in return for just waiting for it. The only other place where it could happen was the prison. Where could he go now? Nowhere. Cows grazing on the slopes far off gave the place an air of sublime stillness. He realized that he had no alternative: he must play the role that Velan had given him. (28)

Raju makes the decision casually, without realizing the serious implication that it might have for the villagers. The villagers of Mangal (at the outskirts of which Raju took shelter in a temple) were as if waiting for a saint to arrive from somewhere, at the very spot where Raju arrives; and when the boy announces that the saint is "back at his post" (37), Raju suddenly finds himself in the midst of a group of children and their teacher eager to listen to his wise words. As in the past, so also now, he rises to the occasion and plays his role admirably well:

> They (the children) had their foreheads smeared with sacred ash, and their slates creaked in the silent night, while the teacher lectured to them, and Raju, seated on his platform, looked on benignly. The teacher was apologetic about the numbers: he could muster only about a dozen boys: "They are afraid of crossing the river in the dark; they have heard of a crocodile hereabouts."
>
> "What can a crocodile do to you if your mind is clear and your conscience is untroubled?" Raju said grandly. (39-40)
>
> "And why do you ask us to recollect all that we have said since daybreak?" Raju himself was not certain why he had advised that, and so he added, "If you do it you will know why." (44)

Raju grows a beard and long hair; offers advice to every villager in his crisis, whatever may be its nature; and prescribes medicine to the sick. He himself is puzzled at his success in the role of the holy man.

The story takes a new turn when Raju decides to throw off the mask of the holy man, which, he realizes, has deprived him of any private life, of the right to "eat like an ordinary human being, shout and sleep like a normal man" (46); and he starts narrating his life story to Velan, with the intention of convincing him that he is not really a holy man. Velan listens to Raju intently, without interruption:

> Raju asked, "Now you have heard me fully?" like a lawyer who has a misgiving that the judge has been wool-gathering.
>
> "Yes, Swami."
>
> Raju was taken aback at still being addressed as "Swami." "What do you think of it?"
>
> Velan looked quite pained at having to answer such a question. "I don't know why you tell me all this, Swami. It's very kind of you to address, at such length, your humble servant." (207–8)

The relationship between Raju and Velan (and Raju and the villagers), after Raju makes the confession, no longer remains simple. Raju is no longer the hypocrite, the fraudulent holy man; nor is Velan any longer the naive peasant who mistook Raju for a holy man. But their relationship as *swami* and *chela* continues. Raju, instead of turning back to normal life, finds himself more involved in the role of the holy man and finally believes in his spiritual powers, and Velan remains throughout a devoted disciple of Swami.

Narayan's treatment of the Velan-Raju relationship is as serious as it is comic. The whole episode of Raju's transformation into a holy man, and eventually, a martyr, may at first seem merely farcical. But the novelist's presentation of the Indian mind and values, in the Velan-Raju relationship and Raju's self-sacrifice, is quite profound. Velan's unflinching devotion to Raju, even after knowing Raju's past, is in the true tradition of the *guru* cult, which emphasizes "faith" and not "logic" as the criterion of choosing one's *guru*. A disciple is not supposed to scrutinize the *guru's* drawbacks, and Velan, as a true disciple, is not concerned with Raju's past life. It is not the strange development of circumstances as much as the values and attitude of Velan and the people of Mangal that transform Raju into a saint and martyr. Obviously, Velan and the people of Mangal were waiting for the arrival of a saint in their lives. The Hindu philosophy recognizes *bhakti* or "devotion" as one of the ways to attain God, and the birth of a godhead in every age. The waiting of Velan and the villagers of Mangal for a saint is symbolically the waiting of the entire Hindu race for an *avatar* (incarnation) to destroy the evil among them. Raju apparently fulfills such a role by sacrificing himself to bring rain. Although the villagers of Mangal may be mistaken in their belief in Raju's sainthood, such a possibility exists as long as one believes in devotion to a *guru* or godhead as a way to salvation, and in the periodic emergence of *avatars* to eradicate evil.

Narayan often introduces characters who are very much involved in worldly affairs, but claim to live like holy men or show great enthusiasm for virtues like asceticism and renunciation. Such characters are neither hypocrites nor simple caricatures. In classical and puranic literature we meet characters who lead the life of the householder yet practice the virtues of asceticism. One such character is Janaka, who is both a king and a sage (*rajarshi*). Among the Vaishnava sect there is a sub-sect known as Grihi-Vaishnava, the members of which marry and live like ordinary men and yet practice asceticism. Even the ancient sages about whose life we learn from works like the *Upanishads*, lived with wives and children and yet practiced asceticism. Hinduism draws no line of demarcation between the life of the householder and that of the holy man. Participating in worldly affairs without being attached to them is a supreme virtue in Hindu philosophy, and Narayan's treatment of characters like the old landlord in *Mr. Sampath* (1949), the priest in *The Dark Room* (1938) and Jagan in *The Vendor of Sweets* (1967) should be viewed in this light.

The landlord in *Mr. Sampath* is an old man who lives away from his children and is supposed to be in the fourth phase of life (*sanyasa*). He lives in a small room that belongs to one of his friends, and his worldly belongings are scanty. Srinivas's chance meeting with the old man reveals the latter's character:

> The very first time Srinivas met him he saw the old man bathing at a street-tap, while a circle of urchins and citizens of Anderson Lane stood around watching the scene. They were all waiting for the tap to be free. But the old man had usurped it and held his place. Srinivas felt attracted to him when he saw him spraying water on the crowd as an answer to their comments. The crowd jeered: he abused it back; when they drew nearer he sprayed the water on them and kept them off, all the while going through his ablutions calmly. Srinivas asked someone in the crowd: "What is the matter?" "Look at him, sir, this is the same story every day. So many of us wait here to fill our vessels, and he spends hours bathing there, performing all his prayers. Why should he come to the tap built for us poor people? We can't even touch it till he has done with it." "Perhaps he has no other place." "No place!" a woman exclaimed. "He is a rich man with many houses and relations!" (8)

The old man is selfish, greedy, and has no love for the neighbors. We also learn from his conversation with Srinivas that he hates his own children and the children of others who call him "grandfather." His only human concern, however, is his granddaughter's marriage. In other words, he is as worldly a person as anyone else: "'Home! Home!' he laughed. 'I have no home. Didn't I tell you that I am a *Sanyasi*, though I don't wear ochre robes?'" (9)

The gulf between the ideal he preaches and his practice in real life makes the old man funny and ridiculous. But Narayan does not portray the character without sympathy. The old man's sudden death when the ball strikes his head heightens the pathos of his situation—lonely and alienated from everyone:

> The old man seemed to sit there in meditation, his fingers clutching the rosary. His little wicker box containing foreheadmarking was open, and his familiar trunk was in its corner. Dusk had gathered and his face was not clear. The boy's ball lay there at his feet. (148)

In both the novels, *The Dark Room* and *The Financial Expert* (1953), Narayan introduces the character of a priest, who, though not a holy man, is supposed to possess virtues like asceticism. The priest of the Maruga temple, who in his miserliness resembles the landlord of Srinivas, agrees to employ Savitri in his temple if Mari repairs, free of cost, three old umbrellas and fixes up iron bands around the grain barrel. The priest in *The Financial Expert* also does not mind spending hours in *puja* in rich people's houses. Both the priests resemble each other so much that they do not emerge as distinct individuals. Both are arrogant and in the habit of bullying people who come to see them. The priest's encounter with Mari (*The Dark Room*) is an exact replica of the priest's meeting with Margayya (*The Financial Expert*):

> "Who are you?" asked the old man, half closing his eyes in his effort to catch the identity of his visitor.
>
> "I am Mari, my master, your humble slave."
>
> "Mari, you are a vile hypocrite," said the old man.
>
> "What sin have I committed to deserve these harsh words?"
>
> "I sent my boy thrice to your place, and thrice have you postponed and lied. It was after all for a petty insignificant repair that I sent for you."
>
> "Nobody came and called me, master. I swear I would have dropped everything and come running if only the lightest whisper had reached me. Whom did you send?"
>
> "Why should I send anyone? After all, some petty repair—I thought I might have a word with you about it if you came to the temple; but you are a godless creature; no wonder your wife is barren. How can you hope to prosper without the grace of Maruga?" (*The Dark Room*, 122–23)
>
> He (Margayya) felt somewhat shy as he said: "I want to acquire wealth. Can you show me a way? I will do anything you suggest."
>
> "Anything?" asked the priest emphatically. Margayya suddenly grew nervous and discreet. "Of course, anything reasonable." Perhaps the man would tell him to walk upside down or some such thing. "You know what I mean," Margayya added pathetically.
>
> "No, I don't know what you mean," said the old man pointblank. "Wealth does not come the way of people who adopt half-hearted measures. It comes only to those who pray for it single-mindedly with no other thought." (*The Financial Expert*, 29)

The conversations easily suggest the authority and importance the priests enjoy in traditional Indian society. In spite of their arrogance and highhandedness, neither of the priests is devoid of kindness and sympathy. The priest of Maruga asks Savitri to live with the womenfolk of his family instead of living alone in the courtyard of the temple. The priest in *The Financial Expert* is hospitable and offers food to Margayya.

In the character of Jagan (*The Vendor of Sweets*), Narayan portrays a prosperous widower, aged sixty, torn between the worldly interest of running a sweetshop and caring about a spoiled child, and the following of the philosophy of the *Bhagavad Gita* and Mahatma Gandhi. There may or may not be a contradiction between worldly interest and the teachings of the *Gita* and Gandhi, but to Jagan (and to every average Indian), the teachings of the *Bhagavad Gita* and Gandhi are not compatible with the pursuits of worldly pleasures. In India, Gandhi is popularly viewed as a holy man, and Jagan, who plans to enter the fourth stage of life (*sanyasa*) when the novel ends, considers Gandhi as his "master":

> "Conquer taste, and you will have conquered the self," said Jagan to his listener, who asked, "Why conquer the self?" Jagan said, "I do not know but all our sages advise us so." (13)

The character of Jagan and his situation are amply suggested in these opening lines of the novel. The prosperous sweet-vendor who claims to have "the biggest sweet shop in the country" (42) quotes the advice of the sages not to succumb to the pleasure of the tongue. He is sincere in quoting the authority, and he himself takes neither sugar nor salt. He makes his toothbrush out of the branch of margossa and does not drink any water except that boiled and reserved in a mud jug exposed to the sky. In other words, he lives like an ascetic and has "conquered taste."

But what Jagan has failed to conquer is his attachment to his only son, and to the sweet shop. Between the father and the son there is no communication. Mali, Jagan's son, shows no interest whatsoever in establishing understanding between himself and his father; rather, he ignores him and all the values and morals he preaches. But Jagan's love for his son, in spite of the teaching of the *Bhagavad Gita* on non-attachment, remains an obsession with him. He even develops a liking for the half-Korean girl, Grace, who lives with his son without getting married to him. When Mali plans to send Grace back to America, Jagan feels unhappy: "He had got used to the presence of Grace in the house and he felt desolate at the thought of losing her" (132).

Narayan treats the character of Jagan in a half-serious, half-comic way. Jagan clearly represents, in his beliefs and values, the generation of Indians who lived in the last phase of the British rule, and, under the influence of Gandhi, believed in *charkha* and nature cure, in contrast with the new generation of the post-Independence period with their enthusiasm for modern science and technology. Jagan is alienated both from his only friend, the cousin, who visits his shop to devour sweets free of charge in return for listening to Jagan's philosophy of "conquering taste," and from his son who plans to write with the aid of a novel-producing machine and lives with a Christian girl. His taking to the life of *sanyasa*, in his circumstances, is more an escape than a genuine withdrawal from the world. Escape in the face of a crisis is a typical Hindu attitude that Narayan suggests in the character of Chandran, turning a holy man, after failing to marry the girl he loves. When Jagan finds it hard to live with his son, the advice offered by the cousin is: "Don't be hasty; go on a pilgrimage to the temples and bathe in the sacred rivers" (99).

In the last chapter of the novel, we find Jagan planning "to go to the forest," but still carrying the back door key with him and worrying about Grace's return to America. We have reason to believe that he will come back again to his house after a few days, through the back door, and again take charge of his sweetshop. Like Chandran's, Jagan's *sanyasa* will perhaps be temporary. Jagan is a portrait of those Indians who are committed to the life of a *sanyasi*, but unable to shake off the attachments of a *grihastha* (householder).

Works Cited

Mehta, Ved. *John is Easy to Please: Encounters with the Written and the Spoken Word.* Harmondsworth: Penguin, 1971.

Narayan, R. K. *The Bachelor of Arts.* 1937. East Lansing: Michigan State University Press, 1954.

_____. *The Dark Room.* 1938. University of Chicago Press, 1981.

_____. *The Financial Expert.* 1953. New York: Time-Life, 1966.

_____. *Gods, Demons, and Others.* New York: Viking, 1964.

_____. *The Guide.* New York: Penguin, 1958.

_____. *Mr. Sampath: The Printer of Malgudi.* 1949. University of Chicago Press, 1981.

_____. *The Vendor of Sweets.* 1967. New York: Penguin, 1983.

Shils, Edward. *The Intellectual Between Tradition and Modernity: The Indian Situation.* London, 1961.

A Meeting in Malgudi:
A Conversation with R. K. Narayan

JOHN LOWE

During the summer of 1983, I had the good fortune to travel across India as a Fulbright Scholar, participating in a program designed to acquaint American educators with Indian literature—including that of living writers. The trip was designed, however, to acquaint the fifteen of us (all teachers from the United States) with the India that had inspired this literature as well, so it was a seminar in transit, including lectures, readings, and literary discussion all over the country. We also saw the more important cultural monuments, like the Taj Mahal, the imperial ghost city of Fatehpur Sikri, the site of the Buddha's first sermon. We went from Delhi to Agra, to Jaipur; saw the carved and painted caves of Ellora and Ajanta; the sights of Bombay and the University of Pune; the mat-makers of Cochin; the rural silk industry of Bagalur village; the rubber plantations of Kerala; the silk shops of Bangalore; the Muslim tombs of Hyderabad; and the amazing artistic hubbub of Calcutta. We took in the scenery from aloft in Indian Airlines jets, from the windows of the mountain-climbing Deccan Express train, and once even saw the hazy peaks of Jaipur from atop elephants, as we made our way up to the Amber Fort. We rose at five o'clock for dawn cruises across Periar lake, where wild animals came to drink in Thekkady, and we rode the rain-swollen sacred Ganges to view the pilgrims coming for their morning ablutions in Varanasi. We had tea in the owner's garden in the misty mountains of South India, while visiting Peermark Tea Plantation.

Always, however, we were talking and thinking about the literature that all of this had inspired. Along with the cultural monuments, we were also visiting literary shrines, such as Tagore's house in Calcutta, or libraries where we would view centuries-old manuscripts and hear about the men who wrote them. We saw major art and folk-art museums in an attempt to understand India's artistic past, but also tried to link it to the artistic and popular culture of the present.

There was a marked emphasis, however, on contemporary literature. A major benefit of the program was thus meeting the various writers and artists who lived on or near our path. In Bombay, for instance, we met the poets Nissim Ezekiel, Rafiqui Baghdadi, and Rajiv Rao, who read from their works. There were meetings with artists in other mediums as well, including artisans in the villages, famed traditional dancers and singers, filmmakers, actors, and actresses. Thus we visited the amazingly active Mehboob Film Studios in Bombay with the famed producer, Johnny Bakshi, as our guide; he showed us the sets, explained the interaction of film writers and directors, and introduced us to the popular character actor Arjoon Aosare. When we were departing Aurangabad, we were amazed to see a seething crowd around the entrance to the airport being held in check by the police. Imagine our surprise to find that movie idols Rajiv and Tina (currently an item, according to our issues of popular Indian magazines) would be on board our flight—and they were, after rushing through a gauntlet of fans. Later, in Calcutta, we would be honored by having tea with the great director, Satyajit Ray, in his apartment.

Despite all this, the highlight of the trip, in many ways, was reached on July 29, when we were staying at the Lalit Mahal Hotel, the luxurious former palace of a now-deposed maharajah. It was indeed an auspicious day. That morning we had driven up the mountain to see the Nadi Bull, and to participate in the Temple of Chamundi Feast, where we were blessed by the local priest.

Our Indian guide for that part of the country was a remarkable man named Stanny Tekaekara, whose family was well known in the area. He used his considerable influence to lure the reclusive R. K. Narayan to our hotel from his nearby home.

Many of us had been buying and reading his novels along the route, whenever a good bookstore came into view. I was packing copies of *The Guide* (1958) and *The Dark Room* (1938). Several of us had of course read some of the Malgudi novels before leaving the states, so we were able to tell the other members of the group about the master's work as we flew, drove, walked, and floated across India.

We gathered together in the conference room some time before the master's scheduled afternoon arrival, comparing notes about the differing books we had read. We also were excited by the fact that we were not only meeting the Master of Malgudi—we were actually *in* Malgudi. And yet, one of the things we had been discussing all along was the unique way that Narayan's novels, set in South Central India, somehow managed to express aspects of an overarching Indian ambiance, even though, as we all now knew so well, India is an incredibly diverse country. Each region and state possesses its own unique culture and, frequently, its own language. Indeed, while in Mysore, we had visited the Indian Language Institute on the University of Mysore campus, where we were reminded about the way English had come to bridge some of these cultures as a literary language, as in Narayan's work.

There was a palpable air of excitement when Stanny led our guest into the room. We all rose, and introductions began. Soon, all of us were being served tea, as we sat around the long conference table with Stanny and the famous writer at its head. Narayan began with a modest disclaimer: "I have nothing much to say—what I say I write." Nevertheless, we plunged in with questions.

Q. *In your travels in the United States, are there moments you remember?*
A. I maintained a journal and wrote in it at night. Every night I wrote in it. I also wrote much of my novel *The Guide* then, which I finished in Berkeley, California. I find Berkeley crowded now with wild men everywhere—it's rather frightening. [Narayan had recently revisited California—he wrote *The Guide* during an earlier trip there].

Q. *Is there anything in* The Guide *that was transformed out of the American experience?*
A. I don't think so. It is totally Indian. In the film and on stage and in a Broadway show they spoiled the whole thing. It is native to this soil. I couldn't dare to write about America—only American writers can write wide geographical novels.

Q. *I read a critical piece on your work once that asserted quite confidently that Malgudi was a fictional place.*
A. Yes, that's often said or assumed in other countries.

Q. *Did the central character in* The Guide *die or just collapse at the end of the novel?*
A. I don't know what happened. I didn't want him to die either.

Q. *In your book* The Painter of Signs, *(1977) I'm particularly interested in the central character. Could you tell us something about him and his background? Was there a real life model for him?*
A. Yes, of course. There was one particular one.

Q. *Which of your many books do you like best?*
A. I think it has to be *A Tiger for Malgudi* (1983). The main character is a tiger. I'm not moved by great group forces but by individual characters, not social history.

Q. *Do you write every day?*

A. Yes, I do, especially when I'm doing a long novel. But I also have long fallow periods when I don't work as hard. Many days during these times I only write one or two hours at most.

Q. *Is there an influence from the Ramayana and the Mahabharata that has affected your novels and your philosophy?*

A. My own versions of the Ramayana and the Mahabharata have been very influential on my fiction. [Narayan has prepared English versions of both these epics for Western publication—in the United States they are published by Penguin]. But then every Indian writer has been influenced by them in many different ways.

Q. *Why are your novels so successful—much more so than those of any other Indian writer?*

A. I don't know; whatever reason there is for this, I'm not responsible for it.

Q. *Do you see your characters as types or as unique characters? [Narayan misunderstands this question and thinks that the questioner is asking about the titles of his books; but his answer is interesting, in that he says that titles are pulled only after the book has been sent to the publisher.]*

Q. *Wasn't much of your first book [*Swami and Friends, *1935] autobiographical?*

A. No, only parts of it were. Fiction can't be created entirely from autobiography, because any individual writer's life is very restricted.

Q. *In your novel* Swami and Friends *I noticed you create tension by describing a very real fear of tigers. As a child, did you experience any moments like that?*

A. What you're describing is part of the area where the characters in that book live. That's not typical for much of India.

Q. *I'd like to get your reaction to the film that was made of your wonderful novel* The Guide.

A. It was really quite terrible. You can't, however, expect a director to feel the same way that you feel about either your story or the characters. Directors are always looking for star values. I would rather not go near them again—they are dishonest, modern versions of demons. On the other hand, it is sometimes possible to do better with filmed versions of my books. *Mr. Sampath* (1949) was much better, partly because it featured an excellent actor. It was done in a Hindi version some time ago. I took the character of that book and rewrote it as a screenplay, so I had much more control over that project.

Q.   *In your visits to America over the years, have you noticed any changes?*
A.   America hasn't really changed all that much in the last twenty-five years. Basic American values seem to me to have remained the same, and you still see the same kinds of people on the streets. You still see hippie-type people in Greenwich Village—they just move faster now. In suburban areas such as New York's Westchester, not much has changed. Everyone now has color TVs instead of black and white, and they're all Japanese instead of American. People all seem to have two sets instead of one, and many people have cable television. Similarly, most of the cars people drive up in Westchester used to be German—now they all seem to be manufactured by the Japanese. I seem to detect a little more fear on Manhattan streets, but we have that here too; that kind of thing is happening all over the world.

Q.   *What are your impressions of Gandhi's values and ideas and their effect on India?*
A.   That is a question that deserves an extended historical answer. I wrote a book called *Waiting for the Mahatma* (1955), which you should read. I didn't know Gandhi personally, but all Indians have of course been influenced by his life.

Q.   *Are you friends with other Indian writers?*
A.   Mulk Raj Anand is here and we are friends, but we don't read each other's books.

Q.   *More than any other Indian writer, you have managed to create complex and fascinating books without relying on long narration. How have you managed this?*
A.   Sheer accident. I have to say, however, that this seems to me to make my books more readable. I don't want to either bore my readers or to get bored myself. I've never wanted to write long books. I go over my manuscripts carefully and do a great deal of editing. I always blue pencil anything that seems at all repetitive.

Q.   *In your book,* The Guide, *the three central figures seem to be allegorical—representative of the Hindu godhead of Brahma the creator, Vishnu the preserver, and Shiva the dancer and destroyer. Did you consciously think of this when you were writing the novel? Were you trying to write an allegory?*
A.   I see what you mean, and I suppose those characters do represent those things.

But I didn't think of it at the time I was writing the novel. I am Indian; any Indian writer will be shaped and influenced by the culture that produced him, and thus to some extent will be writing allegorically.

Q. *Who are the American writers whom you most admire?*

A. I like John Updike, Sinclair Lewis, Theodore Dreiser. I also admire William Faulkner, Arthur Miller, and Tennessee Williams.

Q. *Is the existentialist movement very strong in Indian literature today, and if so, why?*

A. I don't think there is any successful influence of that type in contemporary Indian literature. That way of thinking has not been very influential in this culture.

Q. *As a follow-up to the preceding question—I see your characters as loners, people who are isolated. I think of people such as Srinavas in* Mr. Sampath *as an example.*

A. Family life usually saves an individual from what you are describing. One's family saves one from too much alienation and too much time to brood. There are situations, however, that isolate some individuals. In Bombay, for instance, people are cooped up in apartments. In that kind of place you may be prey to alienation and despair, but virtually nobody writes about it. The people who are currently writing in Bombay are quite different people from the sort you are describing—writers there tend to be very busy.

Q. *Much has been written about your long and close relationship with the British writer Graham Greene. What is it exactly about his work that you find attractive?*

A. I like his technique very much. He is such a versatile writer. Then too, he is very readable, a quality I much admire.

Q. *Which of his novels do you admire most?*

A. I especially like *The Honorary Consul* and *Dr. Fisher's Party*, partly because I frequently like a writer's later books. There is more depth in Greene now. It comes with age.

Q. *Do you think in English or Tamil before you write?*

A. I don't think there is such a thing as a language that one thinks in. That type of creative thought knows no language.

Q. *But does your inspiration ever come in English?*

A. No, just ideas. I'm really not yet that introspective.

Q. *In* The Guide, *as the main character tries to make decisions, things go wrong, but he transcends the events that occur at the end. When he tries to do things for himself, however, he hurts himself. How should we read these aspects of the book?*

A.   It's a long time since I've read my book. But that character is forced to go through all the types of saintly activity. At the beginning he acts—at the end he thinks, "I am going to die of this" and goes through with it anyway. In that book I was concentrating on narration, character, transformation, and transcendence.

At that very appropriate moment, which seemed to offer, at least for most of us, a concise description of virtually all of Narayan's fiction, Stanny rose and said we'd imposed on our guest long enough.

Some Notes on "Reluctant Guru"

WARREN FRENCH WITH JAVAID QAZI

Although I am familiar with all the writings of R.K. Narayan that have been published in the United States and the United Kingdom, I have not had access to many that have appeared only in India. His reminiscence "Reluctant Guru" was unknown to me until by accident I came across a slim collection of memoirs and essays titled for the leading piece and published in New Delhi by Orient Paperbacks in 1974 while I was visiting my former colleague, Thomas L. Warren, at Oklahoma State University during the winter of 1990. We were both surprised and excited to discover that in this seven-page account I find one of Narayan's most perceptive and noteworthy analyses of his experiences in the United States which recalled to us more than two decades later some of the most rewarding experiences of our academic careers. Since then I have found the essay has also been collected more recently and more conveniently in a *A Writer's Nightmare, Selected Essays 1958–1988* (New Delhi: Penguin Books India, 1988).

This brief recollection describes the novelist's bemusing visit to "a certain mid-Western University," as "Visiting Professor," though neither he nor his academic friends had any "concrete or convincing" conception of what this title meant before his arrival on the scene. Then he learned that he had been invited in response to student demands "to brighten up (and also broaden) English literary studies with a lot of interesting, though not relevant, additions to their reading lists." To his dismay he discovered, however, that since he had been summoned from India at a time when many others from this distant land were arriving bearing messages of spiritual comfort for eager disciples that the students assumed he was a mystic because "all Indians are spiritually preoccupied."

Although he protested that this wasn't true, he found himself forced into the position of "reluctant guru," a role not contemplated by those responsible for inviting him. His most cogent remarks in his composite summary of many talks that he gave stress, however, that his countrymen had similar misconceptions of Americans as technicians possessing secrets that the Indians sought for their national development: "Your search is for a 'guru' who can promise you instant mystic elation; whereas your counterpart looks for a Foundation Grant. The younger person in my country would sooner learn how to organize a business or manufacture an atom bomb or an automobile then how to stand on one's head."

I understand why, with his characteristic consideration for the delicacy of other's sensibilities, R.K. Narayan declined to identify his hosts in narrating his experiences; but as one of those alluded to I am delighted with his account and wish only that I could have known of it long before I accidentally discovered it. Perhaps also readers in India would be less concerned with the specific site than with the general principles Narayan drew from his encounters there, but I think that his American following would enjoy a more definite sense of place.

He speaks about his visit to the University of Missouri—Kansas City in Spring 1969—a time of great unrest and soul-searching on all American campuses, when the struggling but greatly respected privately-funded University of Kansas City was making a stressful transition into the state University system. Visitors like Narayan were welcomed because the school, which had been founded during the depression as an offshoot of the University of Chicago, where President Robert Hutchins' "Great Books" program then was the basis of the curriculum, was devoted to the principle of promoting "general" rather than technically specialized education based on fostering international cultural relations.

Even during the difficult early years, distinguished visitors like Russian sculptor Archibald Archipenko and Mexican muralist Miguel Corrovubias left their mark upon the campus developing spaciously on a hillside. A year before Narayan's visit the young C.W.E. Bigsby (now director of the Arthur Miller Center of American Studies at the University of East Anglia) had spent a semester here.

One point needs clarification. Although Bigsby and his successor, Mark Leaf, from the University of Durham were "visiting professors" in the usual sense of temporary appointees offering a schedule of regular courses during a school term, Narayan held a different and less clearly defined position. When early in correspondence he expressed reluctance to become involved in an unfamiliar formal offering that would involve a long visit, it was arranged that he should respond as suited him to requests for individual lectures, discussions, and interviews, while maintaining as nearly as possible on American premises his usual life style at Treadway Hall, a venerable apartment house that the University had inherited as housing for visitors and new appointees, for about three months.

He was not, in fact, a guest of the University itself, but of one of the peculiar institutions that did indeed support his speculations about departures at this school from "universal practice"—the Caroline Benton Cockefair Chair of Continuing Education, which was provided with university facilities but funded by private contributions. A distinctive feature of this adornment to the community's cultural life was that the word chair was not, as generally today, used metaphorically in this title, but referred to an actual piece of furniture intricately carved in a Medieval manner that was introduced at all meetings of the program as a kind of throne that served not, again as generally today, as a memorial to the dedicatee, but was actually occupied by her (the eighty-six year old woman Narayan recalled as a member) as she dynamically and articulately directed proceedings and listened attentively. While Narayan acclimated himself to this arrangement with a calmness that eluded most American visitors, I never felt quite sure that he had realized that this was an unconventional arrangement for American academia. His small number of formal lectures, which were meditations rather than orations, were offered to this Chair and the "largely elderly ladies" who supported it, whom Javaid Qazi recalls as "very senior, almost predisposed to thinking of things mystical in the twilight years of life."

Before commenting on the implications of this observation about one source of the reception that forced upon Narayan the role of "reluctant guru," some further identifications are in order to establish the credentials of the present writers. I was the Chairman of the English Department, and I am deeply honored to find myself recalled by such a distinguished visitor as "a distinguished scholar and critic." However, I must ruefully disclose that the "detailed, deep study," that he graciously says I have made of his writing, has resulted so far only in an essay on *The Vendor of Sweets*, which I developed from a review in the *Kansas City Star* in 1967 for a study of outstanding contemporary fiction, and an introduction I was later privileged to write for a collection of criticism of his work published in India.

I had worked for several years, however, to arrange his visit to the campus in the hope that it would encourage more extensive reading of fiction in English by other than Anglo-American authors and that it would develop in students some sense of responsibility for the influences stressed in *The Vendor of Sweets* that post-World-War-II American life style was beginning to have on other cultures internationally. I had hoped that the fictional world that he had created in his Malgudi novels, comparable to William Faulkner's "Yoknapatawpha County," would make them look beyond their own society to understand the real similarities and differences between it and others that Narayan stresses in his composite report of the talk that he often delivered during this visit; but as he points out that was not the role he was called upon to play.

I should have realized that at the time of his visit "guru hunting" was peaking in the United States. As Javaid Qazi points out, "In those days there was a terrible Guru-need rampant across the land and anyone who could mouth a few appropriate phrases could take up the role easily." On the campus, he goes on, "we young ones made matters worse by being only too eager to chuck the hard realities of jobs and making a living and plunge into the dreamscape of mysticism."

Javaid enters into this account as one of the only two others I can identify who figure prominently in Narayan's account—"the couple of young men from India, doing their postgraduate courses in English, also holding assistantships," who were "extremely popular" with undergraduate students. Actually Javaid is a Pakistani, but Narayan may have made both Indians in order to avoid overcomplicated irrelevancies in his article about the amicable relations on an American campus of nationals of two nations then on antagonistic terms. In his recent letter responding to his first reading of "Reluctant Guru," from which I have been quoting, Javaid spots himself as the one who "left untended his nape-draping tresses," while the other with a "tiny beard" is Hamayun Ali Mirza, truly a native of India. Both had arrived on campus the September before Narayan's spring visit, also as part of a determined effort to provide broad international perspectives in our literature program.

Javaid had come directly from Pakistan, where he had studied at schools following Cambridge University programs and edited an impressive undergraduate literary magazine; Hume (as everyone knew Mirza) had come to the United States as an undergraduate to study engineering, but he had abandoned technical training for literature with a mystical flavor and had become an enthusiastic disciple of the Maharishi Mahesh Yogi, whose Transcendental Meditation movement was then far outstripping the offerings of numerous other visitors bringing consciousness-expanding programs from India in attracting American adherents. (Although Javaid was Hume's roommate for a year, he remained always the sophisticated Cantabridgian skeptically avoiding any cultist attachment.) Although many faculty members were apprehensive about the reaction of Midwestern freshmen to inexperienced young Asian instructors, both were most popular and innovative teachers. Both went on to earn doctorate degrees in English at American institutions, and Javaid is still in California, alternating between doing technical writing in Silicon Valley and teaching the same skills to others in regional colleges. Hume went off to India for two years with the Maharishi's entourage, but returned to complete a provocative dissertation on the mysterious J.D. Salinger. Since then, however, he has disappeared.

Both did manage to spend far more time with our visitor than I could manage during a period of daily campus crises. Javaid reports that Narayan "lived off yogurt and boiled rice mostly," always courteously refusing the temptation of American banquets. He resisted, in fact, most tempting complications of American life. Javaid reports a characteristic episode:

> I remember, one day Mirza and I took him to Penney Plaza and he looked into the possibility of buying an electric shaver. When the issue of voltage problems was raised with the salesclerk, he decided not to buy it after all. He remarked that it seemed silly to purchase this complicated bit of machinery to remove a bit of facial hair, especially when there was no guarantee that it would work in India. Mirza and I heartily applauded the decision. Another victory against unneeded technology.

No mystical escapism here. Perhaps if Narayan played the guru reluctantly, he exercised more practical influence on his American audience than he may have supposed. What struck me particularly about his visit is that unlike many other guests, especially from less distant regions, he never looked upon himself as a celebrity. He succeeded, rather, in becoming involved in life on campus during a critical period in a way that many distinguished visitors, who moved through their residence isolated from the students' routines, never did. The Cockefair elders would have gladly taken up this time with empty ceremonials, but he spent his time in more valuable ways and he perhaps, in gently chiding the "hotchpotch studies" of enthusiastic young teachers, promoted the development of more resourceful and resilient minds than the more studied responses to more schematic programs can.

One "reluctant guru" may have succeeded better in raising consciousness than multitudes who have accepted the role overwillingly.

R. K. Narayan, The Dramatist

M. N. SUNDARARAMAN

Most of the readers of R. K. Narayan may not be aware of the fact that Narayan is a dramatist too. However, this prolific writer of novels, short stories, and essays is, like the single-speech Hamilton, a single-play dramatist. But even this single product reveals his grasp of the genre and the potentialities of his success in the field if he should choose to write more plays. The play "Watchman of the Lake," like Narayan's famous short story "The Restored Arm," forms part of the appendices to *The Emerald Route*, a kind of tourist-guide to Karnataka, written by Narayan and illustrated by his brother, R. K. Laxman. The author in his introductory note to the play says:

> This one-act play is based on a folk theme, the story of a rustic who sacrificed himself in order to save a tank about to breach. I heard this story sometime ago when I traveled by bus from Kadur to Chigmagalur, while the bus halted indefinitely at a wayside stall selling tender coconuts. At this point I noticed a finger post pointing "Sakkerpatna" and made a casual enquiry, which was answered by a fellow passenger with a local anecdote, which I later developed into a one-act play. I have included it in this volume on Karnataka as the folk tradition and the perennial philosophy implicit in the theme are worth our study. (99)

Narayan continues that this Sakkerpatna, which is now an obscure little place on the eastern base of the Bada Buden Hills in the State of Karnataka, was, a thousand or more years ago, the capital of a king called Rukmangada. In the center of this town there is a shrine which "is dedicated not to distant gods or heroes but to a rustic, who was watchman of a lake called Ayyankere, four miles from the town." For the purposes of this little drama, the rustic is called Mara.

The plot of the play is very simple: This Mara has a dream in which the goddess appears and asks him to inform the king that he (the king) should build a lake to dam up the waters of the river, Veda, which sprang up on the spot where "Sanjeevini" (which was brought to Lanka by Hanuman to revive Lakshmanan) once had grown. When Mara tells others about his dream they call him mad and a fool. However, he succeeds in conveying the message to the king and getting the lake built. The king appoints him the watchman of the lake and Mara does his duty sincerely. Many years later, one day, there are torrential rains. Mara gets worried about the safety of the lake and prays to the goddess. She appears before him and asks him to clear out of his hut immediately and declares: "I am going to kick away the miserable stones you have piled up to imprison the water of my Veda. I am going to destroy your tank" (108). When all his pleas with the goddess, who is in a most "terrible and reckless mood of destruction" fail, Mara begs her to wait till he can "come back" after running to the capital and informing the king. The goddess agrees to stay her hand till he comes back. Mara goes to the capital, meets the king but outwits the goddess by asking the king to kill him so that he will not return and the goddess, as per her promise, cannot destroy the lake. In the larger interests of the State, the king, most unwillingly, beheads Mara, but, in appreciation of his noble and supreme sacrifice, builds a temple for Mara and makes the watchmanship of the temple a hereditary right of Mara's family.

Narayan, within a short space of five scenes, has very effectively dramatized this great deed of heroism of a simple rustic. The character of Mara is ably portrayed, though the plot itself does not permit the drawing of a full-length picture. The attitude of others towards Mara's claim about the goddess's command is reflected in the words of the headman who calls him "a worthless dog," "lunatic," and "fool." The headman is eager to keep Mara out of the way when the king passes that place. He first threatens him that he would have him locked up in the cellar, but later tries to coax him: "I will give you a fine gift if you behave yourself" (101). The replay of Mara to this offer of the headman, reveals, at one stroke, his love for his wife and his sense of humour:

> *Headman:* Be off. And like a good fellow keep to your backyard till the king departs. I will give you a fine gift if you behave yourself.
>
> *Mara:* Another person has already given me the greatest gift any man could give.
>
> *Headman:* Oh! Who is that great man?
>
> *Mara:* My father-in-law.

The simplicity and innocence of Mara are revealed when he asserts to the Headman: "I don't feel I am a fool" and also when he believes the words of the bully Bhima, that his mother had given him an "iron decoction" when he was a baby, so much so that it gave him the strength to run up the hill with a large grindstone on his back.

His sincerity of purpose, which moves the hearts of at least a few, is made clear by his efforts to meet the king and convey the message of the goddess. Even Bhima—"a giant in appearance" but with the "soul of a baby"—lets him go when he hears of his dream and the command of the goddess. Mara slips out of the cellar unseen, climbs a tree, hides himself among the leaves and waits for the king's arrival patiently. His piety and complete faith in the stories of the mythologies are quite in keeping with his rustic nature. After the construction of the lake and his appointment as the watchman, he does his duty faithfully with a kind of pious pride:

> This place is sacred and belongs to the goddess; and her command is that nothing that flies or swims or walks in these parts should ever be killed. . . . I am the master of this place. The king made me so. But for me the Veda would have run away and disappeared as she was doing before. I gave her a home, where she stays, and nourishes the fields of thousands of the king's subjects. . . . Even the headman of the village, who once beat and bullied me, will have to beg my permission if he wants to touch the water. Here I am the king; no one can question me. (105)

The king also, though his appearance is very brief, impresses us with certain qualities of his character. He is not led by others, but has a mind of his own. When others say that Mara is unworthy of His Majesty's notice, the king says: "We will hear the man himself speak. Let him be brought forward." After listening to Mara's words about the dream, he comes to the right conclusion: "you have the grace of gods upon you. Your words are weighty. . . .When we return this way tomorrow accompany me to the capital." The king is shocked to hear Mara's suggestion to save the lake: "No, no. What a horrible suggestion." However, later, he is forced to accept the idea on the principle that one life may be sacrificed to save many. The king shows his gratitude to the rustic by erecting a temple in his honor.

We read in the mythologies of the gods outwitting the demons or "Rakshasas" by turning their words against them, but here a simple rustic outwits a goddess by making her promise that she will not indulge in destruction until he returns but prevents the destruction by not returning at all. There is a tragic grandeur in his words to the king: "If Your Majesty's sword is there . . ." and "Or send for the executioner." Again, his last request moves us not only by its simplicity but also by his love of his family: "My last request is this: When I am gone, make him [his son] the watchman of the lake, and after him his son, and then his son's son to the last generation of our family" (109). Above all, there is the irony of one who was called a fool and lunatic coming to be worshipped as a god. The situations and the dialogue are also natural and convincing. Like Narayan's novels and short stories, this play too has in it merits and values that remain hidden under the veil of simplicity in respect of both the theme and the language.

Works Cited

Narayan, R. K. *The Emerald Route.* Mysore: Indian Thought Publications, 1977.

The World of Nagaraj: *Narayan's Metanovel*

RAJINI SRIKANTH

Nagaraj, the protagonist in R.K. Narayan's most recent novel, *The World of Nagaraj*, wishes desperately to write a treatise on the Indian sage Narada. But Nagaraj, though he is obsessed with his idea, and, to be fair to him, takes the initial steps to try to bring it to form, does not succeed. At one level, *The World of Nagaraj* can be read as a parody of the figure of the would-be writer. However, like all of Narayan's comic depictions, the author's portrayal of Nagaraj is sensitive and sympathetic. Narayan perfected the art of deadpan humor many novels ago, and here, as in his other works, the effect of his emotional detachment and neutral posture, as he leads the reader through Nagaraj's bumbling attempts and repeated failures, is vastly funny without the slightest touch of malice or ridicule. But this work throws up issues of a more thought-provoking nature: in particular, the power of fiction, the nature of authorship, and the non-authorial obligations of the aspiring or successful writer in an Indian community.

What fascination does Narada hold for Nagaraj or, more to the point, for Narayan? In *The Talkative Man*, published just two years before *The World of Nagaraj*, the central character introduces himself in the first paragraph of the book thus:

> They call me Talkative Man. Some affectionately shorten it to TM. I have earned this title, I suppose, because I cannot contain myself. . . . I'd choke if I didn't talk, perhaps like Sage Narada of our epics, who for all his brilliance and accomplishments carried a curse on his back that unless he spread a gossip a day, his skull would burst. (1)

The curse is mentioned again, almost verbatim, in *The World of Nagaraj*. Here, as in the earlier work, Narada is referred to as a celestial character whose life depends on his use of words and his proliferation of fictions. His very birth, according to Nagaraj's sources, was the result of potent and magical words, a *mantra*, uttered by the Supreme Lord (124). In his book of Hindu myths retold, *Gods, Demons, and Others*, Narayan reminds us of Narada's pivotal role in the composition of the mythico-religious epic *Ramayana*. It is Narada who, with his story of Rama, moves the poet Valmiki so profoundly that the latter is led into the deepest meditation of Rama and from there to the composition of the 24,000-stanza *Ramayana* (133–36). I will return to Valmiki later for what we can learn from the story of his life about the necessary preparations a poet must undergo before he can narrate.

Narada, then, is an accomplished narrator. All through Hindu mythology, he figures as the traveling raconteur, telling stories with skill as he traverses the worlds above and below the earth and mingles with the gods and humans. He dispenses stories and brings news, often planting distrust and raising suspicion, not with the malicious and destructive intent of an Iago, but with the acumen of a politician or seasoned diplomat looking out for the best interests of whichever party he serves at that moment. It is easy to see why Narayan, himself a powerful storyteller, should find Narada's narrative prowess so enchanting. C. N. Srinath, a personal friend of the author, writes in his retrospective essay on Narayan of the author's deep groundings in Hindu mythology; he mentions Narada as a character whom Narayan found particularly stimulating (419).

By contrast, Nagaraj's preoccupation with Narada finds its source in the former's *limitations* as a verbal artist. The protagonist of this latest Narayan novel is shy and diffident, a poor purveyor of words; he is in awe of Narada's ability to spin stories and he ascribes to the sage's narrative powers the strength of divine weaponry. In fact, Nagaraj's thesis for his proposed book on Narada is that:

> The sage floated along with ease from one world to another among the fourteen worlds above and below this earth, carrying news and gossip, often causing clashes between gods and demons, demons and demons, and gods and gods, and between creatures of the earth. Ultimately, of course, such clashes and destruction proved beneficial in a cosmic perspective. Evil destroyed itself. (3)

The shy and mild Nagaraj sets out to be the great sage Narada's champion. He wants to be the voice that will make Narada famous. Nagaraj concedes that every good Hindu knows about Narada and the stories surrounding him, but Nagaraj envisions a much wider audience for his book: the vast non-Hindu world that stretches far beyond Malgudi.

Nagaraj's literary aspirations do not constitute the only plot of this novel. There is also the story of Tim, Nagaraj's errant nephew, who suddenly intrudes into Nagaraj's peaceful life. Nagaraj's attempts to be author are intricately tied up with Tim's rebellion against a dictatorial father. The more ensconced Tim becomes in Nagaraj's household (even bringing his new bride to his uncle's home), the harder it becomes for Nagaraj to fulfill his aspiration. Nagaraj does not have the luxury of turning his back on his nephew's demands and refusing to become involved in the filial conflict. Nagaraj's predicament bears out the validity of Arun Mukherjee's observation that characters in the novels of Commonwealth countries are not "isolated individuals going on actual or spiritual journeys and finding their own resolutions, but . . . individuals moulded, confronted and interfered with by their social environment at every step in their lives" (347).

As in Narayan's other novels, the drama unfolds in Malgudi, the author's fictitious locale. Often compared in scope and detail to Faulkner's Yoknapatawpha County, Malgudi is the quintessential township in South India. (I refer the reader in particular to Faulkner's *Snopes Trilogy*, the three novels—*The Hamlet, The Town*, and *The Mansion*—in which he gives us an indelible impression of community life and ambience in the Southern United States.) *The World of Nagaraj* has all the characteristic Malgudi flavor: the variegated inhabitants, the neighborhood gossip, the ubiquitous rumors, the bustle of market squares, the dusty streets, the wandering dogs and cows, the cries of hawkers, the outbursts of family feuds, the local legends, and the enticing aroma of freshly brewed coffee mingling with the languid heat of the South Indian afternoon.

Nagaraj is a respected Malgudi citizen. In one sense, he is perfectly placed to be a writer. He and his wife, Sita, live in his family's ancestral home; he is sufficiently provided for and doesn't have to earn a living. Although he works as a volunteer bookkeeper in a friend's business, he has ample leisure to focus his energies on writing. Furthermore, Sita, though mildly amused by his literary zeal, goes along good-naturedly with his demands, keeps him fed, and leaves him alone when he desires.

Nagaraj considers himself to be literary, or at least literarily inclined. Bits of passages from the body of Western literature pop into his mind from time to time. He belongs, he feels, to that privileged group of individuals who are at home with famous texts. "Begone, here he cometh," "Rome was not built in a day," "It is better to have loved and lost than never to have loved at all," are samples of the literary tags that float up to the surface of his mind. Some of Narayan's most delightfully comic descriptions in this book focus on Nagaraj's "familiarity" with English literature.

Qualified though he considers himself to be, Nagaraj can never seem to get started on his project. There are numerous impediments. To begin with, there is the young librarian who scoffs at Nagaraj's interest in a musty old sage and rudely informs him that the library doesn't carry books on antiquated subjects. Then there is the aged scholar who contemptuously dismisses Nagaraj because of the latter's ignorance of Sanskrit, the classical language in which the sacred texts on Narada are written:

> Go and write the fable of the inquisitive monkey who had his balls crushed when he sat on a split log and pulled out the wedge, in any basha (language) you please, but leave grand subjects alone. (99)

Ultimately, Nagaraj finds help from an unexpected source. The local stationer, Bari, a merchant whom Nagaraj had considered a Philistine, reveals that he owns a large epic of Narada. The book is written in Hindi, Bari's native tongue and a language with which Nagaraj is only minimally acquainted. But Bari promises to read a chapter out loud to Nagaraj every night. Delighted, Nagaraj equips himself to take copious notes.

Two obstacles present themselves, however. Tim gets married and returns to Nagaraj's house with his wife, Uma. Uma considers herself a singer, and every day she practices her singing to the accompaniment of the harmonium—an accordion-like instrument. The music drives Nagaraj to distraction and he is unable to concentrate.

The other difficulty is that Bari's book never seems to get to the point. Although the title, *Narad Puran*, promises stores of information about Narada, the merchant's readings night after night deal only with the universal chaos of water and darkness that existed in the beginning of the world. Nagaraj fills ten notebooks with his copious writing, but Bari is still reading about giant waves and total darkness. When does Narada appear, Nagaraj asks anxiously. The merchant calms his fears, and persuades him of the necessity for this protracted preamble and buildup. Nagaraj scribbles furiously, anxious not to miss anything. He takes down information indiscriminately, without thinking, and when he goes home he is often unable to decipher his notes or make sense of what he has written.

The final obstacle, one that totally demolishes Nagaraj's literary spirit, presents itself when Uma, who lands a singing job in a local restaurant, buys a large harmonium, one that sounds twice as loud as its predecessor. The book closes with Nagaraj's resigned attitude toward the new situation. There is poignancy in his capitulation to circumstances:

> I can have no hope of writing any more. You could as well take the notebooks back to the old room, where at least white ants may relish my notes on Narada. . . .And another thing: don't be surprised if I wear the ochre robe when I am at home. It'll force me to remain

silent and not speak out and upset the children (Tim and Uma) and drive then out again. I shall also acquire a lot of cotton wool and try and pack it all in my ear so that even a thunderclap will sound like a whisper. (184–85)

Nagaraj is like the vast majority of Narayan's characters: a simple and uncomplicated hero. He does nothing grand, says nothing magnificent; he is just a kind, decent human being who dreams of a grand gesture but who will continue to survive in his ordinariness and averageness.

In her analysis of Narayan's characters, Manorama Pandit emphasizes the concept of *dharma* or duty and claims that "detachment as a mental state is necessary to enlightenment" for his heroes:

The protagonist comes to be disturbed through his own excessive attachment to something and realizes the problematic nature of the attachment because of the disturbance. The solution comes when in a moment of supreme detachment, the protagonist performs an act for no other consideration than this—that it is the protagonist's *dharma* or duty—the right thing to do.

The focus on *dharma* is appropriate, given that much action among Hindus is informed by it (although distorted interpretation of what constitutes *dharma* in a given situation can result in bewildering behavior). In Nagaraj's case, *dharma* does not lend itself to a straightforward application. Should one see his ultimate suppression of his need to write as a form of detachment, a fulfillment of the *dharma* of a family patriarch, or should one view this literary suppression as an act of failure, an inability to detach himself from the exigencies of family circumstances? The latter, I believe, is the correct perspective.

No individual in India (or in any non-Western culture, for that matter) can hope to detach himself completely from family and community obligations. In recognition of this difficulty, the Hindu *Dharma Shashtras* (the works dealing with the code of conduct a good Hindu must follow) decree that the fourth and final phase of a man's life should consist of *physically removing himself* from the everyday world of demands and desires and meditating on the true meaning of existence. *Sanyas*, this final stage of life, can only be fulfilled by distancing oneself, both physically and mentally, from the community of other individuals. The outside world ceases to exist for the *sanyasi*.

In the context of the author or the artist, however, *dharma* takes on a dialectic twist. The author is in the strange position of having to be both in and out of this world at the same time. He must steep himself in the world around him if he is to write with validity about the people in it;

but without distance between his imagination and the clutter of life, he cannot impose structure, cannot order the world according to his plan. It is not a coincidence that both Valmiki and Vyasa, the composers respectively of Hinduism's two greatest epics, *Ramayana* and *Mahabharatha*, were sages; i.e., individuals who had perfected the ability to detach themselves from the cacophony of living and give their unswerving concentration to the task of composition. Arun Mukherjee points out that "the main motif of Indian epics is exile" (350). But exile in Hindu mythology is not an enervating state or a sterile passage of time in which the exiled individual bemoans his isolation. Quite the contrary. The exiled individual, who is removed from traffic with other human beings, has the time to concentrate inward, gains in strength and resolve, and then re-enters the world better equipped to deal with it.

In this regard, the story of how Valmiki became a poet is illustrative. Valmiki tells how he spent thousands of years in meditation, so engrossed in the incantation of the word "Mara" (which word, when repeated without pause in an endless stream, fuses to become "Rama") that an anthill grew over him. When, eventually, the anthill was broken open and he emerged, he had become a sage, blessed with divine vision. Valmiki explains to Rama himself, "Owing to the potency of your name, I became a sage, able to view the past, present, and future as one" (*Gods, Demons, and Others*, 133).

Nagaraj is no visionary, no poet in a state of grace. He capitulates to circumstances. His escape from what he cannot control is to don the ochre robe of the *sanyasi* in his own home when he does not want to be drawn into the conflicts and calamities of his brother's and nephew's lives. The cosmic chaos and primeval fluidity about which Bari reads can be seen as an externalization of Nagaraj's feeling of helplessness in the sea of everyday life. Nagaraj, unfortunately, does not have the wherewithal or the literary resources to channel this all-encompassing ocean into a recognizable body of water. Instead, he is buffeted about on its waves like an ant in a nutshell. The answer to the thunderclap of everyday life is not to emulate Nagaraj and stuff one's ears with cotton wool in an ineffectual gesture to deaden the sound to a whisper (which with its sibilance is usually more distracting than the normal tones of speech). The answer is to hear in the thunderclap the roll of drums, the clash of cymbals, and the fanfare of trumpets; in other words, to give to amorphous noise the structure of composition.

Narayan is approximately eighty-seven years old. His first work was published in 1935. Since then he has written several works of fiction and nonfiction. One wonders if this latest novel is a well-established and renowned author's humorous as well as nostalgic reminiscence of harder times, of literary dreams, and the difficulties of turning fancies into realities.

Works Cited

Mukherjee, Arun P. "The Vocabulary of the 'Universal': Cultural Imperialism and Western Literary Criticism." *World Literature Written in English* 26, no. 2 (1986): 343–53.

Narayan, R. K. *Gods, Demons, and Others.* New York: Viking, 1964.

_____. *Talkative Man.* New York: Viking, 1986.

_____. *The World of Nagaraj.* New York: Viking, 1990.

Pandit, Manorama. "Detachment and Liberation in the Novels of R. K. Narayan. *Dissertation Abstracts International* 46, no.11 (May 1986): 3355A.

Srinath, C. N. "R. K. Narayan's Comic Vision: Possibilities and Limitations." *World Literature Today: A Literary Quarterly of the University of Oklahoma* 55, no.3 (summer 1981): 416–19.

The Dialectics of Opposing Forces in The World of Nagaraj

PUSHPA N. PAREKH

The central irony in R. K. Narayan's latest novel, *The World of Nagaraj* (1990) is played out in the dramatization of the various internal and external obstacles that obstruct Nagaraj's writing on the Sage Narada, who himself created obstacles through his mischief and gossip among the gods, the demons, as well as the humans. But the point to remember is, as Nagaraj explains to his friend, Jayaraj, "Ultimately, of course, such clashes and destruction proved beneficial in a cosmic perspective. Evil destroyed itself" (3). This theme of evil destroying itself has been explored in Narayan's earlier novels, more specifically in *The Man-Eater of Malgudi* (1961). As the printer's assistant, Sashtri points out, "Vasu, the taxidermist" who is also described as the "rakshasa" or demon, "creates within him, unknown to himself, a tiny seed of self-destruction, and goes up in thin air at a most unexpected moment. Otherwise what is to happen to humanity?" (250). Yet it is in *The World of Nagaraj* that the dialectics of opposing forces work at various plot, thematic, and structural levels, to envision the essential nature of the Malgudi world.

It is Nagaraj's constant confrontation with the obstacles to his writing, his inner conflicts and outer postures, his little successes and apparently gigantic failures that unfold the world of Nagaraj, which is the world of Malgudi—a world of inner dreams and outer realities. Julian Moynahan in "India of the Imagination. . . ," speaks of the "two-stranded comic plot" (8): Nagaraj's mission to write the book on Narada, and the disruption in the life of Nagaraj through the intervention of his nephew, Tim, and his brother, Gopu. These two plot strands unravel parallel concerns with at least two thematic and structural patterns of opposition: internal/external opposition and the active/passive opposition.

Nagaraj's mission in life is to write a book on the Sage Narada,

> the celestial sage who had a curse on his back that unless he spread a gossip a day his head would burst. The sage floated along with

ease from one world to another among the fourteen worlds above
and below this earth, carrying news and gossip, often causing
clashes between gods and demons, demons and demons, and gods
and gods and between creatures of the earth. (3)

The obstacles in the execution of this "grandiloquent plan," ironically
and almost superstitiously, make us aware that after all Nagaraj is planning to write about the sage who creates obstacles (unlike Ganesh who
helps remove or overcome obstacles). These obstacles take opposing
forms: internal and external. At several points they also represent the
blocks in human beings' confrontation with the inner and outer worlds.

Internal obstacles to Nagaraj's writing project constitute Nagaraj's
own life-style and nature—"Facilitated thus by a lack of arrangement,"
Nagaraj worked free at Coomar's Boeing Sari Centre, "without a feeling
of compulsion" (24). This arrangement suited Nagaraj perfectly: "He
loved this work, alternating red ink and black ink while entering figures"
(23). Further it allowed him to be "out of the house as far as possible,
otherwise he might have to arbitrate between his mother and Sita all
day" (24). He brings this "lack of arrangement" to his own writing project, as the author succinctly and ironically points out in the beginning of
the novel:

> Nagaraj fancied himself a man with a mission. If you asked, "What is
> your mission?" he would look away and pretend not to have heard
> your query. He was not quite clear in his mind about his mission,
> but always felt he must be up and doing. (1)

We have further evidence of Nagaraj's indecisive nature—a quality
which has its own appeal:

> He understood his wife's strategy. If she had come out to call him,
> he would have snapped back (he imagined), "Don't disturb me
> now." But Mother's intrusion was different. He stirred himself and
> said mildly, "I know when to bathe, Mother." He knew he sounded
> pompous, while he had only been watching and wool-gathering,
> which were important activities in his scheme of living. Watching
> and brooding had a subtle value which people never realized. Left to
> himself he was prepared to sit on the pyol the whole day, looking on
> the life and movement of Kabir Street. (6–7)

Nagaraj's easy-going nature and life-style allow numerous issues, experiences, reflections and reveries to assume central importance in his daily
activities. As a result, writing the book becomes often peripheral, side-
stepped by other activities and interests: the "laborious search for the
ochre robe and dhoti, acquired finally from a bearded sadhu at the Town

Hall on the lawn" (9); his meditation in the puja room, where "in his ochre robe he felt transformed. . . .It was a state of being dead for some moments each day" (12).

In addition to inner obstacles, there are outer or external obstacles. Nagaraj complains, "There are no authentic references to Narada anywhere and I feel handicapped" (19). Nagaraj's plan is to "write something which will have authority" (19). Ironically, Nagaraj in his personality as well as in his relationships to others, lacks this authority. Therefore, to achieve it in his writing seems all the more imperative. Narayan's good-humored understanding of his protagonist's simple motives invests the world of Nagaraj with psychological realism.

Secondly, Nagaraj's lack of knowledge of Sanskrit is a major obstacle in reading works on Narada himself. Kavu Pundit, the one source recommended by the old librarian at the Town Hall, proves useless as well. His response to Nagaraj's ambitious project is irritatingly ambiguous:

> The pundit said, "Even if you lived through ten births, you would not reach the end of his life story."
>
> "What should I do now?" Nagaraj asked, puzzled by his answer.
>
> "Go and sit on the river step and meditate and the answer will come . . . .You must observe austerity." (97–98)

Nagaraj's attempts at meditation are equally unsuccessful:

> Nagaraj realized when he tried meditation, whatever it meant, his thoughts wandered in all directions, and were in a jumble. Perhaps he should press his fingers to his nostrils, stop breathing and close his eyes. He attempted this course for one second and felt suffocated. (101)

Despite the Talkative Man's persuasion of the pundit to read and explain the Sanskrit volumes for a fee, the pundit only covers "various antiquated subjects," "airing his views on the state of affairs in general" (109).

Family problems constitute a recurring pattern of obstacles to Nagaraj's project. Nagaraj's preoccupation with Tim, his nephew, and his wanderings, threaten the execution of his own writing ambitions:

> At ten, Nagaraj was sitting on the pyol peering into the darkness of the crossroad from the market. The boy was still away. Rather a puzzle what he was doing with himself. He had got into the habit of borrowing neighbor Sambhu's scooter, imitating the Talkative Man. . . .

> Nagaraj speculated, looking at the stars, whether Tim would have
> fallen off the scooter somewhere. (57)

Nagaraj's attempts to hold Tim, even for a moment, to have a serious
discussion about his late home-comings, his smelling of alcohol, and his
dropping out of college, take up quite a bit of his energy, time, and concentration:

> Worry had been a luxury unknown to Nagaraj till now. Nowadays
> when he sat on the pyol he realized that his mind had lost its poise.
> His thoughts constantly revolved round the subject of Tim, with
> many questions unanswered, and he found it exhausting. (61)

Compounding his worries is, of course, Sita's constant egging him on to
talk to Tim, to be firm with him—almost, as it seems to Nagaraj, like
Lady Macbeth or even "like Narada: creating complications between two
parties (himself and Tim)" (67). It is, however, his ability to see the ludicrous even in apparently serious situations, to let his mind wander into
the sidelines, almost like a photographer's eye that can blur out what is
distracting and focus on the foreground or the background at will, that
Nagaraj retains his balance. Therein also lies his ability to accept life with
all its conflicting forces and pressures. Nagaraj's "plans for his magnum
opus on Narada" are often interrupted by Tim's quick appearances and
disappearances. Despite his firm resolve, Nagaraj hesitates to talk to
Tim, and in the meantime "the boy was gone. . .while Nagaraj kept gazing on it, not knowing what to do next, dreading lest Sita should come
before him again with her sinister looks and hissing commands" (67–68).

After Tim is married off to Saroja, fresh problems arise for Nagaraj. By
this time he has gathered enough material, through Bari who owns the
stationery shop at Kalighat Lane, to begin his writing on Narada. His several "ruminations and reminiscences" as well as the puzzling nature of
his notes from Bari's readings (in which "nowhere could he find a mention of Narada") constitute minor obstacles (129). It is Saroja's early
morning activities and harmonium practice that finally frustrate
Nagaraj's literary aspirations. His writing cannot progress beyond the
record of the great deluge. His attempts to plug his ears with cotton wool
(on his wife, Sita's advice) misfire as Sita snatches the package for light-
ing "God's lamp-wicks" (140). His resolution to tell Saroja "to shut up"
miserably fails as did his earlier attempts to talk to Tim. His slinking
away from Saroja's room as she is playing a new piece for him only leads
to further problems. Tim and Saroja leave their home to stay in an out-
house at Kismet. This incident results in Gopu's arrival and the search for
Tim who, when found, simply abandons them. They are left "sitting on

the stone bench," until Gopu follows Tim, telling Nagaraj, "Stay here, I will find out where he lives" (158).

The plot of continuous reversals in action mimes the picaresque tradition; only here the most significant action takes place in Nagaraj's mind, grappling with the futile attempts to please everybody and still fulfill his own dreams. Ironically, as Nagaraj is preparing to occupy the room in which Tim and Saroja lived, for his writing purposes, his wife suggests that he overcome his notion of writing on Narada: "It's only a notion which has somehow got nailed in your brain. Pluck out the nail. Nothing more; get rid of it" (180). While Nagaraj's heart is bleeding at the thought of eliminating Narada, "abandoning a personality who had occupied his thoughts all his working hours for years," the task is done by the sudden arrival of Tim and Saroja. They show up at Nagaraj's doorstep, laden with "two trunks, bedding rolls, a large-sized harmonium (which was known as a "leg harmonium" and which had a stand, the bellows to be operated by a foot pedal, leaving both hands free for the player to produce the maximum noise) and a folding chair" (182–83). Nagaraj, confused and apologetic, can't help the unvoiced aside to his wife, "If you had brought ten pounds of cotton wool to plug his ears, it would not have sufficed, considering the monster you have brought in" (183). Nagaraj's writing project has to be totally abandoned:

> "I wish the police had come and seized the harmonium," Nagaraj said. "I dread that tomorrow morning it will start blaring. I can have no hope of writing any more. You could as well take the notebooks back to the old room, where at least white ants may relish my notes on Narada. . . ." (185)

Thematically, in Nagaraj's life the obstacles to his writing serve a purpose. Ultimately, the family ties take precedence over individual preoccupations. The "logic and unambiguity" of Sita's words to Nagaraj ring true: "It's only a notion which has somehow got nailed in your brain" (180). In R. K. Narayan's Malgudi, the traditional values, even by the most incongruous means, affirm their lasting quality. For a while the protagonist may struggle to assert his individual personality on situations and events, but, in time, the traditional bonds and values, the age-old truths residing in the heart of the Hindu customs and traditions, will emerge stronger: "For Narayan, then, the very conditions of human growth are individual discrepancy and communal collaboration" (Walsh, 139). Meenakshi Mukherjee in *Realism and Reality: The Novel and Society in India* compares Narayan's literary world with that created by Anantha Murthy in *Samskara:*

> Almost all of Narayan's novels present a stable world temporarily
> threatened by disruption yet resilient enough to survive the crisis
> and return to normalcy. On the whole Malgudi has a positive life-
> affirming and abiding quality. Anantha Murthy on the other hand
> intends to depict a decadent structure which, once jolted out of its
> groove, cannot be reintegrated again. (168)

Nagaraj, with all his sarcastic asides and humorous quips, chooses the
wisdom of the conventional, the accepted, and the traditional. His acceptance of Tim, of course, aggravates his conflict with his own brother,
Gopu. However, Nagaraj undermines the brunt of that conflict by
assuming the meek "hangdog air" though smarting inwardly at "Gopu's
superciliousness" (54), or by outright flattery: "He said admiringly, 'You
should have been a detective. How much information you have managed to gather sitting in the village! Clever fellow!'" (87). While Nagaraj
accommodates his own pride in order to avoid further conflicts with his
brother, he does not totally abandon all self-assertion. It is while waiting
for Gopu to return from his mission of following Tim, that Nagaraj
makes some interesting discoveries about himself and his relationship to
his brother. The stench of the garbage heap that almost chokes Nagaraj,
like the stench of the Gobar gas plant which is his brother Gopu's main
life-source, symbolizes the drab reality from which Nagaraj often wishes
to escape. It is this stench that leads Nagaraj to reflect on two puzzling
forces that he has encountered in his own life: toward action and away
from action. His cogitated thoughts run in confusing circles:

> Not an inch of shade anywhere. . . .Horrible place, never suspected
> Malgudi could be so bad. Must talk to someone. Chakravarti, the
> Municipal Chairman, is lazy and indifferent; also I don't know him
> at all, and even if I came face to face with him I wouldn't be able to
> attack him so what is the use of complaining. But whatever may be
> the reason, it's his business to see that garbage doesn't develop into
> a hillock anywhere. But what can anyone do? Quite a lot of junglees
> have invaded the town, attracted by the promise of work on the
> new railway line to Mempi. Too much of a dream; they will not
> take it up in this generation, although ministers make speeches.
> (159)

The question of action and inaction is especially pertinent to Nagaraj's
relationship with Gopu. Nagaraj has always been timid and apprehensive in Gopu's presence. As a young boy he was "spurned" by Gopu,
who "ordered him about" (27). An analogy that their father draws
between the two brothers is significant: "You are like Lakshmana in
the Ramayana, who stood behind Rama, his elder brother, all the time

without a murmur or doubt" (27). Nagaraj's obsequiousness to his older brother is fostered as much by his very nature as by the traditional hierarchy of family members, the Hindu custom of joint-family living arrangements, as well as the archetypes embedded in Hindu myths. On Gopu's wife joining him at their family home, all that Gopu says to Nagaraj is "Boy, leave my room" and Nagaraj moves out with his books and the "dealwood box" (28).

The separation between the brothers comes as a result of their father's death and "the drawing up of a list of assets, properties, possessions and articles" left by their father, resulting in the "partition deed" being signed and registered (33–34). Nagaraj's attachment to Gopu's son, Tim, is broken by this separation. Later, Tim's sudden arrival at Nagaraj's home and his decision to live in the city triggers Gopu's angry accusation of Nagaraj: "You have spoilt him beyond repair: you are Narada, mischief-maker. If he doesn't want to see me, I don't want to see his face either" (44). This accusation, accepted meekly by Nagaraj, becomes, in his mind, a compliment as he dreams of writing about Narada: "Narada created strife, no doubt, by passing disturbing gossip from one quarter to another, but it always proved beneficial in the long run, in an eternal perspective" (44).

Nagaraj, even at this stage, resolves to put into action, through his writing on Narada, the self-assertiveness that he lacks in his brother's presence: "Must write about him from this angle. Must write in English, of course, so that the book is widely read and people understand the concept of Narada" (44). In chronicling the life of Narada, perhaps Nagaraj wishes to chronicle his life, especially to "show" his brother: "'Wait till I write my book.' He addressed his brother mentally, sending his thoughts to the bus stand" (45). It is in describing Narada that Nagaraj describes his own inner desire to be free like Narada, free from the constraints of his brother's power:

> All that mattered was that he was a unique personality, the god of music. He was ever-cheerful and active, always with a song on his lips, and moved with ease among gods and demons. Blessed with extreme mobility, he traversed at a thought the skies and space, through galaxies and the Milky Way, and was welcome in all the fourteen worlds above and below this world. Gods and demons alike were friendly to him, although he was a bearer of gossip from one world to another and created strife. (44–45)

Nagaraj is in many ways the human parallel to the celestial Narada. This parallelism, in Narayan's comedic perspective, is rife with ironic reversals. Nagaraj prides himself on possessing a fairly good ear for music. That is all the more reason Saroja's modern movie songs and music jar his senses. Further, as Narada "was ever-cheerful and active," so Nagaraj's sense of humor is his own saving grace. Now comes the question, in what senses is Nagaraj active or inactive? In terms of physical mobility, Nagaraj is quite active. He rises early and, as stated in the opening part of the book, engages himself in moving from one friend (Jayaraj) to another (Coomar), from acquaintances (Dr. Velu, Bari, Verma of the Boardless, and the Talkative Man), to figures who assume demonic or threatening stature (Gopu and Professor Jesudoss). He can move through difficult situations (steering conversations among his wife, his mother, and himself) which might threaten domestic harmony. Nagaraj is, unlike Narada, quite unaware of the means and methods of gathering news (such as Tim's whereabouts). Gopu has his spies, and Nagaraj disparagingly considers himself superior to these gossip-mongers:

> I was not considered fit for their company. Phew! What a notion! I have survived and they have vanished into thin air. Probably his gang is still here, but fat and old and unrecognizable, and secretly in touch with Gopu in the village spying on me and Tim all the time . . . .(161)

It is in this recognition of his own nature as against Gopu's that Nagaraj "acts." Unlike the Western concept of "action" as man's mark of positive control on life as realized through some acknowledgement of self-will, the Eastern concept of true human action involves the recognition of life's inner action, a spiritual awakening achieved through overcoming the assertions of the self-will. Nagaraj, unlike Raju of *The Guide*, never reaches the spiritual levels of awareness. However, he operates out of an inner moral candor and sincerity which elevates him above Gopu. His introspections, dramatized most effectively in the scene where he is waiting for Gopu to return from following Tim, are morally significant:

> How long should I wait here? He has condemned me to live in this stench and I am powerless to move. I think he casts a spell on an idiot—must have practiced it at his gobar gas farm. Villagers would be up to anything. Otherwise why can't I use my head and rise and walk off? I fear him. If he comes back and doesn't find me, he'll blow up in anger. . . .Let him blow up when he comes back. If he can't find his way home, let him stay where he pleases—will serve him right. . . ."Am I my brother's keeper?" asked Cain, and Gopu is Cain, he has almost killed me. . . . (162)

At this point, it is interesting to notice that besides the Biblical allusion, there is also a version of the Hindu myth of creation from *Vayu Purana* which supports Nagaraj's decision. Significantly, Narada plays an important role in this version:

> The sons of Daksa (son of Brahma, who was instructed by Brahma himself to create progeny), the Haryasvas, who had great heroic powers, assembled, for they wished to create progeny. But Narada said to them, "How childish you are. You do not know the surface of the earth, how far it extends, how high or low; then how will you create progeny. . . .What is the measure of the earth? What is to be created? Without understanding this, how will you create? You would create too little or too much, and this would be a fault." When they heard his words they set out in all directions, following the winds, and they disappeared; even today they have not returned, but are wandering with the winds. Thus the great sages wander on the path of the wind.
>
> When his sons had been destroyed, Daksa. . .begat another thousand sons. . . .They, the Sabalasvas, wishing to increase progeny, were again addressed by Narada as he had spoken before. Heeding his words. . .they too went forth on that path in all directions, and even today they have not returned, like people who have been shipwrecked at sea. From that time forth, a brother who delights in following his brother and sets forth is destroyed; and this should not be done by a wise man. (O'Flaherty, trans. 46–48)

After his mental liberation from his brother, Nagaraj can reminisce, "Ha! Ha! Wonderful brothers. A sister between us would have made some difference. She would have acted as a buffer" (182). In Western terms, this break from his passivity would be seen as a step toward Nagaraj's assertion of self. But not so in Eastern Hindu terms. R. K. Narayan, through his own gentle ironic humor and insight, reveals the nature of the ineluctable forces that balance all odds, all conflicts, all incongruities of life. In his earlier novels, Narayan builds on this Hindu belief. In *Mr. Sampath*, Srinivas observes the futility of action in a cosmic perspective. In *The World of Nagaraj* too, Nagaraj's assertiveness is premature, inconsequential, and, in the long run, as much an aside as have been his several unvoiced repartees to his brother. It collapses totally in the final scene where he apologetically helps Tim and Saroja move into the house, in the face of the fact that this passivity on his part spells death to his writing project.

The fractious nature of human relationships, especially evidenced in family bonds, is no new theme in Narayan's novels. It appears again and again, at first as an underlying motif of sibling rivalry in *Swami and Friends* (between Swami and his new brother). In *The Financial Expert*, the

214 Pushpa N. Parekh

animosity between the brothers reaches such a habitual pattern that any changes are viewed suspiciously by Margayya:

> Through all his grief a ridiculous question (addressed to his brother) kept coming to his mind: "Are we friends now—no longer enemies? What about our feud?" A part of his mind kept wondering how they could live as friends, but the numerous problems connected with this seemed insoluble. (178)

In *The World of Nagaraj*, the study of real and unreal tensions and conflicts between the two brothers provides a riveting comedy, at one level. Julian Moynahan points out another level at which the fraternal conflicts can be viewed: "Their differences are not only those of siblings but also entail the immemorial tension of rustic and townsman, muscleman and intellectual, the doer and the dreamer" (8). Beyond the symbolic level, the fraternal conflicts reflect the psychological realism of Nagaraj's world, the Malgudi world, by extension the Hindu world, and by further extension, the universe as perceived by a non-Western frame of reference. The writer Jaidev, in his article, "India's Comic Master: Exploring Narayan's Art of the Ludicrous," comments:

> Nearly every novel by Narayan is structured around a hero who, partly because of his obsession with self, becomes increasingly alienated from his community. Thus starts a process which brings him anxiety, isolation, and sometimes degradation. The process comes to a comic, consoling end with the hero's tame submission to the will of the community. (62)

This community may appear at times as absurd and dominant; its members at times may seem ridiculously fraught with theatricality, yet Nagaraj realizes, as do all Narayan's heroes, that it is "something real and graceful as well. The individual's dreams and aspirations, in contrast, are bubbles, flimsy and futile" (Jaidev, 62). It is through this kind of comprehension that Nagaraj, like other Narayan heroes, achieves a morally viable synthesis of opposing forces. Even his final words in the novel, however disenchanted, ring with the life-affirming values of his world: "You could as well take the notebooks back to the old room, where at least white ants may relish my notes on Narada. . ." (185). All obstructions, whether internal or external, as well as all human endeavors, active or passive, that Nagaraj has undertaken to overcome those obstructions, find resolution in the final synthesis. This final synthesis is particularly relevant to Narayan as a writer; it affirms for him all the roles he plays: that of doer, thinker, and dreamer. It also assigns meaning to the various kinds of projects he might have undertaken, successful as well as unsuccessful. Human action, even a writer's act of writing, is often parenthetically relevant. Whether he acts or not, life still persists and will do so.

Works Cited

Jaidev. "India's Comic Master: Exploring Narayan's Art of the Ludicrous." *World Press Review* 28 (Nov. 1981): 62.

Moynahan, Julian. "India of the Imagination. . . ." *New York Times Book Review,* 15 July 1990, 8.

Mukherjee, Meenakshi. *Realism and Reality: The Novel and Society in India.* New Delhi: Oxford University Press, 1985.

_____. *The Twice-Born Fiction: Themes and Techniques of the Indian Novel in English.* New Delhi: Heinemann, 1971.

Narayan, R. K. *The Financial Expert.* 1953. New York: Time Incorporated, 1966.

_____. *The Man-Eater of Malgudi.* New York: Viking, 1990.

_____. "Vayu Purana." Trans. Wendy Doniger O'Flaherty. *Hindu Myths: A Sourcebook Translated from the Sanskrit.* New York: Penguin, 1975.

Walsh, William. "Sweet Mangoes and Malt Vinegar: The Novels of R. K. Narayan." *Indo-English Literature.* Ed. K. K. Sharma. New York: Humanities Press, 1982.

Chronology of Some Significant Events in the Life of R. K. Narayan

1906–1926   Born in Madras (10 October 1906). Attends Lutheran Mission School, CRC High School, and Christian College High School, Madras. Family moves to Mysore where Narayan's father serves as Headmaster at Maharajah's College High School, allowing his son special library privileges; young Narayan reads voraciously, mostly in the English classics and literary magazines.

1926   Enters Maharajah's College, Mysore.

1930   Graduates Maharajah's College. Enters briefly into teaching profession, then begins to strictly pursue vocation as novelist while living with his parents and extended family.

1933   Marries (Rajam). Works as reporter with *The Justice*, a Madras paper, reporting from Mysore. This work brings Narayan into "close contact with a variety of men and their activities" (*My Days*, 111).

1935   *Swami and Friends* published; upon its acceptance, Narayan stops work with *The Justice*.

1937   *The Bachelor of Arts* published. Narayan's father dies, leaving the author responsible for rent payment—which he meets by providing articles for various magazines. Somerset Maugham visits Mysore. Narayan's friend urges Maugham to read Narayan's work.

1938   Daughter (Hema) born. *The Dark Room* published. Narayan receives government stipend to write a travel book on Karnataka State. The experience provides him with a wealth of material and images for later works. Publishes *Mysore*.

1939	Begins to write stories and sketches for *The Hindu*, a Madras newspaper (over time, Narayan will provide hundreds of pieces for *The Hindu*). Narayan's wife dies of typhoid in June (the experience of her sickness and death represented autobiographically in *The English Teacher*).
1941	Narayan inaugurates his own publication, *Indian Thought*.
1948	Narayan begins to build his home on the outskirts of Mysore. Takes five years to complete and, once ready, serves at first as the author's retreat for writing while his extended family continues to live in the city.
1949	*Mr. Sampath* published.
1953	*The Financial Expert* published.
1955	*Waiting for the Mahatma* published.
1956	*Lawley Road and Other Stories* published. Receives a grant from the Rockefeller Foundation and travels to the United States. Begins to write *The Guide*. *Next Sunday* published.
1958	*The Guide* published. Narayan receives the National Prize of the Indian Literary Academy.
1960	*My Dateless Diary* published.
1961	*The Man-Eater of Malgudi* published.
1964	Film version of *The Guide* begun, with Narayan's reluctant approval. Narayan receives the Padma Bhushan award.
1965	Receives the National Association of Independent Schools award.
1967	*The Vendor of Sweets* published.
1968	Dramatic adaptation of *The Guide* presented on Broadway.
1970	*A Horse and Two Goats* published.
1972	Narayan's shortened adaptation of the *Ramayana* published.
1974	*Reluctant Guru* and *My Days: A Memoir* published.
1975	Receives English-Speaking Union Book Award for *My Days*.
1976	*The Painter of Signs* published.

1978	Narayan's abbreviated adaptation of the *Mahabharata* published.
1983	*A Tiger for Malgudi* published.
1985	*Under the Banyan Tree* published.
1987	*Talkative Man* published.
1988	*A Writer's Nightmare* published.
1990	*The World of Nagaraj* published.

R. K. Narayan:
A Select Bibliography of His Works

Narayan, R. K. *An Astrologer's Day and Other Stories*. London: Eyre & Spottiswoode, 1947.

_____. *The Bachelor of Arts*. 1937. "Introduction," Graham Greene, Chicago: University of Chicago Press, 1980.

_____. *Cyclone and Other Stories*. Mysore, India: Indian Thought Publications, 1944.

_____. *The Dark Room*. 1938. Chicago: University of Chicago Press, 1981.

_____. *Dodu and Other Stories*. Mysore, India: Indian Thought Publications, 1943.

_____. *The Emerald Route*. Bangalore: Director of Information and Publicity, Government of Karnataka, 1977.

_____. *The English Teacher*. 1945. Chicago: University of Chicago Press, 1978.

_____. *The Financial Expert*. 1953. Chicago: University of Chicago Press, 1981.

_____. *Gods, Demons, and Others*. New York: Viking Press, 1964.

_____. *The Guide*. 1958. New York: Penguin Books, 1980.

_____. *A Horse and Two Goats*. New York: Viking Press, 1970.

_____. *Lawley Road and Other Stories*. 1956. Delhi: Hind Pocket Books, 1972.

_____. *The Mahabharata*. New York: Viking Press, 1978.

_____. *Malgudi Days*. 1941. New York: Viking Press, 1982.

_____. *The Man-Eater of Malgudi*. New York: Viking Press, 1961.

_____. *Mr. Sampath: The Printer of Malgudi*. Chicago: University of Chicago Press, 1949.

_____. *My Dateless Diary: An American Journey*. New York: Penguin Books, 1960.

_____. *My Days*. New York: Viking Press, 1974.

_____. *Next Sunday*. 1956. Delhi: Hind Pocket Books, 1972.

_____. *The Painter of Signs*. New York: Viking Press, 1976.

_____. *The Ramayana: A Shortened Modern Prose Version of the Indian Epic.* 1972. New York: Penguin Books, 1977.

_____. *Reluctant Guru.* Delhi: Hind Pocket Books, 1974.

_____. *A Story-Teller's World.* Introduction, Syd Harrex. New York: Penguin Books, 1989.

_____. *Swami and Friends.* 1935. Chicago: University of Chicago Press, 1980.

_____. *Talkative Man.* New York: Viking Press, 1987.

_____. *A Tiger for Malgudi.* New York: Viking Press, 1983.

_____. *Under the Banyan Tree and Other Stories.* New York, Viking Press, 1985.

_____. *The Vendor of Sweets.* New York: Viking Press, 1967.

_____. *Waiting for the Mahatma.* East Lansing: Michigan State University Press, 1955.

_____. *The World of Nagaraj.* New York: Viking Press, 1990.

_____. *A Writer's Nightmare.* New York: Penguin Books, 1988.

Critical Studies of R.K. Narayan's Literary Contributions: A Select Bibliography

Afzal-Khan, Fawzia, "Genre and Ideology in the Novels of Four Contemporary Indo-Anglian Novelists: R. K. Narayan, Anita Desai,
Kamala Markandaya and Salman Rushdie." *Dissertation Abstracts International* 47, no. 4 (1986): 1328A.

Agnihotri, H. L. "Gandhi and R. K. Narayan." *The Literary Endeavor: A
Quarterly Journal Devoted to English Studies* 3, no. 3–4 (1982): 52–60.

Ahluwalia, Harsharan S. "Narayan's Sense of Audience." *Review of International English Literature* 15, no. 1 (1984): 59–65.

Albertazzi, Silvia. "The Story-Teller and the Talkative Man: Some Conventions of Oral Narrative in R. K. Narayan's Short Stories." *Commonwealth Essays and Studies* 9, no. 2 (1987): 59–64.

Amur, G. S., et al. "The River, The Lotus Pond and the Ruined Temple:
An Essay on Symbolism in R. K. Narayan's Novels." *Indian Readings in
Commonwealth Literature.* New York: Sterling, 1985: 94–105.

Asnani, Shyam M. "The Use of Myth in R. K. Narayan's Novels." *The
Literary Endeavor: A Quarterly Journal Devoted to English Studies* 3, nos.
3–4 (1982): 19–31.

———. "The Central Motif in Narayan's *A Tiger for Malgudi*: A
Mythopoeic Interpretation." *The New Indian Novel in English: A Study
of the 1980s.* Ed. Viney Kirpal. New Delhi: Allied Publishers Ltd.,
1990: 3–10.

———. "The Socio-Political Scene of the 1930s: Its Impact on the Indo-
English Novel." *Commonwealth Quarterly* 6, no. 21 (1981): 14–23.

Atkinson, David W. "Tradition and Transformation in R. K. Narayan's *A
Tiger for Malgudi*." *International Fiction Review* 14, no.1 (1987): 8–14.

Austin, Jacqueline. "Narayan's Hope." *The Village Voice* 30, no. 45 (5
November 1985): 55.

Badal, R. K. *R. K. Narayan: A Study.* India: Prakash Book Depot, 1976.

Beatty, Jack. "Idyll of Loyalty." *The New Republic* 186, no. 3507 (1982):
45–46.

Bhatnagar, O. P. "Love, Non-Violence and Freedom in *Waiting for the Mahatma.*" *The Literary Endeavor: A Quarterly Journal Devoted to English Studies* 3, no. 3–4 (1982): 61–69.

_____. "Playing the Role in *The Guide* and *The Inner Door.*" *Commonwealth Quarterly* 4, no.12 (1979): 71–79.

Bhushan, Kul. "Use of Myth in R. K. Narayan's *The Man-Eater of Malgudi.*" *Magazine of World Writing* 9–10 (1983 Summer-Winter): 81–88.

Biswal, Jayant K. *A Critical Study of the Novels of R. K. Narayan: the Malgudi Comedy.* New Delhi: Nirmal Publishers & Distributors, 1987.

_____. "Commitment to Life: A Study of R. K. Narayan's Major Novels." *Journal of Indian Renaissance* 45, no. 4 (1977): 57–63.

Campbell, Felicia. "Two Gurus—Vonnegut's Bokonon and Narayan's Raju: Teachers Outside the Classroom." *West Virginia University Philological Papers* 36 (1990): 77–81.

Chauhan, P. S. "The Commonwealth of the Imagination: Narayan and Naipaul." *Language and Literature in Multicultural Contexts.* Suva, Fiji: University of South Pacific, 1983: 89–96.

Chellappan, K. "The Apocalypse of the Ordinary: The Comic Myths of R. K. Narayan." *The Literary Endeavor: A Quarterly Journal Devoted to English Studies* 3, nos. 3–4 (1982): 32–38.

Coppola, Carlo. Review of *A Tiger of Malgudi. World Literature Today* 58, no. 2 (1984): 325.

Cronin, Richard. "Quiet Quiet India: The Despair of R. K. Narayan." *Encounter* 64, no. 3 (1985): 52–59.

Dale, James. "Wordsworth and Narayan: Irony in *The English Teacher.*" *ACLALS Bulletin* 4, n no. 5 (1977): 58–65.

Dasenbrock, Red Way. "Intelligibility and Meaningfulness in Multicultural Literature in English." *PMLA.* 102, no.1 (1987): 10–19.

David, P. C. and S. Z. H. Abidi. "Levels of Irony in the Short Stories of R. K. Narayan." *The Literary Endeavor: A Quarterly Journal Devoted to English Studies* 3, no. 3–4 (1982): 39–44.

Desai, Anita. "Malgudi." *London Review of Books* 8, no. 21 (4 December 1986): 23–24.

_____. "R. K. Narayan and the Grand Malgudi Circus." *The Washington Post* "Book World" 4 September 1983, 3, 9.

Fernando, Nihal and Nightingale, Peggy. "Between Cultures: Narayan's Malgudi in *Swami and Friends* and *The Bachelor of Arts.*" *A Sense of Place in the New Literatures in English.* St. Lucia: University of Queensland Press, 1986: 75–85.

Garebian, Keith. "Narayan's Compromise in Comedy." *Literary Half-Yearly* 17, no. 1 (1976): 77–92.

_____. "*The Financial Expert*: Kubera's Myth in a Parable of Life and Death." *International Fiction Review* 3 (1976) 126–32.

_____. "The Spirit of Place in R. K. Narayan." *World Literature Written in English* 14 (1975): 291–99.

Gooneratne, Yasmine. "Traditional Elements in the Fiction of Kamala Markandaya, R. K. Narayan and Ruth Prawer Jhabvala." *World Literature Written in English* 15 (1976): 121–34.

Goyal, Bhagwat S. "From Picaro to Pilgrim: A Perspective on R. K. Narayan's *The Guide*." *Indo-English Literature: A Collection of Critical Essays*. Ghaziabad: Vimal Prakashan, 1977: 141–56.

_____. *R. K. Narayan: A Critical Spectrum*. India: Shalabh Book House, 1982.

Greene, Graham. Introduction to *The Bachelor of Arts*. London: Heinemann, 1978.

Hardin, Nancy Shields. "Mysore/Malgudi: R. K. Narayan's World of South India." *The Missouri Review* 6, no. 3 (1983): 125–38.

Harrex, S. C. *Fire and the Offering: The English Language Novel of India 1935–1970*. Calcutta: Writers Workshop, 1978.

_____. "R. K. Narayan: Some Miscellaneous Writings." *The Journal of Commonwealth Literature* 13, no. 1 (1978): 64–76.

_____. "Mode: Comedy; Type: Rakshasa; Author: R. K. Narayan." *The Commonwealth Review* 2, no.1–2 (1990–1991): 134–43.

Holmstrom, Lakshmi. *The Novels of R. K. Narayan*. Calcutta: Writers Workshop, 1973.

Jayantha, R. A. "*The Man-Eater of Malgudi*: Some Aspects of Its Narrative Strategy." *The Literary Endeavor: A Quarterly Journal Devoted to English Studies* 3, no. 3–4 (1982): 91–101.

Jeurkar, R. K.; Amur, G. S.; Prasad, V. R. N.; Nemade, B. V.; Nihalani, N. H. "Narrative Techniques in the Short Stories of R. K. Narayan." *Indian Readings in Commonwealth Literature*. New York: Sterling, 1985: 106–16.

Jussawala, Feroza. "When 'Sweet Mangoes' Turn to 'Malt Vinegar.'" *International Literature in English: Essays On the Major Writers*. Ed. Robert L. Ross. New York: Garland, 1991: 89–98.

Kirpal, Viney. "Moksha for Raju: The Archetypal Four-Stage Journey." *World Literature Written in English* 28, no. 2 (1988): 356–63.

_____. "An Analysis of Narayan's Technique." *Ariel: A Review of International English Literature* 14, no. 4 (1983): 16–19.

_____. "The Theme of 'Growing Up' in *The Bachelor of Arts*: Chandran's Transition from Adolescence to Adulthood." *Commonwealth Quarterly* 2, no. 6 (1978): 50–65.

Knapp, Bettina L. "Narayan's *The Man-Eater of Malgudi*: The Printing Press and a Secret Meditative Language." *Journal of Evolutionary Psychology* 10, nos. 3–4 (1989): 234–41.

Langran, Phillip. "R. K. Narayan and V. S. Naipaul: A Comparative Study of Some Hindu Aspects of Their Work." *Dissertation Abstracts International* 49, no. 11 (1989): 3356A.

Larson, Charles R. "A Note on R. K. Narayan." *Literature English Commonwealth* 50 (1976): 352–53.

Mahood, M. M. *The Colonial Encounter: A Reading of Six Novels.* London: Collings, 1977.

_____. "The Marriage of Krishna: Narayan's *The Man-Eater of Malgudi.*" *The Colonial Encounter: A Reading of Six Novels.* London: Collings, 1977: 92–114.

Mathur, O. P. "*The Guide*: A Study in Cultural Ambivalence." *The Literary Endeavor: A Quarterly Journal Devoted to English Studies* 3, no. 3–4 (1982): 70–79.

_____. "Two Modern Versions of the Sita Myth: Narayan and Anand." *The Journal of Commonwealth Literature* 21, no. 1 (1986): 16–25.

Moore, Susan. "Comic Novels about India: Neglected Masters, and Others." *Quadrant* 29, no. 9 (1985): 76–79.

Murti, K. V. S. "Bacchus and Buddha: Salman Rushdie and R. K. Narayan. *The Commonwealth Review* 1, no. 2 (1990): 157–68.

Naik, M. K. *The Ironic Vision: A Study of the Fiction of R. K. Narayan.* New Delhi: Sterling Publishers, 1983.

_____. "Irony as Stance and as Vision: A Comparative Study of V. S. Naipaul's *The Mystic Masseur* and R. K. Narayan's *The Guide.*" *Journal of Indian Writing in English* 6, no. 1 (1978): 1–13.

_____. Malgudi Minor: The Short Stories of R. K. Narayan." *The Laurel Bough: Essays Presented in Honour of Professor M. V. Rama Sarma.* Bombay: Blackie & Son, 1983: 193–202.

_____. "R. K. Narayan and 'the Spirit of Place'" *The Literary Endeavor: A Quarterly Devoted to English Studies* 3, nos. 3–4 (1982): 7–18.

_____. "The Signs Are All There." *World Literature Written in English* 16 (1977): 110–14.

_____. "Theme and Form in R. K. Narayan's The Man-Eater of Malgudi." *Journal of Commonwealth Literature* 10, no. 3 (1976): 65–72.

Naipaul, V. S. *India: A Wounded Civilization.* New York: Vintage Books, 1977.

Narasimhaiah, C. D., ed. *Fiction and the Reading Public in India.* Mysore, India: University of Mysore, 1967.

Narasimhaiah, C. D. "Literature in the Global Village: An Inquiry into Problems of Response." *Asian and Western Writers in Dialogue: New Cultural Identities.* London: Macmillan, 1982: 79–98.

Nasimi, Reza Ahmad. *The Language of Mulk Raj Anand, Raja Rao, and R. K. Narayan*. Delhi: Capital Publishing House, 1989.

Olinder, Britta. "Aspects of R. K. Narayan's Narrative Technique." *In Actes du Congres d'Amiens*. Paris: Didier, 1987: 463–72.

_____. "R. K. Narayan's Short Stories: Some Introductory Remarks." *Commonwealth Essays and Studies* 8, no. 1 (1985): 24–29.

_____. "Reality and Myth in R. K. Narayan's Novels." *The Literary Criterion* 20.2 (1985): 8–22.

_____. "Reality and Myth in R. K. Narayan's Novels." *Language and Literature in Multicultural Contexts*. Suva, Fiji: University of South Pacific, 1983: 286–96.

_____. "The World of Malgudi: Indian Society in the Work of R. K. Narayan." *Papers on Language and Literature: Presented to Alvar Ellegard and Erik Frykman*. Goteborg: ACTA University Gothoburgensis, 1985: 303–13.

_____. "Irony in R. K. Narayan's Short Stories." *Proceedings of the Nice Conference of the European Association for Commonwealth Literature and Language Studies*. Nice: Fac. des Lettres & Sciences Humaines de Nice, 1989: 183–87.

Pachegaonkar, Krishna, et al. "A Note on R. K. Narayan's *My Days*." *Indian Readings in Commonwealth Literature*. New York: Sterling, 1985: 181–86.

Pandeya, Shiva M. and Tej Nath Dhar. "R. K. Narayan's *Waiting for the Mahatma*: A Study in Structure and Meaning." *Journal of English 7* (1980): 52–91.

Pandit, Manorma. "Detachment and Liberation in the Novels of R. K. Narayan. *Dissertation Abstracts International* 46, no. 22 (1986): 3355A.

Perrin, Noel. "Conversions to Nonviolence." *The New York Times Book Review* 4 September 1983, 4.

Philip, David Scott. *Perceiving India Through the Works of Nirad C. Chauduri, R. K. Narayan, and Ved Mehta*. New Delhi: Sterling Publishers, 1986.

Pontes, Hilda and Nissim, Ezekiel. *R. K. Narayan*. Atlantic Highlands, New Jersey: Humanities, 1983.

Pousse, Michel. "Grateful to Life and Death." *Commonwealth Essays and Studies* 10, no. 2 (1988): 107–17.

_____. "The West in R. K. Narayan's Novels." *Commonwealth Essays and Studies* 9, no. 2 (1987): 99–108.

_____. "R. K. Narayan as Gandhian Novelist." *The Literary Criterion* 25, no. 4 (1990): 77–90.

Raichura, Suresh. "R. K. Narayan: *The Guide*." *Major Indian Novels: An Evaluation*. Atlantic Highlands, New Jersey: Humanities, 1986: 104–34.

Raizada, Harish. *R. K. Narayan: A Critical Study of His Works.* New Delhi: Young Asia Publications, 1969.

Rama, Atma. *Perspectives on R. K. Narayan.* India: Vimal Prakashan, 1981.

Ramamurti, K. S. "The Title of R. K. Narayan's *The English Teacher.*" *The Literary Endeavor: A Quarterly Journal Devoted to English Studies* 3, nos. 3–4 (1982): 45–51.

Rani, K. Nirupa. "Autobiographical Element in R. K. Narayan's Early Novels." *Journal of Indian Renaissance* 45, no. 3 (1976): 44–48.

Rao, A. V. Krishna. "Identity and Environment: Narayan's *The Guide* and Naipaul's *A House for Mr. Biswas.*" *Newsletter of the South Pacific Association for Commonwealth Literature and Language Studies* 24 (1987): 165–77.

Rao, R. Raj. "God-Consciousness in *The Guide* and *Siddhartha.*" *The Literary Endeavor: A Quarterly Journal Devoted to English Studies* 3, nos. 3–4 (1982): 87–91.

Reddy, K. Venkata. "Point of View, Time and Language in R. K. Narayan's *The Guide. The Literary Endeavor: A Quarterly Journal Devoted to English Studies.* 3, nos. 3–4 (1982): 80–86.

Rothfork, John. "Hindu Mysticism in the Twentieth Century: R. K. Narayan's *The Guide.*" *Philological Quarterly* 62, no. 1 (1983): 31–43.

Sah, Prajapati P. "R. K. Narayan's 'Gateman's Gift': The Central Theme." *The Literary Criterion* 15, no. 1 (1980): 37–48.

Sales-Pontes, A. Hilda. *R. K. Narayan.* New Delhi: Concept, 1983.

Sant, Arvindra. "From Reluctant Guru to Popular Hero: The Cinematic Commercialization of R. K. Narayan's *The Guide.*" *Transformations: From Literature to Film.* Kent State University, 1987: 104–8.

Shack, Neville. "A Vocation for Enchantment." *The Times Literary Supplement* 4307 (18 October 1985): 1168.

Sharrad, Paul. "Tradition and Tragedy: Anita Desai and R. K. Narayan." *The Commonwealth Review* 2, nos. 1–2 (1990–1991): 181–82.

Singh, Balbir. "The Theme of Art and Immortality in R. K. Narayan's *The Guide.*" *The Literary Criterion* 25, no. 2 (1990): 36–46.

Singh, Ram Sewak. *R. K. Narayan: The Guide; Some Aspects.* Delhi, Doaba House, 1971.

Singh, Satyanarain. "A Note on the World View of R. K. Narayan." *Indian Literature* 24, no. 1 (1981): 104–9.

Sinha, U. P. *Patterns of Myth and Reality; A Study in R. K. Narayan's Novels.* Delhi: Sandarbh Publishers, 1988.

Srinath, C. N. "R. K. Narayan's Comic Vision: Possibilities and Limitations. *World Literature Today: A Literary Quarterly of the University of Oklahoma* 55, no. 3 (1981): 416–19.

Strandgaard, Henrik. "The Novels of R. K. Narayan." *Angles on the English Speaking World.* 1 (1986): 38–50.

Sundaram, P. S. "Malgudi: The World of R. K. Narayan." *Indian P.E.N.* 43, i–ii: 1–10; iii–iv: 1–8.1977

_____. *R. K. Narayan.* New Delhi: Arnold-Heinemann India, 1973.

_____. *R. K. Narayan as a Novelist.* Delhi: D. K. Publishers Distributors, 1988.

Sunitha, K. T. "The Theme of Childhood In *The Castle of My Skin* and *Swami and Friends.*" *World Literature Written in English* 27, no. 2 (1987): 291–96.

Towers, Robert. "The Old Country." *The New York Review of Books* 29, no. 5 (1 April 1982): 21–22.

Trivedi, H. K. and N. C. Soni. "Mysore: R. K. Narayan's Little-Known Idyll." *Banasthali Patrika* 20 (1976): 37–44.

Updike, John. "Alive and Free from Employment." *The New Yorker* 50, no. 28 (1974): 80–82.

_____. "India Going On." *The New Yorker* 58, no. 24 (2 August 1982): 84–86.

Vanden Driesen, Cynthia. "The Achievement of R. K. Narayan." *East & West* 21, nos. 1–4 (1977): 51–64.

_____. "From Rogue to Redeemer: R. K. Narayan's *The Guide.*" *International Fiction Review* 6 (1979): 166–70.

_____. *The Novels of R. K. Narayan.* Nedlands, Australia: Centre for South and Southeast Asian Studies, University of Western Australia, 1986.

_____. "R. K. Narayan's Neglected Novel: *Waiting for the Mahatma.*" *World Literature Written in English* 26, no. 2 (1986): 362–69.

Varma, R. M. *Some Aspects of Indo-English Fiction.* New Delhi: Jainsons Publications, 1985.

Walker, Steven F. "Literal Truth and Soul-Making Fiction in R. K. Narayan's Noel *The English Teacher:* Spiritualist Fantasy versus Jungian Psychology?" *Weber Studies: An Interdisciplinary Humanities Journal* 6, no. 2 (1989): 43–52.

Walsh, William. "The Intricate Alliance: The Novels of R. K. Narayan." *A Review of English Literature* 2, no.4 (1961): 91–99.

_____. *R. K. Narayan.* England: Longman for the British Council, 1971.

_____. *R. K. Narayan: A Critical Appreciation.* Chicago: University of Chicago Press, 1982.

_____. "R. K. Narayan: The Unobtrusive Novelist." *Review of National Literatures* 10 (1979): 59–69.

Weir, Ann Lowry and Braj Kachru B. "Style Range in New English Literature." *The Other Tongue: English Across Cultures.* Urbana: University of Illinois Press, 1982: 307–22.

Westbrook, Perry D. "The Short Stories of R. K. Narayan." *Journal of Commonwealth Literature* 5 (1968): 41–51.

Woodcock, George. Two Great Commonwealth Novelists: R. K. Narayan and V. S. Naipaul." *Sewanee Review* 87 (Winter 1979): 1–28.
_____. "The Maker of Malgudi: Notes on R. K. Narayan." *Tamarack Review* 73 (1978): 82–95.

Index

A

ablutions, 19, 21, 22, 159, 174, 179
acceptance, 2, 5, 6, 43, 63, 76, 156,
    158, 210
affirmation, 6, 103, 134, 155, 164
aggression, 134, 142, 143, 145-48,
    150, 151, 152, 156, 158
ahimsa, 70
alienation, 64, 75, 137, 152, 162, 184
Alphonse, 111
altruism, 67, 142
ambiguity, 6, 83, 113
ambition, 167
America, 176, 181, 183
Anand, Mulk Raj, 11, 53, 73, 76, 79,
    86, 168, 169, 183
Ananthamurthy, U.R., 52
Anglo-Indian, 23
anima, 158
Annamalai, 51
anti-British, 32
anti-eroticism, 164
anti-Muslim, 164
anti-patriotic, 26-27
appetite, 6, 101, 104-5, 106, 109, 110,
    111, 112
archetype, 45, 46n.7, 59, 211
art, 3, 7, 15, 22, 42-45, 59, 60-63, 65,
    74, 79, 85, 89, 94-95, 98, 104, 132,
    144, 167, 179-80, 197, 214, 215
ascetic, 73, 113, 164, 165-68, 169, 176
asceticism, 108, 112, 128, 167, 173,
    174
astrologers, 67, 95, 97, 169
Atkinson, David, 112
autobiography, 46, 182

avatars, 65, 173
Ayyankere, 193
Aziz, 126

B

Babu, 12
The Bachelor of Arts, 7, 65, 74, 169-70,
    177, 217
Bagalur, 179
Balu, 50, 92, 97, 98
Bandopadhyaya, 10
Bangalore, 47, 179, 217
Bari, 200, 202, 208, 212
Barthes, Roland, 34, 36, 116
Basham, A. L., 162, 165
Benares, 118
Bengal, 164
Bhabha, Homi K., 26, 29, 33, 34-
    35n.4, 132, 134, 137-38
Bhagiratha, 14
bhakti (devotion), 64, 173
Bharat, Natyam, 89, 156
Bharata, 168
Bharati, 102, 103
Bharatiyar, 35n.6
Bharracharya, 73
Bhasmasura, 11, 19
Bhima, 195
Bhogopakaranam, 116-17, 121, 123n.6
Bible, 81, 212
Bombay, 179, 184
Brahma, 13, 14, 109, 113, 157-58,
    159, 168, 183, 213
Brahman, 15

maya, 117, 167, 171
meditation, 76, 158, 174, 190, 198,
   202, 207
Mehta, Ved, 86n.2, 169
Mempi, 111, 147, 149, 155, 159, 210
metaphor, 27, 30, 34
metaphysical, 6, 15, 18, 45, 53, 75,
   76, 121
metaphysics, 44, 98
Mirza, Hamayun Ali, 190, 191
money, 12, 62, 63, 71, 75, 81, 90-92,
   93-98, 102, 104, 105, 159, 163
Mother, 27-28, 43, 45, 51, 59, 61-62,
   76, 120, 157-58, 170, 206
Mother-divinity, 158
Mother-goddess, 164
Motherhood, 116, 117, 120
Mr. Sampath, 2, 7, 173, 182, 184, 213,
   218
Mukherjee, Meenakshi, 10, 11, 141,
   209
Mukherjee, Arun P., 199, 202
Muni, 51, 59
Munoo, 86
Muslim, 164, 179
Muslim-Hindu, 164
My Days, 40, 43, 46n.5, 72, 217, 218
Myadas, Loony, 10
Mysore, 181,
Mysore, 217
mystic, 91, 188
mystical, 44, 46n.6, 76, 108, 189, 190,
   191
mysticism, 67, 108, 156, 164, 190
myth, 11, 13, 14, 22n.3, 93, 103, 117,
   120, 121, 132, 138, 155, 212-13
mythico-religious, 198
mythological, 62, 160
mythology, 156-57, 158, 165, 197-98,
   201

N

Naipaul, V.S., 3, 4, 101, 153
Nalini, 62, 63, 104, 105

Narasimhaiah, C.D., 7, 22n.2, 23n.7,
   43, 57, 66-67, 68, 71, 72
narration, 26, 45, 183, 184
narrative, 6, 9, 10, 11, 12, 15, 16, 18,
   19, 25, 28, 31-33, 34, 46n.5, 89, 92,
   94, 96, 98, 101, 109, 112, 130, 132,
   141, 142, 150-51, 153, 165, 198
narrator, 13, 15, 16, 18, 19-22, 23n.7,
   40, 43, 44, 98, 130, 141, 142, 150,
   198
Nataraj, 13, 16, 17-19, 141-152, 155,
   156, 158-163, 165
Nataraja, 107
neocolonialist, 144
Nirvana, 76
non-aggression, 156
non-attachment, 176
non-Malgudian, 116
non-mimeticm, 37, 43-44, 45
non-violence, 70, 163, 165, 168

O

O'Flaherty, Wendy Doniger, 160, 213
Oedipal, 27, 30
Oedipus, 103
Olinder, Britta, 108
oppositional, 25, 159
oppression, 19, 27, 32
ordinariness, 76, 201
outcastes, 50

P

The Painter of Signs, 2, 5, 51, 81, 85,
   115, 121, 125, 127, 135, 136, 138,
   181, 218
Pakistan, 190
Dr. Pal, 90, 94-95
Panigrahi, K.C., 10
pan-Indian, 52
Pandit, 21, 22, 201, 203
paradox, 6, 35n.10, 137, 138
Parasara, 15-16, 18
parody, 46, 197